SOCIAL CRITICISM IN POPULAR RELIGIOUS LITERATURE OF THE SIXTEENTH CENTURY

D0170825

Social Criticism in Popular Religious Literature of the Sixteenth Century

by

Helen C. White

OCTAGON BOOKS

A DIVISION OF FARRAR, STRAUS AND GIROUX

New York   1973

Reprinted 1965
by special arrangement with The Macmillan Company

Second Octagon printing 1973

OCTAGON BOOKS
A Division of Farrar, Straus & Giroux, Inc.
19 Union Square West
New York, N. Y. 10003

Library of Congress Catalog Card Number: 65-25892
ISBN 0-374-98455-7

Printed in USA by
Thomson-Shore,Inc.
Dexter, Michigan

To

HARRIET

with my thanks

ACKNOWLEDGMENTS

FIRST of all, I wish to express my gratitude to the Henry E. Huntington Library and Art Gallery for the fellowship that made it possible for me to spend the year 1939–1940 working on the magnificent collection of sixteenth-century English books at the Huntington Library. This book is the fruit of that year's research. My thanks are due, too, to the University of Wisconsin for the research grant that enabled me to return to the Huntington Library in the summer of 1941 to check my manuscript.

It is a pleasure to express my indebtedness to a number of sixteenth-century scholars who have aided me with advice and suggestions, Mr. Louis B. Wright of the Huntington Library, Dean George C. Sellery and Mr. Merritt Y. Hughes of the University of Wisconsin, Mr. Edwin F. Gay, Mr. Godfrey Davies, and Mr. Edward A. Whitney of the Huntington Library, Mr. R. F. Jones of George Washington University, Mr. William Haller of Barnard College, Mr. Stanley Pargellis of the Newberry Library, and my sister, Miss Olive B. White of Bradley College. I am especially indebted to my sister Harriet for her generous help in checking the citations.

It gives me pleasure, too, to express my warm appreciation of the constant kindness and helpfulness of all the staff of the Huntington Library. Finally, I wish to thank for many courtesies the authorities of Harvard College Library, the Folger Library, the Newberry Library, the Columbia University Libraries, and the Library of the University of Wisconsin.

A word should be added as to the principles followed in the citations from sixteenth-century texts. Titles have been given in as brief a form as possible, with the spelling and, as far as feasible, the punctuation of the original retained, but the type has been standardized, and so has the capitalization. In the citations both the original spelling and punctuation have been kept with the following exceptions: all contractions have been extended, purely typographical peculiarities of sixteenth-century printing have been disregarded, and the varieties of type employed have been reduced to two, roman and italic, with the italic reserved for special purposes.

H. C. W.

The University of Wisconsin
June 1, 1943

CONTENTS

SOCIAL CRITICISM IN POPULAR
RELIGIOUS LITERATURE
OF THE SIXTEENTH CENTURY

CHAPTER I

THE PIERS PLOWMAN TRADITION

WHETHER religion in general, and the Christian religion in particular is to be regarded as basically an instrument of social stimulation and disturbance, or as a means of social reconciliation and stabilization, is a question at least as old as Christianity. Probably, they are right who find in the very early days of the church evidence of the presence of both points of view. Later, it is quite easy to see in certain periods of church history the triumph of the stabilizers and in certain movements the protests of those who were not satisfied with that general attitude.[1] But it would be a mistake to take one attitude as the tradition and the other as the innovation in the sixteenth century or any other century. For both have their place in the tradition.

We are today accustomed to think of regard for tradition and attention to tradition as in itself a characteristic of the conservative and the conformist. As a matter of fact, the reformer is often very much alive to the advantages of the appeal to tradition, and, if often far from comprehensive in his appropriations, nevertheless ready to turn to his use the help it affords. Indeed, he is often very generous in his readiness to make the most of a congenial suggestion and to carry it to conclusions that would have surprised the original author. This is especially true of a time like the sixteenth century in England when the solid regard for the tried and established maintained a firm hold in most men's consciences even when they were sensitive to the challenge of the up-to-date.

In fact, as Mr. Owst has so brilliantly shown in his *Literature and Pulpit in Medieval England*,[2] the sixteenth-century social and

1

religious reformer had at his disposal a singularly rich store of congenial criticism, by no means so systematically accessible to him as Mr. Owst has made it to us, but nonetheless immediately pervasive and effective as only a continuous and living tradition can be. True, as we shall see presently, the sixteenth-century reformer was, often enough, going to use this criticism for ends of which the earlier preachers and writers had hardly dreamed, for the destruction of institutions which they believed essential and only wanted to see reformed. That is the risk which the reformer always runs at the hands of the revolutionary in the history of all institutions. The important point for us is that the sixteenth-century reformers inherited a tradition of social-religious criticism from which they made their own selections, and which they carried on to their own ends, often, in all probability, not entirely aware of what they were doing. For they were not interested in history but in the solution of the problems of their own time; their obligations were not to scholarship but to the accomplishment of the contemporary purposes to which they had dedicated themselves.

Their task of appropriation was made easier by two facts. The first was that already alluded to above, namely, that convinced supporters of the established religious order had made criticisms of the way in which that order was functioning that left little to be desired by the revolutionary either in severity or in range of condemnation. The second was that side by side with the criticism of practice was a criticism of basic theory that at many points of illustration and application ran parallel to it, that, in fact, to a man primarily interested not in theory but in practice was hardly distinguishable from it, and that in many literary instances intermingled with the orthodox criticism of practice in a highly confusing manner. A good many examples could probably be found, but one is so striking that it may serve as a type for all. It is the transformation which the work of Langland underwent mainly through the influence of that of his great contemporary, John Wycliff.

The Vision of William concerning Piers the Plowman is a poem, of course, and not a work of original or systematic thought in the philosophical sense, but after the *Canterbury Tales* of Chaucer, it is probably the most comprehensive literary expression of medieval England. Since our interest is in the ideas expressed rather than in the poem for its own sake, there is no need of going into the problems of authorship. If it could be proved that the poem was the work of several authors, it would only heighten its representative character; it would certainly in no way detract from its importance as an expression of the tradition we are studying. To assume that it is the work of one man, Langland, is merely a convenience. For in spite of some differences of opinion on details, some differences of emphasis on various elements in the situation, and certain differences with regard to hope and expectation, it still remains true that the same approach to the basic problems of religion and society, the same scale of values, social and religious, the same basic purposes govern all three of the existing versions of the poem. In that sense, for all the very complicated textual problems involved, the work may be regarded as a unit, and will be so regarded here.

The highly critical attitude of the author of *Piers the Plowman* to the church and society of his day has been noted by every student of the work. But the character of his criticism has not always been fully appreciated. For that reason it is worthwhile to recapitulate its main lines. The central issue for Langland is the problem of poverty. On the negative side, that involves a failure of two of the basic requirements of the Christian life, justice and charity. On the positive, it involves an appreciation of the meaning of poverty for the social aspects of the Christian life. Poverty is the touchstone of the existing order in church and society; it is both the explanation of the problem of the world's wrong and the solution to it. Of course, this sounds paradoxical, but the paradox rests on a perfectly serious and quite viable interpretation of Christian theory, that, as we shall see presently, is by no means peculiar to Langland in his own time or later.

Langland is not, of course, writing a scientific treatise, or an objective criticism, or even a satire. What he is writing is a prophet's vision in which the light of the professions of a whole society is turned upon its performance with devastating results.

But one thing should be noted here. It is that that light would be visible only to those who share the professions. To one who was indifferent to them there would be nothing to bother about. Of course it would be quite possible for one who did not share those aspirations to measure the profession and the performance and to point out the discrepancies dispassionately, cynically, or contemptuously. There is nothing of that in Langland. The discrepancy is for him a matter of outrage and of heart-break. The very bitterness of his criticism is understandable only in the light of his allegiance to the basic principles that his fellow Christians have violated. He has not only the radical idealism of the mystic who cannot rest content with the shows of things, but the thoroughgoing tenacity of the mystic whose very impatience with illusion has made him proof against disillusionment.

The very word "idealism" is in this context dangerously misleading. For there is a very practical side to the idealism of Langland as of so many mystics. To him the symbol and the reality are intimately bound up in a relation that gives the symbol, on the one hand, merely an intermediary validity and, on the other, a scope and significance of wider and more nearly final validity. It must be remembered, too, that he is not a philosopher, but an artist, that he is working, not through definition and analysis, but through the direct and immediate presentment of the data on which he is operating. The result is that the forefront of his work will be held not by the outlines of his analysis but by the fully-drawn figures of his illustrations. That is why his indictment of the world's wrong has so taken the eye of his readers that it is easier to remember the dramatic figures of the Plowman and of Mede than the ideas which they embody. That is why the wrath and the grief of the visionary are usually appreciated more fully than his faith.

There is no mistaking the grim intensity with which Langland beheld the particular forms which the world's immemorial wrong took in his day, nor the grim intensity with which he portrayed them. For instance, he concludes one of the most eloquent descriptions of the miseries of the poor in this wry world by saying that those who take such woe with patience have their penance and their purgatory on this earth, not only a lively comfort to the victims of such misfortune but also an equally lively comment on the intensity of the sufferings portrayed.[3]

Langland had no doubt as to the human agencies responsible for such suffering. The root was the love of personal and material gain which Langland found the prime cause of the world's injustice. It is that which betrays all fealties to the seduction of Mede, or bribery. The terms in which Conscience repudiates the King's offer of Mede as a bride is one of the most vivid indictments on record of the swath which the love of wealth cuts in all human relations. She corrupts women and so marriage and the family; she corrupts the church from the pope down; she corrupts justice from the local officers, the sheriffs, up.[4] She is the fitting bride for that Falsehood who is the father of the world's wrong. "The Worlde is a wykked wynde · to hem that wolden treuthe," cried the dreamer to Piers.[5]

As for the specific forms of the world's injustice, the indictment against the rich may be summed up in two words: oppression and waste. Langland's admonition to the friars to refuse gifts made out of the unjust exactions of landlords from their tenants and to bid the would-be pious to make proper restitution points to one of the commoner forms of injustice, involving, in his eyes, not only the perpetrator and the sufferer but the churchman who connives at injustice.[6] In the same spirit, Langland asserts that if priests were perfect, they would not take either payment for religious services or gifts for their support from usurers.[7] The notion of tainted money seems very deep-ingrained in his thought, and responsibility for the acceptance of a gift apparently extends to the way in which the resources for the gift were obtained. An analogous responsibility is enjoined upon mayors to see that when they grant the freedom of a craft to a man he be neither a usurer nor a huckster.[8]

It is eminently characteristic of Langland that his attack upon the problem of the behavior of the church is soon revealed to be only the spearhead of his attack on all the social problems of the day. For instance, some of his sharpest invective is devoted to the cheating of merchants as described at length in the confession of

Avarice. In that inclusive confession he does not hesitate to particularize with graphic detail of the devices of the clothmakers for stretching cloth.[9]

For, unlike some of his successors, Langland was aware of small sinners as well as great. He saw the world's exploiters in the greedy nobles and the grasping landlords and the oppressive magistrates, but he saw, also, the small fry, the bandits of the village, as it were, the brewers and the bakers, the butchers and the cooks, who took their toll of the poor who must buy in small quantities, and he asked for them punishment on the appropriate scale, pillories and "pynynge-stoles." [10]

But cheating and oppression are only one side of the injustice of the controlling order of society. The other is waste. Again, waste is not confined to one class. It is revealed in the luxury of the rich, but it is revealed, also, in the idleness of the poor, and the frivolity of the rascal. Worst of all is waste of time, clearly because waste of time is waste of opportunity to win immortal life.[11] It is significant that when the knight offers his service, Piers enthusiastically undertakes to support him in order that he may keep holy church and himself from the wasters and the wicked men that destroy the world.[12] For Piers works for them all, the wasting and the wicked.[13]

The medieval character of Langland's whole approach to the social problem is of course apparent in this diagnosis of the ills of society in terms of the seven deadly sins. But the medieval character is also apparent in the remedy he suggests, essentially a spiritual one. "Love is leche of lyf." [14] To do as the law requires is "dowel," but to love friend and foe is "dobet." [15] Pious works are vain without kindness to one's fellow man.[16] Chastity without charity is like an unlighted lamp.[17] None is so poor or so wretched that he may not love his fellow and give kindness to all sorts of men.[18]

But still more medieval is this inclusion of the poor in the prescription of the remedy for social ill. For Langland the poor are neither a cause nor an object. They have their faults, and he is as unsparing in his indictment of them as of the faults of the rich. He is as severe on the false beggar as on any other rogue.

For he defrauds the needy as well as deceives the charitable.[19] And even the large charity of Piers draws the line at a lot of rascals, some of whom, from the modern point of view, would not seem nearly so much of a threat to general society as others, a juggler, a prostitute, a dice-player, a bawd, a vagabond. But they waste the substance of society, contributing nothing but frivolity and corruption—such are the main lines of Langland's attack upon them.[20]

This distinction between the worthy and the unworthy poor concerns more than the problems of relief for which it later became so important. Rather it is essential to something of more profound and intrinsic importance. That is Langland's insistence that the poor man should be worthy of his calling because that calling is so high. Poverty is kin to God himself and so to his saints.[21] Clerks and learned men have God much in their mouths, but the humble have him in their hearts.[22] Once, contemplating the physical sufferings of the poor on this hard earth, Langland prayed that Christ would send to those who had had such lack here in this world, summer and some sort of joy when they left it for another.[23] But in general he thought the poor had better prospects than the rich. Turning to those of the latter group who were wont to invite minstrels to those feasts which they gave to other rich men, he advised them to invite rather the beggars who are God's minstrels, for their prayers would be comfort to them in the hour of their own dying.[24]

Indeed, when it came to the comparative prospects of the rich and the poor, Langland had little doubt. It was not just that he who was an underling now on earth might have a worthier place in heaven,[25] a possibility of which he vigorously reminded the landlord who was tempted to take gifts from the poor which they could not afford and to which he had no right. Rather it is that poverty is spared some of the temptations that afflict the rich. It was much in Langland's thought that the founder of Christianity himself had made some reflections on the savableness of the rich, reflections which Scripture, in a characteristically extreme form, put even more discouragingly.[26] Certainly, as Patience pointed out, pride is not so likely to be found among the poor as the rich, nor is the perilous duty of judgment of other men. The poor man is not so apt to cheat his neighbors, nor is he furnished with the means to commit folly against sobriety, nor to corrupt himself with dissipation. He is not worried for fear someone will take his possessions; not facing the temptation of treasure, he is more apt to speak the truth. He is a faithful worker who would not take more than is coming to him. Finally the life of a poor man is a blessed thing in itself in its freedom from care.[27] No wonder, as Patience told Activa Vita, the rich dread death more than the poor, for they are in arrears to their maker. But the poor by right claim the joy of heaven from a just judge.[28] So the dreamer hopes that it is for the best that some are rich and some poor.[29] No wonder he concludes that a good plowman can be saved as soon as any.[30] Indeed, in view of what Langland makes of the symbol of Piers it may be concluded that a good plowman will be saved sooner than most.

It should never be forgotten in considering all this social criticism of the clergy that it is the work of an intellectual, and though intellectuals are doubtless as disposed as any other group to defend the interests of their guild in their more aggressive moments, in their moments of discouragement, they are perhaps more alive than most groups to their generic shortcomings. For it is one of the penalties of the strain of the mind that it should lose confidence in its own operations. Probably this aspect of the ecclesiastical criticism of the time should be given more attention than it has hitherto received. Certainly, Langland is running true to form when he points out that no one is sooner taken from the true belief than the clerk.[31] And still more so, when Liberum Arbitrium in a moving description of charity says that it is not to the clerks that the dreamer should go for the desired knowledge of charity but to Piers, for he sees deeper than the words and works out of which the knowledge of clerks is made.[32] It is soon after that conclusion that the revelation is finally made, and it is known that it is Christ who is speaking in the Plowman.[33]

With such a glorification of poverty itself it is hardly surprising that there is no call to revolt in Langland. Patience is what he enjoins upon the suffering. The basis of this prescription is, of course, the belief that one's station and fortune in life are appointed by the will of God:

> "Loke thou grucche not on god · thauჳ he the ჳeve luytel,
> Beo payed with thi porcion · porore or ricchore." [34]

But Langland's conception of patience has a positive side, quite in keeping with his whole respect for poverty, and this is made clear when he declares that "Poure pacient · is parfitest lif of alle." [35] And when this brief life is over,

> ". . . al pore paciente is · may claymen and asken
> After her endynge here · hevene-riche blisse." [36]

The responsibility of the church for the social evils of the day is probably the most persistent and the most famous of the themes of *Piers the Plowman*. The sharpness of Langland's arraignment of the friars is one of the sources of the dramatic interest of the work, hardly exceeded even by the colorful pictures of the seven deadly sins which inspire some of the best writing in the whole poem. There is the fuller satiric indictment like the advice of Covetyse-of-eyes to Recchelesnes:

> ". . . 'have no conscience · how thow come to gode;
> Go confesse the to som frere · and shewe hym thi synnes.
> For whiles Fortune is thi frende · freres will the lovye.' " [37]

There is the swift thrust, all the more effective for its brevity, of that passage in which Langland says that once Charity was found in a friar's frock, but it was a long time ago in Saint Francis' time.[38] And then there is the repeated and continued indictment of the easy penances of the friars,[39] of their money-seeking, and their neglect of the poor. In all this one hears the voice of a widespread and sustained criticism of the mendicant orders.

But Langland's protest against the behavior of churchmen is not confined to the friars. He finds in the corruption and weakness of the clergy at large one of the great sources of social ill, just as he sees in devotion to the ideals which they preach the great hope of the restoration of the peoples of christendom and the hope of the conversion of the heathen.[40]

Especially did he arraign the less satisfactory bishops of the time when he drew up his specifications for the ideal bishop:

"Bisshopes yblessed · if thei ben as thei sholde,
 Leel and ful of love · and no lord dreden,
 Merciable to meek · and mylde to the goode,
 And bytynge on badde men · bote yf thei wolde amende,
 And dredeth nat for no deth · to distruye, by here powere,
 Lecherie a-mong lordes · and hure luther customes,
 And sitthen lyve as thei lereth men · oure lord treuthe hem graunteth
 To be peeres to a-posteles · alle puple to ruele,
 And deme with hem at domes day · bothe quike and ded." [41]

But it is significant that here as in the indictment of the friars, it is discrimination between the poor and the rich, the powerful and the weak, that is the basic object of the criticism. In the friars that discrimination led to the courting and the coddling of the rich to the neglect of the poor. In the bishops it led to severity to the humble and indulgence to the powerful, even submissiveness in matters in which the church should preserve its spiritual authority. In both the social basis of the criticism of the church is clear. This does not mean that Langland on occasion does not criticize the church of his day on other grounds. For instance, as in the passage above, he is very severe on those clerics who do not do their best to maintain high moral standards in their charges. But in general his criticisms of the church and of churchmen tend to gravitate to a social center.

For Langland, however critical, was a convinced and loyal member of his church, as were probably most of the critics of his day. The instruction of Wit is thoroughly representative of his creator's position:

"Bi counseil of Conscience · a-cordynge with holy churche,
 Loke thou wisse thi wit · and thi werkes aftur." [42]

Or, to approach the problem from another angle, as good a test of orthodoxy as any is the treatment of the monastic ideal, an ideal the social significance of which was so soon to be lost among many of the critics of the church. Langland's attitude is revealed in the very fact that when Piers called the pilgrims to the journey to Truth, "on heihte Actif" began to find excuses like a Biblical wedding guest, but Contemplation immediately embraced the way which Piers held out:

> "Quath Contemplacion, 'by Crist · thauh ich care suffre,
> Famyn and defaute · folwen ich wolle Peers.' " [43]

When Grace gave to each group of men the power to fulfill their function in the Christian community, the service of the monastic life was fully recognized:

> "And some he lered to lyve · in longynge to ben hennes,
> In poverte and in penaunce · to preye for alle Crystene." [44]

Above all, it was in the cloister or the school that Clergy found heaven on earth if it was to be anywhere found.[45] In other words what Piers sought was the fulfilment of the religious professions of his day and not their rejection.

Much the same thing is true of his intentions in the sphere of secular life. The ideal society of which he dreams is not organized on a different plan from the one he knows. Rather it is made up of pretty much the existing classes and groups of his day. It is the spirit of the organization that is different. For it is a society in which all classes coöperate, each making its contribution to the whole. The lovely ladies with their long fingers are to make silken chasubles for the clergy, while the wives and widows of lesser rank spin wool and flax for the clothing of the poor and their own satisfaction. This allotment is made by the plowman himself who will sweat and sow for the support of all society.[46] Peace and co-operation for the common good is the pattern, such a state as was in heaven until Lucifer decided that he was wiser and worthier than his master.[47]

But there is in all this no thought of having all things common in the England of his day. That such a doctrine was preached by some of the friars seems clear, for the author represents Envye as sending the friars to school to learn how to preach to men out of Plato and prove their preaching by Seneca: "That alle thinges under hevene· ouȝte to ben in comune." [48] It is clear that Piers' creator regarded such a point of view as at once the fruit and the source of envy. It is clear, too, that Langland was quite aware of something that was to trouble later writers a good deal, the fact that the layman was often misled by an unwise curate.[49]

Now this social-religious position was not something peculiar to Langland. Rather *The Vision of William concerning Piers the Plowman* expresses in a powerful way a central tradition of social criticism, for as Mr. Owst has so brilliantly pointed out, far from being unique, the tone of thought of *Piers the Plowman* is in perfect accord with that of the ordinary orthodox preachers of the period, "indeed a perfect echo in every respect of the Church's message to the world." [50] Far from being an isolated or extraordinary phenomenon, *The Vision concerning Piers the Plowman* was actually in the main stream of a tradition of moral and social denunciation pouring from the pulpit itself. And this tradition of thoroughly orthodox condemnation continued, with, of course, its tribute to the psychology of another age, through the next century, to find with the invention of printing even wider circulation and influence upon public opinion in still another century.

At first sight there is much in common between Langland and Wyclif, particularly in what the two men have to say of the havoc which the spirit of greed for wealth has wrought upon the spiritual life of the Christian world. But it should be noted at the start that Wyclif's arraignment of the spirit of the time is more limited in the area which it covers. For the most part he concentrates upon the clergy, and among the clergy he concentrates especially upon the friars. Wyclif's own university career [51] would, of course, account for his dislike of the friars, but his attack upon them is not only thorough-going but systematic. They fail in hospitality especially to the poor,[52] they steal children, especially poor men's children,[53] doubtless a reference to a habit of recruiting among the exceedingly young scholars of the university of the time. They give letters of fraternity to the rich that are supposed to make them sharers in the works of piety of the friars,[54] a practice which Wyclif flatly denominates blasphemy.[55] But these attacks are incidental.

In the *Vae Octuplex* he characteristically applies an exposition of a text, the twenty-third chapter of Matthew concerning the woes with which Christ threatened the Pharisees and Scribes, to the friars. And in so doing he sums up his case against them once for all under eight headings, condemning them first "Because they do not follow Christ themselves, and prevent others from following Him," second, "Because they deceive and despoil the laity," third, "Because the friars entice children to join their orders," fourth, "Because the power of dispensing with vows, and of giving absolution is abused by prelates and friars for the sake of gain," fifth, "Because they practically set rules and ordinances of their own framing above the gospel," sixth, "Because they have a specious outside, while inwardly corrupt," seventh, "Because they value their habits and other externals, and care not for the pride and hypocrisy within them," and eighth, "Because by quenching of gospel truth they slay Christ in His members while pretending zeal for Him." [56] These eight indictments are then followed by an attack on the doctrine which the friars teach on the subject of the Eucharist, transubstantiation, in the teeth of what God has ordained, Wyclif's own realist view, "Goddis bodi in fourme of breed," [57] and an attack on the authority of the pope.[58] He ends this discussion on the quite orthodox note that each man should "in generalte bileve alle the treuthis that God wole, and muse not in specialte aboute treuthis that God wole hide," [59] here as always implying that it is the friars who stir up speculation and indulge in novelties, while he and his poor priests keep to the path of ancient and established and God-given truth.

But the most interesting portion of this attack on the friars from our point of view is that which concerns their wealth. For that is a part of a larger and even more important matter, and that is his attack on the wealth of the church in general. Especially he attacked those arrangements which had assured the church of steady and independent provision for material wants as well as for the luxury which he arraigned. Those perpetual alms which supported the abbeys he condemned precisely because they supported those institutions which he termed "nestis of the fend." [60] In general he pronounced the "dowinge of the Church with lordship of the world, as it is now dowid," heresy.[61] For church endowments drew priests to the love of worldly things, and so from the love of Christ,[62] with the result that they were "cooldid with temporal goods."[63] And, on the other hand, the system of "impropriating" parochial tithes for the benefit of bishops and abbots deprived the parishes of the proper kind of curates.[64] Even the use of parish funds to support clerical students at the university was to be condemned on the same ground.[65]

For Wyclif believed that the poverty of Christ was the proper model for all the clergy.[66] Priests should live on the tithe and on alms [67] without any supplementary gifts and endowments. The tithe should be regarded as alms freely given, not as something exacted.[68] As for the people, "ther goode wishes shulden move to ʒyve hem freeli that were nede." [69] Moreover, "it semith to trewe men that God wolde that dymes weren partid bitwixe prestis and othere pore men that weren feble, lame or blynd." [70] So priests would have a better chance of achieving their ideal, which once at least he defined at some length as "morenesse of mekenesse and morenesse in service." [71] And the result would be freedom from worldly care and gladness.[72]

Some of his bitterest scorn fell upon the clerical "possessioners," the name he usually gave to the monks,[73] here following the example of the Spiritual Franciscans with whose position he seems to have had much sympathy.[74] But in this area, as elsewhere, he reserved his bitterest scorn for "the beggers," the friars, whom he habitually accused of hypocrisy and extortion.[75] Their professions of poverty he repudiated on the grounds of their rich houses and churches,[76] and their begging he found only a pretext to escape work; complaining that "many freris taken her stait to lyve lustli in this world, for ellis thei shulden be laborers, and lyve hard lyf in lewid stait." [77] Even their acknowledged popularity in preaching was an offense to Wyclif, who had no illusions about the argument from numbers: "And sith ther ben fewe wise men, and foolis ben withouten noumbre, assent of more part of men makith evydence that it were foli." [78] For with their jests and their fables they flatter vulgar taste,[79] and sell their preaching for their gifts and their collections.[80]

In all this the possessioners and the beggers alike contravene the law of Christ,[81] but this is not by any means the only ground on which Wyclif condemns them. This greed of the orders also has its social consequences, as may be seen in his explanation of the malice of Christians in his day: "And rote of this malice is coveitise of preestis, and levynge of Goddis lawe, and hiȝhyng of mannis lawe. Bi this is the comynalte of puple maad pore, and swepte as the pament from hilyyng of stree, and coldid in charite, bothe thei and preestis." [82] This might be taken to mean mainly spiritual damage, but actually Wyclif believed that it involved a good deal of material damage. In this giving to the friars the goods needed by the poor were wasted.[83] Worse, in a time of dearth and privation like that of Wyclif's preaching, the burdens of the poor were doubled:

> "What shulde mefe Anticrist to double tho rentis of tho pore puple in suche yvel tyme? Ffor byfore that freris comen by cautel of tho fende, tho puple gaf no more rente for so myche to hor lordes. And al thinge acountid, thei gyven nowe to tho ordiris wel nyhe als myche as thei did to hor lordes." [84]

It is not surprising, then, that Wyclif promises that if the realm of England were relieved of the four sects, "than myȝte the rewme dispende many hundrid thousand marke more than it dispendith now, alȝif thes sectis weren avoidid." [85] This is a line of argument of which we shall hear more in the sixteenth century.

As for what should be done with the money so saved, Wyclif has some very definite suggestions to offer. In the passage from which the above is taken, it would be given in charity to the poor. But there were other possibilities, as may be seen in the treatise on church temporalities, where in the third chapter Wyclif takes up the problem of disposing of the secular lordships which are such a source of corruption and distraction to the clergy: "And seculer lordischipis, that clerkis han ful falsly aȝenst Goddis lawe, and spende hem so wickedly, schulden be ȝoven wisly bi the kyng and witti lordis to pore gentilmen, that wolden justli governe the peple, and meyntene the lond aȝenst enemyes; and than myȝte oure lond be strengere by many thousand men of armes than it is now, withouten ony newe cost of lordis, or taliage of the pore comyns, [and] be dischargid of gret hevy rente, and wickid customes brou3t up bi coveitouse clerkis, and of many talliagis and extorsions, bi whiche thei ben now cruely pillid and robbid." [86]

Again, this is an idea which we shall encounter frequently in the sixteenth century, the history of which has probably not been taken into account as much as it should have been in judging the operations of Henry VIII. This suggestion for lay use of church property is in line with Wyclif's estimate of the relation of civil and religious power. It rests on two basic notions. The first is that

"the chief lordshipe in this lond of alle temporalties, bothe of seculer men and religious, perteyneth to the kyng of his general governynge. . . . Also it perteyneth to the kyng, the while a bishop or an abbotis see is voyde, to have in his hond al here temporaltees, and at his owne wille to 3eve hem to prelatis. Therfore the kyng may take awey thes temporaltees from prelatis, whan laweful cause exitith." [87]

Even the popes should be subject to kings as both Christ and Peter were.[88] For kings and lords are "mynystris and vikeris of God, to venge synne and ponysche mysdoeris, and preise goode doeris." [89] That is Wyclif's first principle as to the relations between priest and king.

His second goes farther. Kings and lords have the duty of "keeping" Christ's church.[90] Therefore, when priests and monks neglect their obligation to lead a holy life, lords have the duty of compelling them to do so.[91] One form of help they could give the church without too much difficulty, and that is to withdraw their support from the friars.[92] Wyclif admits that it would be harder to put down the possessioners or monks, but the friars are more recently and less well established.[93] Indeed, it would be for the spiritual welfare of the friars themselves to withhold goods from them.[94] Once, at least, Wyclif goes even farther, suggesting that it would be charity to withdraw some of the goods which the church in general possesses, for that would be to relieve the un-

worthy priests as well as the friars of the means of harming themselves:

"For what man wolde bi resoun, kepyng a man in frenesie, 3yve him
a swerd or a knyf bi which he wolde slee himsilf? . . . so, sith preestis
have goodis of men bothe of lordis and comouns, and thei disusen
hem thus, thei my3ten and shulden by charite withdrawe thes brondis
that thus done harme to preestis, and in mesure and manere 3yve thes
goodis to preestis that he himself hath ordeyned him and hise to have
siche goodis." [95]

As for the priests thus relieved, Wyclif reminds them that Christ
paid tribute, and from that example concludes: "And here mai
men see bi resoun, that Cristis preestis shulden not grutche 3if
men token ther temporaltes; for oure Jesus grutchide not." [96]

This suggestion that men might safely and even meritoriously
withdraw their support of bad priests would seem to be a somewhat risky suggestion in a world so closely articulated as that of
the Middle Ages, and so it seems to have proved, for we find
Wyclif protesting as "a feyned word of Anticristis clerkis" the
conclusion that because the poor can withdraw their tithes from
the support of bad clergy, they may also withdraw them from the
support of bad lords:

"But 3it summe men that ben out of charité sclaundren pore prestis
with this errour, that servauntis or tenauntis may lawefully withholde
rentis and servyce fro here lordis whanne lordis ben opynly wickid in
here lyvynge. And thei maken this false lesyngis upon pore prestis to
make lordis to hate them, and not to meynteyne treuthe of Goddis lawe
that thei techen opynly for worschipe of God and profit of the reume
and stablynge of the kyngis pouer and distroynge of synne. For thes
pore prestis distroien most bi Goddis lawe rebelté of servauntis a3enst
lordis, and charge servauntis to be su3et thou3 lordis ben tirauntis,
for Seynt Petir techith thus: 'Be ye servantis suget to lordis in alle
manere of drede, not only to goode lordis and bonere, but also to tirauntis, or siche that drawen fro Goddis scole.' . . .

"And this is a feyned word of Anticristis clerkis that, 3if sugetis may
leffully withdrawe tithes and offryngis fro curatis that openly lyven
in lecherie and don not here office, than servauntis and tenauntis may

withdrawe here servyce and rentis fro here lordis that lyven opynly a cursed lif." [97]

Wyclif's own sermons bear out his claim. He believed in and supported the feudal system of his day as by God established:

". . . it is knowun bi Goddis lawe, that ther ben in the Chirche thre statis that God hathe ordeyned: state of prestis, and state of knyȝtis, and the thridd is staat of comunys. And to thes three ben thre othere, comyn and leeful bi Goddis lawe,—state of virgyns, and state of wedloke, and the state of widewis. State of virgyns is the hiest, bi witnesse of Crist and seyntis in Hevene. Sum state is here good for o man, and sum is good for another; and God moveth a man to his best state ȝif he lette not bi his synne." [98]

The commons are to serve God and their lords; [99] servants have the basic obligation of faithfulness: [100] "For as Poul techith, serv-auntis shulden serve to thes lordis as to God; and so, bi service goostli and bodili, shulden thei serve, *not oonly to good lordis and resonable* to ther servauntis, *but also unto tirauntis,* that distrien Cristis scole, as diden bothe Heroud and Pilat; *for certeyne this is grace in Jesus Crist that is oure Lord.*" [101]

This does not mean that Wyclif had nothing to say to the lord. The relation between lord and subject was one of mutual obligation; as he summed it up at the end of his treatise *Of Servants and Lords:* "Lordis schullen traveile als faste to kunne Holi Writt and do treuthe and equité and meyntene riȝt of pore men, and reste and pees, as pore men ben bisi to labore for here owene liflode and to paye here rentis to lordis." [102] And though Wyclif granted that in the gospel there was no requirement [103] of universal poverty, he did remind the lord that "costli metis and gay garmentis, whan thei ben taken over mesure, thei maken lordis bisi for hem, and spoilen wrongli ther pore tenauntis." [104] He has something to say, too, of the deceits of merchants, as Langland had,[105] and of the injustices of lawyers.[106] He accuses the guilds of conspiring to their own profit at the expense of the rest of the community.[107] Finally, he adjures all Christians without discrimi-nation of class or state to cast their "bisynesse" on God, and not to be too preoccupied with worldly things.[108] But in general

Wyclif was less troubled by the sins of the lay world than by those of the church. Once he went so far as to say that "feith and good religioun stondith in seculer men, and in preestis been wordis withouten good dede." [109] On the whole, then, in the social sphere Wyclif is fairly conservative.

But in what he has to say on religion, his note is distinctly revolutionary, if we remember that revolutionary psychology may in different circumstances take different directions. In the first place, like his fellows, Wyclif clearly thought of himself as a loyal and orthodox member of the church. As regards doctrine, he is in the main. There is in his English works none of that anti-Marian animus, for instance, that is to be so marked a feature of sixteenth-century developments. In spite of his attacks on friars and monks and his asking "ʒif a man be closid in a cloistre, what profitith he, bi Cristis ordenance, to make liʒt to his brother that felith not of his profit?" [110] he had no doubt that contemplative life was the best, citing not only the words but the example of Christ: "For, alʒif Crist dide ertheli workes, netheles he dide on sich mesure that his soule was ever fed in contemplacioun of God." [111] Therefore, priests should give themselves to contemplation.[112]

Again, although in both his Latin works and in his English he yielded perhaps more to the predestination side of that great debate on man's free will that so engaged the medieval mind than would most orthodox thinkers,[113] yet in his English preaching he took pains to hold the balance. To those who argued that what must be must be, he urged that we should "enforse aʒens yvel," and pray for good because God had ordained that the coming of good or evil should be unknown to men.[114] Even if Wyclif laid it down as a basic principle that "riʒt as Goddis children may not do but good thing, so children of the fend may not do but harmful thing," [115] still he concluded his sermon by urging good living on the ground that "worchyng bi riʒt lyf, endid after Goddis wille, makith a man Goddis child and come to the blisse of hevene." [116] And though his explanation of how free will is conserved in his theory is rather obscure, there is no mistaking the intention of the conclusion he draws: "And preie thou God that he drawe thee, for worthinesse of thi liif; for man mai be so unclene that God wole not leie hond on him." [117]

On the sacraments, however, Wyclif's position was different. His thesis that the absolution of the priest had no effect unless God had already forgiven the sin raised but did not answer the question as to just what his conception of the sacrament was.[118] There could hardly be any doubt when in the treatise *Of Confession* he said of private confession: "And it semeth that it is not nedful, but brouʒt in late be the fend." [119]

Even severer was his attack on the orthodox doctrine of the Eucharist. He did not question the fact of the Real Presence, but, as we have seen, he attacked the doctrine of transubstantiation. It was in its origins a quarrel in scholastic philosophy. It was Wyclif the realist who refused to grant that the appearances of bread and wine could be present without the substance: [120] "Bot accydente withouten sugette nowther knowes mon ne God, as Austin teches and resoun proves." [121] In that sentence spoke the scholastic philosopher. In the more homely terms of the popular preacher he pronounced it in his confession "heresye to trowe that this sacrament is Gods body and no bred; for hit is bothe togedir." [122]

The attack on the doctrine of transubstantiation, whether or not it was the cause of his final loss of the friars' support, certainly reenforced his attack on the friars and the pope.[123] For he declared that the doctrine of transubstantiation was grounded on the authority of the pope and the cardinals and not on Christ's teachings.[124] And he did not hesitate in his turn to charge the friars who supported this doctrine with being heretics.[125]

This was not mere polemic. Today we are accustomed to having change commended to us as new good for ancient evil. Wyclif's age was rather of the opinion that what was old was more likely to be right than what was new. At any rate, the accusation of novelty seems to have been one to which he was especially sensitive, and he was anxious to throw it back on his adversaries.[126] The orders he habitually called "new religions" and their members and supporters "new religious." [127] And he charged that all these new religions were full of heresy,[128] and that they were responsible for the discord in the church.[129]

His most basic attack upon the friars is, then, that they constitute a schism in the whole body of Christianity.[130] Christ made one sect and set his law against the making of sects.[131] But the friars constitute private sects against the religion of Christ,[132] new sects, Wyclif insists, shrewdly retorting upon the established order that charge of novelty which he as a reformer in an established order had found so heavy to meet.[133] And of course he was in no doubt as to where to look for their source. Antichrist was the root and explanation of their novelties,[134] the fiend himself, the author of their ways.[135] He claimed that his own teaching and the teaching of his poor priests, so often under suspicion of heresy, was but a return to the teaching of Christ. The sect he made was Christ's sect. As for the others, pope, cardinals, bishops, monks and friars, he regarded their opposition as the touchstone of their true character.[136] It was not his poor priests but Christ's church which he prayed might be protected from these enemies.[137] For back of all the disputes what was at issue was the difference between God's law and man's, one of Wyclif's favorite dichotomies.[138]

In the light of that distinction, Wyclif bitterly censured the prelates for worldliness and wasting of spiritual goods.[139] Christ's law demands that Christians should follow good prelates and flee from evil ones.[140] But since he had already in the same sermon pointed out that in his day prelates followed a very different pattern of life from Saint Paul's, and it was not wise to follow them lest they lead their followers to hell, there was not much room for choice.[141] It is not surprising, therefore, that he concluded that the church could get along very well without prelates, as it did in the time of the apostles when the church prospered without prelates "as Goddis lawe techith." [142] Priests and deacons are all that the church really needs.[143]

The immediate crime of the bishops is, of course, clear; they hindered Wyclif's poor priests from preaching.[144] Wyclif might encourage them by telling them and his lay listeners that "if

prechours holden hem prechinge in Cristis name, thei han ful
autorite more than prelatis moun ȝyve hem." [145] But the prelates
remain second only to the friars in the book of his wrath. For
preaching to Wyclif was the highest work possible to man on
earth.[146] He was very contemptuous of the emphasis on liturgical
observance, seeing in it an unworthy supplanter of the study of
scripture.[147] Even singing was a distraction.[148] The essential thing
was study and preaching of the gospel.[149]

In another direction, too, Wyclif may be said to anticipate the
reformers of the sixteenth century. That is in his reiterated use
of the word "freedom." The church is in thrall to man's law.[150]
"And here mai men opynli see how myche Anticrist is to blame,
that after the fre lawe of Crist ȝyveth another contrarye lawe;
for it lettith keping of Cristis lawe, and puttith men fro fredom
of Crist." [151]

In other words Wyclif raises some very fundamental doubts
about the dependability of church authority such as should have
done much to undermine lay confidence in the authorities which
they had been taught to trust and respect. Especially is this true
of what he has to say of the pope. Wyclif's sermons run pretty
nearly the whole gamut of attack, from the bare suggestion, on
which one would have thought there would be little argument,
that Christ was to be trusted rather than many Pope Joan's,[152] to
the full development of the dramatic possibility that the present
regime of the pope was one of the signs that Antichrist had
established his rule, presaging the immediate coming of "dome." [153]
After such a general indictment, the more detailed charges are
hardly surprising. Pride is one of the most frequent.[154] Then, too,
the pope may err and sin; [155] papal pardons to the undeserving
are blasphemies,[156] papal censures hurt only the guilty.[157]

But it is not so much the specific charge as the cumulative effect
of these attacks that is impressive. For though the English sermons
of Wyclif follow the basic lines of the liturgical year, taking up
the perennial themes and problems of Christian life upon appropriate occasions, still certain basic preoccupations are apparent on
almost every page. Indeed, on the most classic themes where one
would have thought that there was little room for special pleading,

Wyclif manages to bring in the two main objects of his attack, the pope and the friars. For instance, on the old scriptural warning to beware of false prophets, he cites the false friars as a timely illustration.[158] The standard reference to the high priests and the Pharisees gives him a chance to compare false prelates and friars to those ancient objects of divine opprobrium.[159] Even so relatively innocuous an allusion as one to the good and perfect gifts from above gives the preacher a chance to cite the privileges given by the pope as gifts from the opposite direction.[160] Whenever a gloss or an illustration for a text of condemnation is needed, Wyclif has the pope, the prelates, the friars ready to hand. And as he once cited Christ's example to defend scornful language in a good cause,[161] one may be sure that the original condemnation of Scripture suffers no attenuation in the gloss or the illustration. Some measure of Wyclif's competence in the genre may be taken from his description of monasteries and colleges as "dennes of theves and nestis of serpentis, and homely housis of quyc devels." [162]

But the important thing about these incidental attacks as about the more sustained and systematic arraignment is that Wyclif draws up an indictment of the monastic orders and the hierarchy that offers striking point-for-point parallels to the sixteenth-century attack upon the established organization and government of the church. As we have seen, he quite whole-heartedly shared the horror which his age felt at heresy, and retorted the charge with great freedom and spirit upon his adversaries. But it is nonetheless true that at certain key points, whatever his intention, he opened the way for the changes that were to come, and still more for the changes that were to be attempted and hoped for in the sixteenth century and in some cases not realized until the seventeenth. For as the most recent biographer of Wyclif, Workman, has suggested, he is not so much the precursor of the Elizabethan Settlement and of the Established Church as of the Nonconformist movements of the seventeenth century.[163]

For his own time, however, it is probable that the revolutionary aspects of his message derived much of their effectiveness from the fact that they were so intimately associated with that criticism of the wealth of the "possessioners" and the friars to which we have already become accustomed in so orthodox a writer as Langland. Certainly in the development of the social-religious criticism of the next two centuries that criticism became one of the most important vehicles for the dissemination of attitudes which, if not to be altogether attributed to Wyclif's teaching, are still unmistakably indebted to his continuing influence. One of the most dramatic illustrations of this phenomenon is to be seen in what the sixteenth-century writers made of Langland's great work.

Indeed, the sixteenth-century writers saw in Langland primarily a co-worker with Wyclif in the work of reform. This is not surprising. One could hardly expect the sixteenth century to appreciate the orthodoxy of Langland. Rather it valued him because it saw in his work the foreshadowings of its own revolt. This is clear in the first edition of *Piers the Plowman* printed, that of 1550,[164] the work of a very remarkable man whose own prophetic activities we shall presently have occasion to study in some detail. For the present we shall simply recall that Robert Crowley in the course of a very active career in the cause of social and religious reform was by turns printer and preacher. It is easy to see why he was interested enough in *Piers the Plowman* to reprint it for the benefit of his own age, from what he says in the explanatory note to the reader which he prefixed to Langland's text. He has just completed a brief account of the author and come to the work itself. He concludes it was first written after 1350 and before 1409, in the time of King Edward III:

"In whose tyme it pleased God to open the eyes of many to se hys truth, geving them boldenes of herte, to open their mouthes and crye out agaynste the worckes of darckenes, as did John wicklefe, who also in those dayes translated the holye Bible into the Englische tonge, and this writer who in reportynge certaine visions and dreames, that he fayned him selfe to have dreamed: doeth moste christianlye enstruct the weake, and sharply rebuke the obstinate blynde. There is no maner of vice, that reigneth in anye estate of men, whiche this wryter hath not godly, learnedlye, and wittilye rebuked." [165]

The effect of this approach is still further strengthened by the summary of the principal points of the book with which he prefaced the second printing of this work, also in the same year of 1550.[166] A couple of sentences from the summary of the initial vision will show how Crowley selects and underscores the elements which he thinks important:

"The vision begynneth the fyrste leafe, and continueth to the fourth, declaryng fyrste the diverse studies that menne folow. . . .

"Than it declareth the great wyckednes of the byshoppes, that spared not to hange their seales at every Pardoners proxes, and what shameful Simonye ragneth in the church.

"Nexte it declareth somewhat of the powre and office of Kinges and Princes, and than secretly in latine verses it rebuketh their cruelnes and tyranny: Than under the parable of Rattons and mise, it rebuketh the folye of the commune people that cluster togythers in conspiracies agaynste such as god hath called to office under their Prince," etc.[167]

Crowley has another means of pointing up the text of his author to bring out the truths which he thinks his writer intended to set forth and to guard against possible misinterpretation, and that is the marginal note so popular at this time. For instance, against what is probably one of the most optimistic declarations of faith on record,

"I Conscience know this, for kind wit, me it tauȝt
That reason shall rayne, and realmes governe,"

he writes, "This is no prophecy, but a resonable gathering," that is from Scripture.[168] Against

"And how dowel at ye day of dome, is dignely underfongen
And passeth al the pardon, of S. Peters church
Now hath the pope power, pardon to graunt the people"

he writes: "Note howe he scorneth the auctority of Popes." [169]

These marginal notes are interesting for another reason. Sometimes the wisdom which the reformer had learned from the disestablishment of the monasteries or some other of the recent changes leaps out of a marginal comment, as in what he puts against one of Langland's diatribes against unworthy clerks,

"That they came for covetise, to have cure of soule," a classic arraignment that one would have expected Crowley to underscore with enthusiasm. What he actually writes is, "Curates oughte to have a competent lyvyng certayne." [170] But in general Crowley's comments stick close to his primary purpose of using Langland to reënforce a good cause to which Crowley believed the old author was devoted in the forefront of the awakening time.

By and large, that is the position of those writers who in the sixteenth century made use of the central figure of Langland's vision and the tradition of social criticism it represented. Typical is the variety of forms assumed by the central character of Langland's poem, that evolving mystical figure that in the fashion of so many symbolic figures, grows with the progress of the story from the humble plowman of his first appearance to the redeeming Christ of the possible Christian society at the end. The most impressive is probably the oldest, written not long after Langland's own poem, *The Praier and Complaynte of the Ploweman unto Christe,* first published in 1531.[171] This work must be pretty nearly the most searching of its genre in its challenge to the common acceptances of contemporary secular society, for in a passage like the following it goes to the root of basic economic relationships:

"O Lorde these rych men seggen that they done moch for thy love. For many pore laborers ben yfounde by hem, that schulden fare febelich ne were not they and her redinesse for soth me thinketh that pore laborers geveth to these rych men more then they geven hem ageyn warde. For the pore man mote gone to hys laboure in colde and in hete, in wete and drye, and spende his flesch and hys bloude in the rych mennes workes apon gods grounde to fynde the rych man in ese, and in lykynge, and in good fare of mete and of drinke and of clothinge. Here ys a gret gifte of the pore man. For he geveth his own body. But what geveth the rych man hym ageynwarde? Sertes febele mete, and febele drinke, and feble clothinge. What ever they seggen soch be her werkes, and here ys litel love." [172]

This indictment of the illusions of the employing class is universal in its objective and in its revelation of a very sharply defined class-consciousness. But it speedily focusses upon the friars and their pretensions to poverty. Now, as we have seen, there was nothing original in this line of attack in itself. The hypocrisy of the friars' pretensions to poverty was an ancient theme of their critics. And it was long to continue in the anti-monastic literature of the years to come. There is, for instance, in the Piers literature of the fifteenth century a classic example of such an arraignment in *Pierce the Ploughmans Crede,* which was probably composed some time near the end of the fifteenth century and published first in the middle of the sixteenth (1553).[173] This work is a very vigorous and sustained assault upon the friars for their gluttony and their elaborate church adornment as well as their morals, and their haunting of taverns, and their quarreling. There is, then, nothing original or unique in the attack which *The Praier and Complaynte of the Ploweman unto Christe* made upon the luxury of the friars.

What is distinctive is the source to which this old charge is attributed. That is the working or peasant class which the friars have forsaken in their efforts at self-advancement: "O Lorde thou ne tauȝtest not a man forsaken a poore astaate and traveyle to ben afterwarde a lorde of hys brethren or ben a Lordes felaw and dwellinge with Lordes as doth men of these newe religions." [174] The class feeling of such a passage is unmistakable. It must be more than a dramatic assumption of a role, and yet it would be rash to take it too literally as an expression of a widespread popular attitude. Probably it is something of both, a sharpened personal statement of a latent resentment. Whatever it is, it is certainly thoroughgoing, for the author goes on to suggest that the old associates of the friars feel that they must bear the cost of the advancement they so much resent: "But Lorde thou ne tauȝtest not a man to forsaken the travelouse lyvinge in porenesse in the worlde to lyven in ese with rychesse by other mennes traveyle and have lordshupe on her brethren." [175]

But interesting as this class-desertion line of attack upon the friars is in itself, it becomes still more significant when viewed in the light of the very radical theory of the nature of property which this unknown author apparently held. It is in his objections to the church's insistence upon the repayment of debts that he expresses it most clearly:

"For who that beth in charite possesseth thy goodes in commune and nat in propre at hys neȝboures nede. And then schall there none of hem seggen thys ys myne, but it is goodes that god graunteth to us to spenden it to hys worschupe. And so ȝif any of hem boroweth a porcion of thilke goodes, and dispendeth hem to gods worschupe, God ys apayed of this spendinge, and aloweth hym for his trew doinge. And ȝif god ys apayed of that disspendinge that ys the principall lorde of thilke goodes, how darre any of his servauntes agen there of acountes other chalengen it for dette? . . . And ȝif my brother spendeth amys the goodes that I take hym, Ich am dyscharged of my delyveraunce of the goodes, ȝif I take hym in charite thilke goodes at his nede. And ych am yholde to ben sory of hys yvell dispendinge ne I maye not axen the goodes, that I toke hym to his nede in forms of dette. For at hys nede they weren hys as well as myne." [176]

That is for any age a radical version of the stewardship theory of possession. That joined with the sharp class-consciousness of the writer made his drive upon the existing order an impressive one. And though like so many of his contemporaries he focused this general attack on wealth upon the wealth of churchmen, especially the religious orders, there were elements in this criticism that were much too widely based to be satisfied by the accomplishment of the dissolution of the monasteries.

One finds evidence of their persistence in a tract of the middle of the sixteenth century that in many ways resembles the social complaints of Robert Crowley at the same date, *Pyers Plowmans Exhortation, unto the Lordes, Knightes and Burgoysses of the Parlyamenthouse.*[177] This time Piers like Crowley has turned his attention to the members of Parliament, and in so doing he has brought into the light of the traditional social criticism a class of society that had not by any means passed unscathed in the earlier literature, but which had hitherto received less attention than more influential offenders, and that is the merchant class. Moreover, the unknown author of this tract seems to be as aware as Crowley that the "possessioners" and exploiters do not remain entirely constant from age to age. For he draws a parallel that, when the non-evolutionary habits of thought of the age are con-

sidered, is surprisingly suggestive of a perception of certain underlying relationships:

"Nevertheles even as in the time of oure greatest errour and ignoraunce, the fatte priestes wold never confesse that any thing concerninge
our religion was amis, worthy to be reformed, even so now at this daye
there be many fatte marchauntes which wold have no reformation in the
comon wealth affirming that therin al thinges be wel, but he that
wyll be conversaunt with the comen sorte of the poore comens, shal
(if he stop not his eares, nor hyde not his eyes) both heare se and per-
ceyve the case to be farre other wise. He shal heare tel that a fewe
richemen have ingrossed up so many fermes and shepe pastures, and
have decayed so many whole townes, that thousands of the poore comens
can not get so muche as one ferme, nor scant any litell house to put
their head in. It is not agreable with the gospel that a fewe parsons
shall lyve in so great aboundaunce of wealth and suffer so many their
christen brothers to lyve in extreme povertie." [178]

But the important thing about this essay is that it brings the
ancient Piers Plowman attack upon the greed and covetousness
that have wasted society up to date. It is the psychology of a new
time. Indeed, even the disillusionment of the new time is to be
found in *Pyers Plowmans Exhortation*. For there is much to
suggest that the author like Crowley, as we shall see presently,
had been disappointed in his expectations of the good to be reaped
from the suppression of the monasteries. Indeed, he has some very
interesting things to say about the economic effects of the suppression. The first is a fairly common complaint of the time, namely,
that there are more people for whom work is to be found now
that the monasteries are abolished.[179] The second is a curious one
in view of some of the common charges of the opponents of the
monasteries, namely, that now that the monks have married, there
is a serious increase in the population to the consequent intensification of the problem of support of the nation.[180]

As we shall see presently, this disillusionment over the disestablishment of the monasteries is typical of the time. So, too, is a
certain increase in caution. For this same author, however severe
he may be in his criticism of the oppressors of his age, is anxious,

like so many of his contemporaries, that he should not be misunderstood as supporting what he would regard as dangerously radical ideas of social reform. Again, the spectre of communism rises, and he hastens to lay it: "I wol[d] not that those ydell membres of this realm[e] which for the mayntenaunce of their ydeln[es] wold have al thinges in commen, shuld thin[k] that I do now harpe of that string: far[r] be such madnes fro me, for that confusio[n] wold utterly extinguish all industry unt[o] all maner of good artes and qualities, and reduce us unto a bestly trade of life." [181]

This note of caution is typical of the Piers literature of this period. It is to be caught in the handling of other controversial issues of the time. For complicated as it was, the distribution of wealth was not the only point at issue between the various groups of society. There is one perhaps still more fundamental, and that is the issue of authority as represented by the magistracy. Some of the Christian social radicals of the time, especially among the Anabaptists, were for the abolition of the magistracy. Probably the number of thoroughgoing anarchists of this type was pretty limited, for all the impression they made upon contemporary European opinion. Certainly in this Piers Plowman literature there is little evidence of the anti-magisterial aspect of Anabaptist teaching. In one book much later in the century some of the basic issues are raised but in a very limited and conservative form. It is Francis Thynne's *Newes from the North* of 1579,[182] presenting a conversation between Simon Certain, the godly keeper of the inn at the sign of the Greek Omega at Ripon in Yorkshire, and his neighbor, Pierce Plowman, who comes into the inn with an armful of unbound books, "Billes, Answers, Replications, Rejoinders, Copies of Depositions, and such like," which apparently he has just bought in London for a good deal more than they are worth.[183] Piers is wondering why magistrates, judges and other officers exact such charges for what is worth so little.[184] The area involved is mainly that of the law and the magistracy, but the attitude of Piers Plowman is one that is going to be met again in the field of religion as well. For when Certain attempts to defend the lawyer's and the magistrate's fees and charges and other rewards on the familiar ground of the necessity of preserving law and order,[185] Piers defends his competence to express a contrary opinion: "I am no Schoole man, Neighbour quoth hee, but yet some reason I have and some experience I have seen, and some heed I have taken thereof,"[186] and proceeds with his attack on the lawyers and the magistrates for their impositions on the poor.

In the course of this discussion Piers asks a number of decidedly leading questions, of which probably the most important and most interesting is, "why poore men are not called to office of estate and government in common welths but evermore the rich and welthy." This question the host of the Greek Omega answers in pretty conservative terms, defending existing practice on the ground that

"the poore would be rich and so are not content with their present estate, but desire alteration and chaunge and all such persones are more meet to be commaunded then to commaund in a common welth. But of the rich and welthie it is clean otherwise, for they are alredy that which the poore have desire to be, and therfore content, and consequently Freends and furtherers of peace and unitie which is never nor never wil be where they have authoritie in their hands that are not content with their owne present state, and so great hazard of the common peace lyeth therin."[187]

This is one of the clearest defenses of the theory of the ruling class to be found in the literature of the time.

In general, where the bitterer note of social protest is still to be heard in the Piers literature, it will usually be found that the social attack ends up in an onslaught on the church. This is true of an anonymous piece first published about 1550 but, to judge from allusions to certain Henrician executions, probably composed some years earlier, *I Playne Piers*.[188] The keynote of this work is struck in a jingle on the title-page:

> "I playne Piers which
>   can not flatter
> A plowe man men me call
> My speche is fowlle, yet
>   marke the matter
> Howe thynges may hap to fall."

The ensuing treatise combines a plea for the free circulation of the Scriptures in English with a general attack on the old religious order and on the wealthy. The somewhat threatening tone of the jingle on the title-page is borne out by the development of these themes, as may be seen in the following consolation which Piers gives to his fellow poor men:

"And I say again to you poore caytyffes, there is an other worlde besyde this, and we can paciently abyde the lordes workynge, there is no sede can brynge greate gayne but he be deed, thys we se playne in oure yerely sowynge, besyde thys we paciently abyde .vii. monethes longe, tho we suffer at home much hunger and wronge, oure whete or we can gether why sholde we not than, goddes workynge ken in savyng us with then, yea here me dere bretherne hoggeherdes sheperhedes and all youre sorte dyspysed, hathe not God chosen the pore of this world, to be rich in fayth, and heires of the kyngdom, whiche he promised to al them of whom he was loved, that howe can youre bysshoppes hate then thus pore and be the Apostelles successours, for they did comfort the pore all." [189]

That the effect of that last sentence was not lost upon the enemies of the bishops is to be seen in some fragmentary proofs of a Marprelate tract which seems to have been interrupted in the printing somewhere about 1590. From what has survived it is clear that this was to be a reprint of *I Playne Piers* with editorial interpolations that would make the most of its possibilities for the support of the Puritan attack on the prelacy.[190] This development is characteristic of the sixteenth-century history of the Piers tradition. The note of social criticism is still to be heard, but the main thrust is not against the civil "possessioners" but against the church.

Especially does the tradition of the plain man Piers prove useful in rousing the simple man to protest against the pretensions and exactions of the learned in the field of religion. This line of attack was to continue through the century with various objectives. But in the first third of the century it was a very inviting, albeit in the end somewhat hazardous, weapon for the advocates of Scriptural study among the masses. *A Godly Dyalogue and Dysputacyon betwene Pyers Plowman, and a Popysh Preest concernyng the*

Supper of the Lorde [191] is a notable example of this appeal to the unlearned for the defense of the new order against the old. The text on the title-page, as so often, defines the point of view from which the author proceeds: "God hath chosen the weake thinges of the worlde to confounde thynges whyche are myghtye, yea thynges of no reputacyon for to bryng to nought thynges of reputacion, that no flesh shuld presume in his sight," certainly an expression of one of the most widely popular sources of appeal in Christian tradition. As so often in this literature, the discussion is given a specific dramatic setting and occasion. It begins with "simple Pyers plowman" arriving at a house where a dinner was in progress with four priests in attendance. One, according to the author, tried to impress the simple people present as being more learned than his fellows. The reader's general impression of the highly popular character of the appeal of this work is confirmed by the emphasis on the pretentiousness of the priest and by the form in which it is expressed. That is simply a very elementary statement of the orthodox doctrine of transubstantiation, and must have been at once apparent as such to any man of any degree of theological training, whatever his attitude to the issues involved. For the priest simply "sayde and declared ther that the sacrament was the very body and bloud of Chryste Alleagynge further that great daunger yt was to receyve yet unworthely." [192]

The response of Piers and the terms in which that response is couched are significant for a point of view of which we are going to hear a good deal more in the next century. Piers was not awed by the theological pretensions of the priest, but "encouraged hym selfe yea was rathere boldened and encouraged by the secret motyon of the holy goost" [193] to ask a question. This "secret motyon of the holy goost" is in the future going to play a large part in lay challenges to theologians who would not be alarmed by Piers' inability to accept the doctrine of transubstantiation. Piers' question as to whether the body to be received at the approaching Easter would be the very same which the Virgin conceived was, so far as can be judged from the literature of the time, a very common one in sixteenth-century popular discussions, much exploited by those who held the point of view which Piers is represented as defending, namely, that the body in the sacrament is "onelye a remembrance of the same." [194] But the "secret motyon of the holy goost" was to lead very soon to the asking of questions not so popular and the delivery of answers not so acceptable to those who first applauded Piers' scepticism and his obedience to the Inner Light.

The conclusion of this essay is, also, interesting not so much for what it says as for what it implies. On the surface, it is a gibe at the professional pride and exclusiveness of the old clergy. In reality it not only adds to the evidence we have from other sources as to the prevalence of amateur theologizing at this time, but it suggests that in certain quarters at least there was a good deal of encouragement of this theologizing of the unlearned. Later we shall find much concern among responsible men as to the possible spiritual consequences of popular theologizing, but the author of this satire can see only material caste-interest in the reaction of his caricature priests:

> "The other .iii. prestes sayd If these hobbes and rusticals be suffred to be thus busy, in readynge of English heresy and to dyspute after this maner wyth us, which are sperytual men we shalbe fayne, to learne some other occupacion or els we are lyke to have but a colde broth."

To this Piers responded significantly, "Amen." [195]

Such use of Piers Plowman to voice the aspirations of those who wish to change the teachings and practice of the church is thoroughly characteristic of this later development of the work of Langland. Indeed, one may say that Langland's creation is used to present a point of view more like Wyclif's than like that of its original author. Its main lines may be summed up in certain charges that occur over and over again. First and foremost, there is the attack on the friars.[196] Then there is the attack on the pope and the power of the keys [197] and the long reign of Antichrist.[198] There is the attack, too, on the images and the alleged giving of gifts to images, when the image of God in the poor is in need.[199] There is the attack on the Real Presence [200] and on confession.[201] And again and again the demand for the free circulation of the Scriptures in English, coupled with the defense of what is called "the New Learning." [202] Indeed, it is difficult to avoid the conclusion that in the minds of these later authors the accomplishment of the changes involved in both the correction of the foregoing abuses and the securing of the desired remedies has come to overshadow the social relief which the poor craved.

That is no less true of another branch of this Piers tradition which remains to be examined. This is the curious blending of the Piers Plowman tradition with the apocryphal Chaucer tradition. Some slight trace of such a blending is to be discovered in Francis Thynne's *The Debate betweene Pride and Lowlines* of 1570.[203] The Chaucerian contribution is apparent especially in the opening description of the fair May world of the dream, a more poetic and romantic setting than one would expect for so grotesquely prosaic a vision as that which it introduces, the two pairs of breeches, the cloth and the velvet, rolling separately down the hill.[204] In the debate which ensues one may catch far-off echoes of Langland, for Velvet Breeches, the protagonist of Pride, challenged the Plowman's competence to serve as a member of the jury which would decide the issue on the ground that he was too simple, that he did not have the education or experience to judge of such a matter as that under consideration, that is the relative importance of the velvet and the cloth breeches, which symbolized pride and lowliness respectively, and, finally, that he did not have a freehold of forty shillings' value. But Cloth Breeches defended the plowman by pointing out that husbandry is very important to society and takes a good deal of intelligence.[205]

But this is little more than ingenious trifling. Much more central to both traditions are two apochryphal Chaucerian compositions. The first, *The Plowmans Tale,* was published some time in the middle of the sixteenth century (1545?) by William Hill,[206] and later republished in 1606, Malone suggests in a note in the front of the Bodleian Library copy,[207] because of the Gunpowder Plot. The second, *Jack up Lande,* was published without any date some time in the middle of the sixteenth century (perhaps about 1540).[208] Its contents would indicate, however, that it was composed before the disestablishment of the monasteries. Both were published as the work of Chaucer.

Of the two, the second, *Jack up Lande,* is of much less interest and may be disposed of in a few words. It is a fairly conventional indictment of the friars, but it does contain one very striking sentence which may go to the root of the strong resentment, felt among religious writers at least, against the friars: "And all men knowen wel that they ben not obedient to bysshoppes, ne lege men to kynges, nether they tyllen, ne sowen, weden, ne repen woode, corn, ne grasse, nether nething that men shuld helpe, but only hem selves her lyfes to susteyn." [209] This picture of the friars as a species of independent order in a society that was firmly coagulating is probably a much more important clue to their unpopularity than some of the charges more frequently preferred against them.

But the treatise abounds in the familiar objections. Why do they seek to bury the rich among them if they consider that they themselves are most holy because of their poverty? [210] The unidentified author, about whom we know nothing except that he is not Chaucer, attacks their begging,[211] their courting of the rich,[212] their charging for religious services,[213] their permitting their rich penitents to persist in their sins of lechery and oppression of their poor tenants [214] and concludes, not surprisingly, that they should be abolished for their sins of both commission and omission.[215]

The Plowmans Tale is a much more extensive undertaking. Like *Jack up Lande* it is certainly not by Chaucer, though it is clearly an effort to exploit the popularity of the *Canterbury Tales* in an imitation of many features of Chaucer's form and style. The author says he has said what he had to say about friars before in "a makynge of a Crede," [216] and there is nothing in the point of view or style of the two works to make it impossible that the same author is responsible for this poem and *Pierce the Ploughmans Crede.* At any rate the indebtedness to Langland is no less clear than to Chaucer, and though the spirit of the whole composition is not so alien to that of *Piers the Plowman* as to that of the *Canterbury Tales,* yet there are certain differences in fundamental point of view that make it just as remote from Langland's work as from Chaucer's. This is to be seen most clearly in a comparison between the pseudo-Chaucerian Plowman's attitude toward the place of the poor in society and that of Langland's Piers. The plowman of Langland is, as we have seen, bitterly critical of the wasters and the rogues who batten upon society, lay as well as clerical. On the other hand, he is quite willing to work to support the right kind of knight and the right kind of priest to do their work in society.[217] But in the pseudo-Chaucerian tale the resentment of the laborer against the idlers who take the best of everything at the expense of the man who lives by the sweat of his brow is focused almost exclusively upon the clergy. The plowman has just identified himself as one who earns his living by the sweat of his brow when he adds his complaint, "But we leude men bene full blynde," [218] and proceeds to complain that the clerks insist that the laity should work to support them, with the result that, "They have the corne and we the duste." [219]

The reaction of the host is perhaps the most Chaucerian touch of the first part of the tale, "What man quoth our host, canst thou preach." [220] The plowman accepts his challenge and begins his arraignment of the clergy. The world of his day he sees as a struggle between two groups of men, defined as follows:

> "That one syde is that I of tel
> Popes, cardynals and prelates
> Parsons, monkes, and freers fell
> Priours, abbotes of greate estates
> Of hevyn and hell they kepe the yeates
> And Peters successours they ben all
> This is demed by olde dates
> But falshed foule mought it befall
>
> The other syde ben poore and pale
> And people put oute of prease
> And seme caytyffes sore a cale
> And ever in one without encrease
> I clepeth lollers and londlese
> Who toteth on hem they bene untall
> They ben arayed all for the peace,
> But falshed foule mote it befall." [221]

He is particularly severe on the pride and splendor of the monks
for a reason that reminds the reader of *The Praier and Complaynte
of the Ploweman unto Christe.*[222] For he charges that they are
mostly of lowly origin and enter religion to better themselves
materially:

> "Had they ben out of relygion
> They must have hanged at the plowe
> Threshyng and dykinge fro towne to towne
> Wyht sory mete, and not halfe ynow
> Therfore they han this all forsake
> And taken to ryches, pryde, and ease
> And few for god woll monkes hem make." [223]

It is significant of a certain respect for the tradition of the church
that this author takes pains to point out that Saint Benedict would
not have had it so.[224] And the same respect is shown in what he
has to say of the Real Presence—Christ is there in the sacrament
as he was when in this life, and there is no need to dispute as to
just how he is there.[225] And something of the same unwillingness
to be regarded as going too far from tradition is to be seen in what
is said of the pope. The basic notions of the succession and the
power of the keys are attacked in moderately contemptuous
terms,[226] but when the Pelican, who may fairly be said to defend
what the author holds to be the truth, is accused of trying to raise
the people against the pope, he defends him by saying that he
does not despise the pope but hopes for the best in the way of
reform.[227] One possible direction which that reform may take is
suggested in one of the charges against the pride and power of the
higher clergy, namely, that they have more power in England than
the king and his law.[228] The king does not tax his people without
the assent of the commons, but the officers of the prelates do as
they wish.[229]

What all this probably amounts to is a pretty fair sample of a
transitional position in which the author now and then glances in
directions which he is probably not as yet entirely willing to take.
But whatever his disclaimers, there can hardly be any question
but that the author of *The Plowmans Tale* challenges the whole

church system in a very eloquent passage that raises the question as to how far he envisaged the possibility of extensive preaching by people like the plowman. It may well be that it is another form of his attack on the wealth of the clergy, but it should not be forgotten that the memory of the first poor fishermen called to the preaching of the gospel was to prove in later times one of the commonest defenses of the lay preachers and still later of the "mechanick" preachers. One wonders just how far the man who wrote the following would go:

> "Christ sente the poore for to preche
> The royall ryche he dyd nat so
> Now dare no poore the people teache
> For antichrist is over all her foe
> Amonge the people he mote go
> He hath bydden, all suche suspende
> Some hath he hente, and thynketh yet mo
> But all thys god may well amende." [230]

What is quite clear is that for this writer as for the authors of the Piers pamphlets and books we have been looking at, the social problem has been pretty much absorbed into the religious. It was therefore possible for the early seventeenth-century editor to present his work exclusively in terms of the attack on the church; indeed, the description on the title-page carries the anti-ecclesiastical bias to an extreme hardly justified by the contents of the book, "*The Plough-mans Tale.* Shewing by the doctrine and lives of the Romish Clergie, that the Pope is Anti-christ and they his Ministers." [231]

This absorption of the social issue into the religious is thoroughly typical of the later Piers literature. True, in those works that first appeared in the middle of the century, and in the notes and comments which sixteenth-century editors of the time appended to earlier works, there do occur, as we have seen, some signs of disappointment in the results of the execution of the program laid out in the foregoing books. The disestablishment of the monasteries, for instance, had created some fresh problems,[232] and new monopolizers of the nation's wealth had appeared in the places of the old,[233] but most of these writers seem to have had no misgivings. Presently we shall see that views very much like those which we have been summing up were widely shared by the preachers of the first half of the century and even later. One wonders if the writers of the anonymous tracts that we have been studying were clerics, likewise. If they were, their professional preoccupations would explain why the religious reforms desired seemed the paramount issue, why other sources of social relief were not more widely explored, why most social discussions came back to religious reformation.

CHAPTER II

THE UTOPIA AND COMMONWEALTH
TRADITION

THOUGH the most important, this religious tradition of social criticism was not by any means the only stimulus to deliberate and self-conscious social thinking in the sixteenth century. There is another, which though not of such immediate importance as the specifically religious, is yet of enduring and pervasive influence upon the thinking of the whole century. And that is the commonwealth tradition which, if not always stemming directly from *Utopia,* yet owes much of its occasion and direction to that work. To term it secular does not connote any opposition to the religious tradition which we are studying. It was by profession, and, so far as we can tell, by conviction, just as basically and thoroughly committed to the Christian orientation as the work of the religious writers of the time. But it was, on the whole, secular in the main preoccupations of its authors and in the motives of its consideration of contemporary problems. As we shall see, presently, it had other models in mind besides the social and economic organization of the primitive church, for its authors were aware not only of the admonitions of the Gospel but also of the speculations of Plato.

Particularly is this true of the work which may be taken as at once the fountainhead and the masterpiece of the tradition, Sir Thomas More's *Utopia.* Probably every great work of the human mind has in its time relations something of the trimurtic quality of those three-faced images of the Hindu trinity beloved of the Brahmanic artists. Certainly this is true in a preëminent degree of *Utopia.* It gathers up much of the medieval tradition which we

41

have been studying, not only in the basic allegiances of its author but, as we shall see, in its fundamental approach to the problems of the age. Yet it is at the same time one of the most characteristic manifestations of its own period, both in its eclecticism and in its emancipation. Finally, it is destined to become one of the most popular and one of the most persistent, though always incalculable, influences on the social speculation of the future. Like the *Piers Plowman* literature it may be regarded as a bridge over which some of the most stimulating ideas of the past carry into a new age. For though Thomas More's *Utopia* belongs by date of its completion to the year 1516, and by spirit and objective to the new learning which was at that time taking over the old medieval world, it still remains true that on certain key issues the author carries on the tradition of Langland.

Superficially, of course, no two works could be more unlike than *Piers the Plowman* and *Utopia*. The one is a prophetic work by a man whose main orientation is clerical, whatever the precise degree of his position in the ecclesiastical hierarchy of his time, and moral, and basically and profoundly religious. The genesis of the other work is much more complicated, and its precise purpose is still the subject of discussion. There can be no question that Langland in *Piers the Plowman* meant with profound earnestness and even literalness every detail and implication of his great vision. But there is still room for a good deal of uncertainty as to how much of the account of the strange new-world land of Utopia was intended as a picture of an ideal commonwealth such as the author's sixteenth-century editors, doubtless influenced by the acknowledged relation to Plato, took it for, and how much of it was a characteristic humanist jeu d'esprit. Probably not many will be found today to disagree with the late Professor R. W. Chambers' suggestion that it is not quite either but rather a construction in a sort of non-Euclidean social geometry.[1] One thing all of its students from that time to this will agree on, and that is that there can be no question of the seriousness of the criticism of his own age implicit in that dialogue between More and the returned traveler, Raphaell Hythlodaye. And it is that rather than the question of how far *Utopia* expresses More's idealism and how far his ingenuity, that is important for our first approach to this work that was to exert such a great influence on the thinking, if not the practice, of succeeding times.

Nothing better sums up the very different orientation of *Utopia* from that of the works we have been studying than the terms in which this dialogue is launched. The reporter of this new world kingdom was first presented to More by his friend Peter Gyles as a man who better than any other could satisfy More's known desire to hear tell of strange lands and peoples and ways of living.[2] That curiosity itself, to begin with, suggests not so much a medieval as a Renaissance attitude. It should be noted, too, that the opening of the dialogue in the travelers' meeting at Our Lady's Church in Antwerp [3] is managed with all the ease and sophistication for which More and his humanist friends were noted.

More represents this whole episode as coming to pass during a visit which he made to the Continent in the service of his King, and so it is not surprising that with the concerns of state-craft very much in his thoughts he should begin with the sug-gestion that such a man as his new friend ought likewise to be engaged in the business of kings.[4] This is the attitude one would expect from a man who accepts the framework of his world and tries to function within it. The reply of Hythlodaye shows al-ready a very different approach. He is not a part of the great world of his day; so he sees no prospect of so functioning. More-over, it is quite clear that he has no confidence in the fundamental values and purposes of that great world. Such is the clear purport of his disclaimer of his new acquaintance's suggestion, a dis-claimer made ostensibly on the ground that kings and princes are more interested in feats of war than in feats of peace.[5] His attitude is rather that of the philosopher or wise man who feels that he has the remedy of the world's ills, but that there is no prospect of anyone's listening to him. At the very outset his potential contribution is thus plainly defined as academic rather than prophetic. And this impression is reënforced by the present invocation of the name of Plato [6] and by various references to his authority and example.[7]

But Hythlodaye's approach to the problems of society is very different from Plato's, indeed, much more like that of Langland. For it is not only with the world's unreason that he is preoccupied, but, still more important, with the world's wrong. The first question he raises concerns a practical issue of More's own day, a question superficially of penology but basically of social value, the exploration of which leads to a probing of the foundations of contemporary society.[8] Again the approach is easy, suave, the usual reminiscence of contacts with a stranger's country leading to an account of the incident that sets off the whole dialogue. That is the discussion on penology supposed to have taken place long ago in the presence of More's own youthful patron, Cardinal Morton. In response to the lawyer who boasted of the severe penalties that had been enacted for the repression of stealing, Hythlodaye suggests that it would be better to provide a way in which thieves could honestly earn their living.[9] That precipitates a lively discussion as to the conditions which produce thieves.

More is very clear as to the reality of the plight of the victims of these conditions. There are people in the England of his day who have no honest way of earning their living. Some of them are the cast-off followers of idle gentlemen, who in the time of their prosperity never learned any proper way to earn their living. Then when their masters die, or they fall sick themselves, they are thrust upon a world that does not have any place for them. Nothing in the picture of the time is more specific, more compassionately imaginative than the description of their plight which More puts into the mouth of Hythlodaye: "When they have wandred abrode so longe untyll they have worne threde bare their apparell and also appayred their health, then gentlemen because of their pale and sicke faces and patched cotes wyll not take them into servyce."[10] On the other hand, the husbandmen in the country do not dare to offer them work, for they have obviously become accustomed to a more delicate way of life and can hardly be expected to weather the unaccustomed rigors of agricultural labor.[11]

But they are not the only victims of the economic ills of the time of whose plight More draws a compassionately lively picture. There are, also, the victims of the enclosures:

"For looke in what partes of the realme doth growe the fynyst, and therfore dearist woll, there noble men, and gentlemen; yea and certeyn Abbottes, holy men god wote, not contenting them selfes with the yearely revennues and profyttes that were wont to grow to theyr fore-fathers and predecessours of their landes, nor beynge content that they live in rest and pleasure nothyng profytyng ye muche noyinge the weale publique: leave no grounde for tyllage: they enclose all in pastures: they throw downe houses: they plucke downe townes, and leave nothing stondynge but only the churche to make of it a shepe-howse." [12]

So they who once lived in the vanished town are driven out on the world. If there were time, they might sell their scant household stuff for something, but, forced to dispose of it at once, they sell it for little or nothing.

"And when they have wanderynge about sone spent that, what can they els do but steale, and then justelye God wote behanged, or els go about a beggyng? And yet then also they be cast in prison as vaga-boundes, because they go about and worke not: whom no man will set a worke, though they never so willingly offer them selfes therto." [13]

It is this practical compassion that binds *Utopia* more closely to Langland than to Plato. And yet there are certain elements in which the orientation of *Utopia* is much closer to Plato, and here one is reminded of those friars of whom Langland complained, who went to the university in his day and plucked communism out of Plato to preach it through the countryside, doubtless to the confusing of the simple.[14] In his urging of Hythlodaye to service in some prince's council, More represents himself as quoting Plato's famous dictum that commonweals will have felicity only if philosophers be made kings or if the kings give themselves to the study of philosophy.[15] That citation is typical of the whole orientation of *Utopia*. It is the work of a man who believes in learning. The only people in his commonweal who have perpetual exemption from labor are the learned, and out of their order are chosen the ambassadors and the representatives, the priests and the magistrates, and finally the prince himself.[16] While Langland shows respect for learning, it will be remembered that he puts his final faith in the good husbandmen, not the clerk. But *Utopia* is the work of the intellectual par excellence. Even when it comes to pleasure, to which the Utopians certainly have no ascetic aversion, appreciating finely the delight of music and sweet odors and beautiful rites, still they "imbrace chiefly the pleasures of the mind." [17] And though the idea of lectures as an adult entertainment, like the pleasure of sermons, had not been so well-worn by the abuse of excess as in the intervening centuries since, still it remains true that only a thorough-going intellectual would conceive of the general population of any country getting up early day after day in order to listen to lectures before going off to their morning labors, just for the pleasure of it.[18]

Yet More expressly repudiates what he styles a school philosophy. For example, when Hythlodaye rebuffs his insistence on the necessity of philosophy to the affairs of kings by denying that it has any place in them, More agrees, with one important qualification:

"In dede (quod I) this schole philosophie hath not: whiche thinketh all thinges mete for every place. But ther is an other philosophye more cyvyle, whyche knoweth as ye wolde saye her own stage, and thereafter orderynge and behavynge herselfe in the playe that she hathe in hande, playethe her parte accordynglye wyth comlynes, utterynge nothynge owte of dewe ordre and fassyan." [19]

This recalls More's own dramatic pictures of the arguments over the penology of the time in the household of Cardinal Morton, with all the amusing touches that show his sensitive and amused perception of the way the world goes. There is, for instance, that delightful moment, when in the discussion of provision for vagabonds the Cardinal's jester has taunted the argumentative friar with the classic layman's jest as to the friars being the greatest vagabonds in the world. All the company watch to see how the Cardinal will take this very unecclesiastical joke, and then when they see that he is not going to disapprove of it, they all join in the laugh except the friar, whose loyalty to his order is much keener than his sense of humor.[20] It is the wisdom of the man of the world that is More's ideal.

And it should never be forgotten, of the man of the great world, of the world of the philosopher-statesman himself. Here, of course, More is closest to Plato and farthest from Langland. For More moves with obvious freedom in the sphere of the rulers of this world. He knows other spheres; he is not bound by this one, but this is the world out of which he approaches the problems of government. He knows the ambitions and the greeds of rulers, and though he thinks them foolish and ruinously costly, still he knows that they are to be reckoned with. So he raises the issues that will engage the rulers' interest and meet their decidedly this-world point of view. War,[21] the relations of kings and councils,[22] the stability [23] and the prosperity of kingdoms,[24] these are his preoccupation, as they are theirs. And he does this in no cynical spirit of accommodation but with full appreciation of the necessity of rule, and with sympathy for those who bear its responsibilities. With Hythlodaye he asks, "who be bolder stomaked to brynge all in hurlieburlie (therby trustyng to get sum wyndfall) then they that have nowe nothing to leese?" [25] This same spirit is revealed in the provisions for the maintenance of husbandry even at the expense of what to a later age would seem a good deal of commandeering of citizens' time and effort [26] and for the maintenance of the stability of crafts even at the expense of the family life which is the basis of his patriarchal social organization,[27] and, above all, in the discussion of the application of human energy in the analysis of the problem of the idle.[28] Even though these elements in the picture are expressly attributed to Hythlodaye, still the fullness and the zest with which they are worked out shows the statesman's concern for the order and the stability of the organized whole. The very practical amplification of ways and means modifies and gives reality to the academic speculation and underlines the statesmanlike character of the whole.

Again, it is the combination of the interests of the philosopher and of the statesman which prompts his emphasis on the need of education and open-mindedness to new ideas for social improvement. Indeed, Hythlodaye avers that the chief reason why the com-

monweal of Utopia is better governed than that of England is that
the Utopians are much quicker to learn from someone who does
something better than they do than are the English.[29] For though
one of the most striking features of life in Utopia is that only
a few of the citizens are exempted from the ordinary labors of
the community to devote themselves exclusively to learning, yet
all are given some learning,[30] and through a system of representatives all are given a share in the responsibility for the government.[31]
Furthermore, it is provided that the learned man who abuses
his exemption from the common lot of labor with idleness or lack
of serious application is sent back into the ranks while the handi-
craftsman who in his leisure devotes himself to learning with
conspicuous profit is admitted to the privileged leisure of the
learned.[32] This again underscores the notion of improvement as
against the rather static class conceptions of Plato. It is a point
of view, different again from Langland's, perhaps a notion not
possible for the times of either, though the socially flexible recruiting of the clergy may have had something to do with its
inspiration. The idea that the flexibility should work both ways
is an original touch of More's, one of many that pay tribute alike
to his flexibility of mind and his ingenuity.

But the central issue of *Utopia* both from the point of view
of its author and of its readers in succeeding generations is the
issue of communism. Here More sets forth expressly his obligation to Plato, who seems to have been an important fountainhead
for such ideas at least among intellectuals, throughout the Middle
Ages.[33] It is through the lips of Hythlodaye that More makes
this basic acknowledgment, significantly enough as a conclusion
drawn from the practical experience outlined above:

"Thies thynges (I say) when I consider with me selfe, I holde well
with Plato, and doo no thynge marveyll that he wolde make no lawes
for them that refused those lawes, wherby all men shoulde have and
enjoye equall portions of welthes and commodites. For the wise man
dyd easely forsee, that thys is the one and onlye waye to the wealthe
of a communaltye, yf equalytye of all thynges sholde be broughte in
and stablyshed. Whyche I thynke is not possible to be observed where
everye mans gooddes be proper and peculyare to him selfe. For where

everye man under certeyne tytles and pretences draweth and plucketh
to himselfe asmuch as he can, and so a fewe devide amonge themselfes
all the riches that there is, be there never so muche abundaunce and
stoore, there to the resydewe is lefte lacke and povertye." [34]

The superiority of the Utopian order to the European' in this
respect is revealed not only in the welfare of the individual, but in
the attention which the interests of the state as a whole received:
"Here where nothynge is pryvate, the commen affayres be earnestly
loked upon." [35]

So far the debt to Plato is clear. But as Hythlodaye proceeds,
he moves farther and farther from Plato. For instance, in what
Hythlodaye says of the disturbing effect of greed upon the commonwealth there is a respect for the poor and their relative value
in the total scheme of things, and a compassion for their sufferings, that is foreign to Plato. Here one is reminded of Langland,
though the actual tone of the passage is less idealistic, less mystical
in its basic orientation, and more practical than Langland:

"And for the moste parte yt chaunceth that thys latter sort is more
worthye to enjoye that state of wealth, than the other be: bycause
the rych men be covetous craftye and unprofytable. On the other parte
the poore be lowlye symple, and by their daily labour more profyt-
able to the common welthe then to them selfes. Thus I doo fullye
persuade me selfe, that no equall and juste distrybutyon of thynges
can be made, nor that perfecte wealthe shall ever be among men, onles
this propriety be exiled and bannished. But so long as it shal con-
tynew, so long shal remayne among the most and best part of men,
the hevy, and inevitable burden of poverty and wretchednes." [36]

It is this interest in the misery of the poor, this eloquence in the
voicing of their wrongs that gives to More's work a character
quite foreign to that of Plato, and much more like that of *Piers
the Plowman* and the Langland tradition. There is nowhere in
the Langland tradition to be found a sharper arraignment of the
injustice of which the poor are the victims than in what Hythlodaye has to say of the other nations in the world that do not
subscribe to communism:

"I forsake God, if I can fynde any signe or token of equitie and justice. For what justice is this, that a ryche goldsmythe or an userer, or to be shorte any of them, whyche other doo nothyng at all, or els that whiche they do is suche, that it is not very necessary to the common wealthe, should have a pleasaunt and a welthy lyvynge, other by Idilnes, or by unnecessary busynes? When in the meane tyme poore labourers, carters, yronsmythes, carpenters, and plowmen, by so great and continual toyle as drawyng and bearyng beastes be skant able to susteine, and agayn so necessary toyle that with out it no commen wealth were able to continewe and endure one yere, do yet get so harde and poore a lyving and lyve so wretched and miserable a lyfe, that the state and condition of the labouring beastes maye seme muche better and welthier. For they be not put to so contynuall laboure, nor theire lyvynge is not muche worse, yea to them much pleasaunter, takynge no thowghte in the meane season for the tyme to come. But thies seilie poor wretches be presently tormented with barreyne and unfrute-full labour. And the remembraunce of theire poore indigent and be-gerlye olde age kylleth them up. For theire dayly wages is so lytle that it will not suffice for the same daye, muche lesse it yeldeth any overplus, that may dayly be layde up for the relyefe of olde age." [37]

This is sharp enough, but still sharper is to come, a direct and personal arraignment of the rich oppressors for their part in the misery of the poor, that Langland had never surpassed for severity or completeness:

"And yet besides this the riche men not only by private fraud, but also by commen lawes do every day plucke and snatche away from the poore some parte of their daily living. So where as it semed before unjuste to recompense with unkindnes their paynes that have bene beneficiall to the publique weale, nowe they have to this their wrong and unjuste dealinge (whiche is yet a muche worse pointe) geven the name of justice, yea and that by force of a law." [38]

The conclusion of this indictment is an arraignment of the social order that has seldom been equalled by any but an anarchist or a leveller in the white heat of revolution. For a sober reflection of a responsible member of society it is hardly to be equalled in the Christian tradition of social protest, certainly in England:

"Therfore when I consider and way in my mind all thies commen wealthes which now a dayes anywhere do florish, so god helpe me, I can perceave nothing but a certain conspiracy of riche men procuringe theire owne commodities under the name and title of the commen wealth." [39] After so summary an impeachment of the prevailing social order of the day, the detailed amplification, in the familiarity of its details comes a little in the nature of an anticlimax: "They invent and devise all meanes craftes first how to kipe safely without feare of lesing that they have unjustly gathered together, and next how to hire and abuse the woorke and labour of the poore for as litle money as may be." [40]

The light of More's solicitude for the rights of the working man is turned upon the social hierarchy of the day with equally startling results. The fear of idleness was one of the commonest of the sociological fears of the time. As might be expected, one finds more concern about the idleness of the poor than of the rich, even though Langland had already insisted that every member of society must labor in his degree.[41] Hythlodaye approaches this delicate problem from a characteristically fresh angle. He has just been explaining how the citizens of Utopia produce all that is needed by six hours of labor apiece. Of course, he realizes that his auditors will be wondering how it is possible for such limited hours of labor to support all of the state in the comfort which he has already claimed for Utopia; so he assures his listeners that this brief working day is quite long enough when every citizen but the few exempt for public interest works at something for the common good.

To drive his point home he reminds his listeners how many citizens in other countries are really idle. Almost all the women, first of all (probably another example of the inability of man to count homemaking among the productive occupations of society). That is challenging enough, but more is to come: "Besides thys how great, and howe ydle a companye ys theyr of prystes, and relygyous men, as they call them?" [42] One of the familiar complaints of the time, as we have already seen, is this of the idleness of the monastic orders, but Raphaell follows it up with one with which, we may be sure, it was not generally associated, or the history of the succeeding period would have been very different, when he suggests that we

"put there to all ryche men, speciallye all landed men, whyche comonly be called gentylmen, and noble men. Take into this numbre also their servauntes. I meane all that flocke of stout bragging russhe bucklers. Joyne to them also sturdy and valiaunt beggers, cloking their idle lesse under the colour of some disease or sickenes. And truely you shall find them much fewer then you thought, by whose labour all these thynges be gotten, that men use and lyve bye." [43]

That is a fairly central attack on the foundations of society as it was known in More's day. True, it is attributed to Hythlodaye, and More takes it upon himself to rebut the argument in terms with which most of his contemporaries would have agreed:

"But I am of a contrary opinion (quod I) for me thynketh that men shal never ther lyve wealthelye, where all thynges be commen. For how can there be abundaunce of gooddes, or of any thing where every man with draweth his hande from labour? Whom the regarde of his owne gaines driveth not to woorke? and the hoope that he hath in other mens travayles maketh hym slowthfull." [44]

That is the strongest objection More offers.

This Hythlodaye receives courteously but points out that it is only natural that More, knowing no more of how the Utopians managed things, should think so. His real answer to More's inability to see how communism would work is his explanation of how it does work in Utopia.[45] But even when he has finished his account of life in Utopia, More still insists that he has his objections and that it was only out of consideration for Raphaell that he forbore to urge them at the time. It is significant that he goes on to explain that he disagreed "chieffely in that which is the principall fondacion of al their ordinaunces, that is to saye in the communitie of theire liffe and livinge, without anny occupieng of money, by the whyche thynge onelye all nobilitie, magnificence wourship honour and majestie, the true ornamentes and honoures as the common opinion is of a common wealth utterly be overthrowen and destroyed." [46]

This is about what most of his contemporaries would have said, and we may be sure that not many people would have seen any need of saying more. But nothing could be in sharper contrast with More's attitude than the usual disclaimer of any sympathy with communism as beyond the pale of a rational or godly man's attention, with which we are already familiar, and which with the passage of the century will grow shriller.

Still more significant is the fact that More does not at the time or later challenge the account which Hythlodaye and his companions seem to have given the Utopians of Christianity: "Howe be it I thynke this was no smal healpe and furtheraunce in the matter that they harde us saye that Christ instytuted amonge hys all thynges commen: and that the same communitie dothe yet remayne amongest the rightest Christian companies." [47] Of course, this was before the Kingdom of God at Münster, and before the dissolution of the monasteries. But certainly, the presentation of this key point without any effort to challenge it implies a very different attitude from that which actuated the passionate disclaimers of so many other orthodox Christian students of Plato. Still more is this true of the rather ambiguous close of the book that has so much puzzled More's readers ever since:

"In the mean time as I can not agree and consent to all thinges that he said, being els without dowte a man singularly well learned, and also in all wordely matters exactly and profoundely experienced, so must I nedes confesse and graunt that many thinges be in the utopian weal publique, which in our cities I may rather wisshe for then hoope after." [48]

Now the plainest sense of that passage is that More thinks that all this would be very nice if it were possible, but he does not see much chance of its being possible in the world he is familiar with. There are, however, a number of things to suggest that even that much of approval is not to be too lightly assumed. More was famous for his wit, and the fascination of that wit, as may be seen in the history of his work after its author's death, lingered long among men who had scant sympathy for the views More presumably held.

One of the most exhilarating qualities of the wit of More's time was its capacity for trying on points of view without any responsibility for rejection or adoption. It is one of the lasting qualities of wit of all time, no less apparent three-quarters of a century later in a scion of More's own family, though a man of a very different character, John Donne. More was a serious-minded lawyer, who took the responsibilities of his profession seriously, and, it should be added, did not do badly with its opportunities. But he has a number of gibes at the law and lawyers, of which the most telling is probably that there were so few laws in Utopia that every man could be his own effective lawyer,[49] a quite reasonable expression of what every lawyer in moments of weariness with the inevitable irrationalities of any profession must sometime have felt, but hardly to be taken as a serious suggestion for a program of reform.

Another evidence of the same light-hearted imaginative emancipation is to be seen in Raphaell's account of the religious position of the Utopians. That position is best to be described as midway between what the theologians conceived natural religion to be and what the deists of the seventeenth century turned to for a way out of the turmoil of controversy that religion in practice had too often become.

With not a few side glances at the classic controversies of the day, the religious position of the Utopians is defined as follows:

"But the moste and the wysest parte beleve that there is a certayne Godlie powre unknowen, everlastyng, incomprehensible, inexplicable, farre above the capacitie and retche of mans witte, dispersed through out all the world, not in bygnes, but in vertue and powre. Hym they call the father of all. To hym allone they attrybute the begynnynges, the encreasynges, the procedynges, the chaunges, and the endes of all thynges. Nother they gyve devine honours to any other then to him. Yea all the other also, though they be in divers opinions, yet in this pointe they agree all togethers with the wisest sort in belevynge that there is one chiefe and pryncipall God the maker and ruler of the hole worlde: whome they all commonly in theire countrey language call Mythra. But in this they disagre that amonge some he is counted one, and amonge some an other. For every one of them, whatsoever that is whiche he taketh for the chiefe God, thynketh it to be the very same nature, to whose onlye devyne myght and majestie the som and soveraintie of al thinges by the consent of all people is attributed and geven." [50]

There is no reason to believe that More was any more a deist when he wrote that passage than when he went to the scaffold. It is not so much the position that he takes on controversial issues as the approach that is important. That is rational, humane, and, again, in a larger sense statesmanlike. On those few doctrines on which he represented the Utopians as insistent, he yet emphasizes this basic point of view: "Though thies be perteyning to religion, yet they thynke it mete that they shoulde be beleved and graunted by profes of reason." [51]

That is at the root of all they have to say of what is the most practical preoccupation of religion:

"For they define vertue to be a life ordered according to nature, and that we be hereunto ordeined of god. And that he doth followe the course of nature, which in desiering and refusyng thynges is ruled by reason. Furthermore that reason doth chiefelie and pryncipallye kendle in men the love and veneration of the devyne majestie. Of whoes goodnes it is that we be, and that we be inpossibilitie to attayne felicite. And that secondarely it moveth and provoketh us to leade our lyfe out of care in joye and myrth, and to helpe all other in respecte of the sosiete of nature to obteyne the same." [52]

That is the platform of Christian humanism. The same spirit is responsible for the Utopian insistence on the immortality of the soul on the ground that to think that the soul could perish is to fail to do justice to its excellence and the importance of man, for King Utopus long ago charged them "that no man shoulde conceave so vile and base an opinion of the dignitie of mans nature as to thinke that the sowles do dye and perishe with the body." [53]

The only other dogmatic prescription of the easy-going Utopians is of the same order, namely the belief in Providence, for they stress that on the ground that they do not find it reasonable to believe that the world runs by chance.[54]

Now the interesting thing about one at least of these two points which the Utopians insist on, the immortality of the soul, is that their emphasis on this doctrine is the result of a quite different debate from that which has been agitating the Langland or the Langland-Chaucer tradition. That debate is neither Lollard nor pre-Protestant, neither Protestant nor Catholic. It would be rash to say it had nothing to do with the Reformation controversies, but it emphatically belongs to a different context, that of Renaissance speculation and scepticism. More was familiar with this dispute and took a decided position on it.[55] In other words, one at least of the two points on which the Utopians most insisted involved issues that belonged to a very different area of speculation from that which concerned most of the religious-social critics of this time and later.

On the actual controversies of his day, especially those which had become most intimately tangled with social speculation, the implications of *Utopia* are best to be described as moderate. It is significant, for instance, that on the controverted issue of the religious orders it is the custom of the Utopians that those who are most devoted to religion express their devotion by the undertaking of the most hard and mean service of their fellows. There is something of More's own spirit in what Hythlodaye says of the attitude of these zealots: "They nother reprove other mens lives nor glorye in theire owne." [56] And there is something of the same spirit of mediation in the position which the Utopians take on the vexed issue of celibacy.

Of what may be called their religious orders, one sect eschew marriage as they eschew all the pleasures of this life; the other sect marry and give up no pleasures that do not keep them from labor. "The Utopians count this secte the wiser, but the other the hollier." [57] As for the priests, they marry.[58] Probably the important point for More was that they were few in number and very carefully chosen.[59] And for the proper Utopian touch some of them were women, widows and old women.[60]

These are More's main contributions to the religious controversy of the day. Clearly, if one judge from nothing more than the relative proportions devoted to various subjects, More in *Utopia* was more interested in the social problems involved than the religious. And even when he did turn to the religious problems, the example of Utopia could hardly be regarded as encouraging to the controversial spirit of the day. Certainly, the story of the zealous convert who began to condemn all religions but his own new-found Christianity and was consequently exiled for sedition, was the kind of story that would make more of an appeal to the supporters of the status quo than to those who suddenly found themselves in possession of the one idea needed to save Christianity.[61] For King Utopus did not forget that the main reason for his easy conquest of the Utopians was the religious dissension which had prevailed in the island before his advent. He, therefore, left every man free to believe as his conscience directed him and gave him the right to try to persuade his neighbor peaceably to his opinion, but forbade all violence and contention even of a verbal nature.[62] Apparently he believed that if the discussion were managed in a reasonable and peaceable fashion, truth would come to light: "But if contention and debate in that behalfe shoulde continuallye be used, as the woorste men be moste obstynate and stubburne, and in theire evell opynion moste constante: he perceaved that then the beste and holyest religion woulde be troden under foote and destroyed by moste vayne superstitions, even as good corne is by thornes and weydes overgrowen and choked."[63] The only exception to this universal tolerance was the man who did not believe in an after-life, and he was forbidden to discuss his belief with anyone but the priests and the learned. He was thus discriminated against on the ground that he was not a safe citizen.[64]

Indeed, all of the Utopian handling of religion seems to be motivated more by a desire to assure the civic peace than any overwhelming passion for the immediate establishment of the one and only faith. It is hardly surprising, then, that the most passionately earnest sentences of the dialogue are devoted not to the condemnation of the contemporary religious order but to the arraignment of the social order. It would be, as we have seen, risky to assume that Hythlodaye spoke at any point for More. But the man who wrote some of those speeches of protest of Hythlodaye's had felt the impact not only of the world's unreason as had Plato but also the impact of the world's injustice as Plato had not and Langland had. In this More is the heir of the medieval preachers.

But it is also true that like those curates of whom Langland complained,[65] More had in his studies found Plato, and had turned to him for part at least of the answer to the world's wrong. Indeed, like the medieval communists he had found in Plato a realization of a neglected aspect of the Christian gospel; an aspect of the Christian gospel which men had not dared or cared to face. But there is one profund difference between More's approach to Plato and that of the medieval communists. The latter had taken Plato as a text for revolution, as a reënforcement of the latent and never entirely submerged social radicalism of the Christian tradition. It is not easy to tell how far the medieval communists intended to go. Langland, who was sensitive to the justice of their arraignment of what Christians had let Christian society become, clearly drew back from the violence he felt in their mob-raising and, sympathetic as he was with their demands for justice and mercy, he had clearly a very different objective from theirs. It is at this point that More is farthest away from the Middle Ages, most clearly of his own time.

For Langland in his vision, quite as much as the curates whose revolutionary agitation he feared, was driving toward a practical objective of individual and social reform. His was the prophet's call to action just as much as theirs was. But More's was not. His was a speculative suggestion, a free and emancipated discussion of basic principles, in which an idea the strength of which he clearly felt, whether or not he would ultimately decide for it, held for the time his extraordinarily flexible and ranging and ingenious mind. It was one of the distinctions of More's intellect that he could free himself from the hold of the existent world of his day and imagine what another world would be like, not completely, of course, but to an extraordinary degree. He could let his mind play with the possibilities opened up in this way with a moral and intellectual detachment impossible to, say, Langland. One has only to compare the latter's agonized wrestling with the problem of the good heathen [66] with More's casual exploration of the consequences of communism for the family,[67] to see the difference between the man for whom the intellectual possibility was almost a moral crisis and the man for whom it was the springboard to fresh speculation. This does not for a moment suggest that More was a man for whom the foundations of social life were only the playthings of speculation. But it was possible for More to let his mind so play about a subject as it was not possible for Langland. In other words, one was a medieval prophet, the other a Renaissance philosopher and wit, at least so far as this work is concerned. For all its passion of sympathy and arraignment, *Utopia* is no more a revolutionary manifesto than the *Republic* or the *Laws* of Plato. But there is an intellectual challenge to the mind of man in it that on its smaller scale is no less haunting than that of the *Republic*.

That this is the right moral and intellectual estimate of the *Utopia* is, I think borne out by the very title of the first English translation from More's Latin which Raphe Robynson, citizen and goldsmith of London, published "at the procurement, and earnest request of George Tadlowe Citezein and Haberdassher of thesame Citie," in 1551. The title is "A Fruteful and Pleasaunt Worke of the Beste State of a Publyque Weale, and of the Newe Yle called Utopia." Robynson is modest about his own excellent version but assures the reader that anyone who goes to the original Latin will find delight in "the swete eloquence of the writer, and al so in the wittie invencion, and fine conveiaunce, or disposition of the matter: but most of all in the good, and holsome lessons, which be there in great plenty, and aboundaunce." [68] The book was dedicated to Cecil whom Robynson claimed for an old schoolfellow.[69] And as the sponsor of such an undertaking might have been expected to do when presenting the work of a man who had been beheaded by the father of the reigning sovereign to "one of the twoo principal secretaries" [70] of that sovereign, Robynson expresses his regret that a man of such parts as More could not, or rather would not, see the light on some of the essential issues of the faith but obstinately persevered in error to the very death.[71] But though it is clear that Robynson was definitely not of the opinion of the Utopians that it is not within any man's power to believe just because he wants to believe,[72] still he expressed his admiration of More's parts so generously and his condemnation of his stubbornness so regretfully that one can but sympathize with the delicacy of his position.

That, however original, *Utopia* was not in its basic interest a unique phenomenon is to be seen in another treatise of the commonweal of roughly the same period, certainly composed some time before 1535, for a reference to the pope's "shavelinges in this Realm" in the body of the text [73] dates it before the suppression of the monasteries. It is an anonymous work, published by Anthony Scoloker without any date under the significant title of *The Prayse and Commendacion of Suche as Sought Comen Welthes: and to the Contrary, the Ende and Discommendacion of Such as Sought Private Welthes.* A straightforward exhortation, it has yet something of the eclectic character of *Utopia* and of the humanism of the time, for on the title-page, it acknowledges its sources: "Gathered both out of the Scripture and Phylozophers." [74] Stoic in its mainsprings rather than Platonic, it is an interesting blending of Greek civic spirit, of Roman pride in manly simplicity, and Christian contempt for the perishable goods of this world. At the top of his table of contents the unknown author has put a sentence of Epicurus: "Yf a man having goods in aboundaunce, do not repute it suffycyente, he is but a wretche and a catyfe, although he were lorde over the whole worlde." [75] In his development of the theme of the folly of covetousness the author then proceeds to draw upon Ovid, Bede, Vincent of Beauvais, and Ecclesiasticus for support in a single brief page.[76] Then he reminds those who have devoted their efforts to the seeking of their own private wealth rather than the common wealth of what "Saynct James in the second chapt. of his Epistle sayth: harken my dere beloved brethern: Hath not God chosen the poore of this woorlde, which are ryche in fayth, and are heyres of the kingdome whiche he promised to them that love him?" [77] This is certainly a note in the old Piers Plowman tradition. So is his indictment of the rich as those who oppress the poor and draw them before judges, and his bitter prayer, "Wolde to God that in these dayes men wolde be as carefull for their pore brethern, as they are for their dogges," a prayer which he documents by citing the sums which the city of London is willing to spend on dogs when they will not give for the succor of the poor.[78] He even goes so far, with the help of a saying of Marcus Aurelius, as to suggest that it is the higher powers who are to blame.[79]

In the manner of the Piers Plowman tradition he attacks the luxurious display of the bishops and tells a good story at the expense of the pope and his cardinals, having for its point the classical contrast between the splendor of the present heads of the church and the poverty of the apostles,[80] from which he draws the appropriate conclusion:

"Wherefore the pope nor hys cardynalles, neyther yet his shavelinges in this Realme, no nor yet unsaciable covetous men which seke private welthes to the decay of the commen weale, unles they repent, may not entre into heaven, although they beare the name of Christians, neyther yet may they be compared to the famous gentyles which sought fame in this woorlde, in spending their goods and adventuring their parsones for the comen weale, of which sorte Marcus Aurelius was one." [81]

But unlike the writers of the later Piers Plowman tradition this author goes on to take up the delinquencies of the royal officials, certainly the most lay and worldly of offenders. For after he has recounted how Marcus Aurelius used to check up on the way his officials treated his subjects, he delivers a direct challenge to the administration of his own time and country:

"Lorde, if in this Reame the kinges majestie wold appoynt but a faythfull counseller to go thorow this Realme, thinke ye there wolde be no complayntes? yes, yes, to many, God amend it. I dare not wryte for offendinge: But this dare I wryte, that, if dyvers officers within this realme shulde shewe their accountes from yere to yere how they have gotten their goods, as marchauntes maye do, it shulde be founde that it were no marvayle though the Kinges majestie lacked money, and his pore comons complayne." [82]

But this practical and timely consideration yields to the contemplation of a series of Gentile models of public-spirited poverty and simplicity, principally Roman, who have sought the common well-being rather than private prosperity.[83] From them he turns to consider the fates of those "which have so loved the world," [84] and from that theme the treatise plunges into the large and gloomy contemplation of the vanity of the world's splendor,[85] on which classical note it ends. Probably composed not much, if any later, than *Utopia* itself, it is an interesting blending of all the streams of social criticism and social reflection current at the time, except, perhaps, it should be admitted, that new world note that is so impressive in *Utopia*. In spite of its emphasis on the common wealth as distinguished from the private wealth, much of it is concerned with the question of the relations between the Christian and the world, a topic related to but by no means inseparable from the question of the Christian and society, a topic which had been the stuff of innumerable medieval sermons and was to be a favorite topic of innumerable sixteenth- and seventeenth-century discourses.

A further evidence of the interest of the first third of the century in discussion of the commonwealth is afforded by a work which though completed in 1538 was not published until almost our own day, the famous *Dialogue* of Thomas Starkey.[86] In one sense this book hardly belongs in this chapter, because it is the work of a cleric, supposedly reporting a series of discussions between two other clerics. But as regards the content of those discussions, it does. For in certain important respects this book may be regarded as an evidence, albeit indirect, of the influence of More's work. There are a good many respects in which the later work recalls the earlier. To begin with, it is a dialogue, and a dialogue between a man of experience and competence in large affairs of state, Cardinal Pole, and a scholar, Thomas Lupset, "Lecturer in Rhetoric at Oxford," and Chaplain to the King. There is no need for our purposes of inquiring into the extent to which the views attributed to Cardinal Pole are his or an expression of the author's. The history of the two men would suggest the former. For our purposes it is enough to note that Starkey like More was familiar enough with the great world to know whereof he spoke. Like More he had been in the service of the king,[87] though his service brought him neither the honor nor the disaster which it brought More. And this was altogether fitting, for Starkey's career suggests that he was not so much a reformer as a conformer. But what remains of his work shows that his claims to be a friend of the humanist Pole were justified,[88] for there are many evidences of humanist interest and temper in the dialogue.

A good example is to be found in the speech almost at the beginning in which Lupset urges Pole to consider the state of the commonweal, especially that sentence in which he pleads that "though hyt be so that lernyng and knolege of nature be a plesaunt thyng, and a hye perfectyon of mannys mynd and nature, yet yf you sundurly compare hyt wyth justyce and pollycy, undowtedly hyt ys not to be preferryd therto as a thyng rather to be chosen and folowyd." [89] This emphasis on practical statesmanlike action is, as we have seen, typical of More's point of view. So is the rational empiricism of Pole's approach to the problem of theft, reminiscent of More's own approach to the very same problem. For when Lupset asks Pole what is to be done for theft and treason, Pole replies that to remove the cause is the way to find the remedy.[90] He would not hang the thief, but rather put him to work for the common good.[91]

This practicality of approach is, however, carried further than in More, or, rather, it is accompanied by a distaste for speculation, a want of faith in the value of speculation perhaps, that is quite foreign to More's temper. This is especially true of those speeches attributed to Lupset. Quite early in the dialogue he alludes to Plato's commonweal, observing that no people could attain to it, and therefore it is reputed of many people to be only a dream.[92] And later on, when Lupset suggests that there is no use looking for such heads of the state as Plato describes, for they are not likely to be found, Pole agrees with him, suggesting that he will be content if they can find men who will put the common good before anything else.[93]

Indeed, the interest of the *Dialogue* is much narrower and more specialized than that of either the *Republic* or *Utopia*. Neither Starkey's Pole nor his Lupset is interested in the more speculative reaches of Plato or More. Both of the participants in the discussion are too much preoccupied with the ills of the England they know, and the specific remedies for them for that. In general, one may say that Lupset is more inclined to dwell on the social and

economic ills of the time, and Pole on the political and governmental.[94] There is probably more of complaint in Lupset, and
more of device for remedy in Pole, as one might expect from their
respective ranks in society.

On most issues, Pole is more complacent about the existing
order than More. For instance, although he admits that the present
state of Christendom is not perfect, he regards Christendom as
the best form of society that has been established among men.
Perhaps it should be added that the main ground for this opinion
is that Christendom helps its members to the attainment of eternal
life,[95] an opinion with which, when based on such grounds, More
could hardly have quarreled, though his agreement would probably have been more qualified. Certainly, More would hardly have
made the concessions to the existing order which Pole did when
he defined the public weal as "ryches and convenyent abundaunce
of al wordly thyngs, mete to the mayntennance of every mannys
state, accordyng to hys degre." [96]

One of the most interesting points at which the thoroughly
clerical Starkey-Pole agrees with the lay More is in criticism of
the existing order in the church, particularly the monasteries.
Like More he is distressed by the number of idle and unsuitable
people among priests, monks, friars, and canons.[97] But he does not
any more than More want to see the abbeys abolished. He wants
to see them reformed. His ideas of the direction which reform
should take are very much like More's. He would not have young
men in them at all. Only men who are really moved by religion
to flee the world would be admitted.[98] His contribution to the
vexed subject of clerical wealth is similar as may be seen in his
suggestions for the disposition of the wealth of the bishops. For
remedy he invokes the provisions of "the commyn law of the
Church . . . that byshoppys schold dyvyde theyr possessyonys
in iiij partys to the use appoyntyd by the authoryte of the law: the
fyrst to byld churchys and tempullys ruynate in theyr dyocesys; the
second to manteyne the pore youth in study; the thryd to the pore
maydys and other poverty; and the ferth to fynd hymselfe and hys
household wyth a mean nombur convenyent to hys dygnyte." [99]

Pole's attitude toward social and economic matters is represented as on the whole much more conservative than More's. He draws almost as graphic pictures of the sufferings of the age, but his whole attitude is different. He gives some very vivid glimpses of the agricultural penury and desolation of the time,[100] but he finds the idleness in the land a greater sickness even than the want of people.[101] Here his attitude is more like that of Langland than of the later sixteenth- and seventeenth-century writers on idleness, for he condemns not only the idle plowmen and crafts-men,[102] and the idle religious, but even more vigorously the idle rout which nobles and bishops and prelates keep in their houses. Indeed, he goes so far as to estimate that a third of the people are living in idleness.[103]

But his attitude on some other economic matters is distinctly more of his time, even more sophisticated than that of most preachers of the latter half of the century. What he has to say on the theme of enclosures is a good example. For Pole defends en-closures on the ground that the land must have cattle for food and sheep for wool, and that these needs cannot be met without pastures,[104] thus giving the arguments of pasture-men a much more sympathetic hearing than they usually received at the hands of writers on the theme of the commonwealth. Much the same atti-tude is apparent in what Pole has to say on the much-mooted theme of the spiritual prospects of the rich: "And lyke wyse wordly felycyte and prosperouse state in thys lyfe present, ex-cludyth not man from the most hye felycyte of the lyfe to come, but rather, yf he use hyt wel, hyt ys also a mean wherby he the bettur may attayne to the same." [105]

But vivid as are many of the glimpses of the troubles of the time in the dialogue, the chief interest of Pole is clearly in govern-ment. As he sees it, the main purpose of the dialogue is to "serch out the commyn errorys, fautys, and defectys in our polytyke rule." [106] The conception of the state that underlies the whole dialogue is actually put into words by Lupset when he says that "hyt ys not to be dowtyd but the cyvyle lyfe ys a polytyke ordur of man conspyryng togyddur in vertue and honesty, of such sort as by nature ys convenyent to the dygnyte of man." [107] This is traditional enough, but there is a distinctly humanist touch to the terms in which Pole defines the national welfare, when he concludes that "a cuntrey, cyte, or towne, hathe hys commyn wele and most perfayt state, when fyrst the multytude of pepul and polytyke body ys helthy, beutyful, and strong, abul to defend themselfys from utward injurys: and then plentuously nuryschyd wyth abundance of al thyngys necessary and plesaunt for the sustentatyon and quyetnes of mannys lyfe,—and so, thyrdly, lyve togyddur in cyvyle ordur, quyetly, and peasybly passyng theyr lyfe, ych one lovyng other as partys of one body, every parte dowyng hys duty and offyce requyryd therto." [108]

As for the best means of securing the government that will assure this happy state, Pole insists on two things. On the first, Sir Thomas More like most of the men of his time would have agreed with Pole when he pleaded for public spirit: "Overmuch regard of pryvat and partycular wele ever destroyth the commyn, as mean and convenyent regard therof maynteynyth the same." [109] Devotion to the public interest was not so common a thing in that day but it might well be urged by a man of large mind. The second contribution of Pole is more original, and to this More could hardly have agreed. True, he would not have quarreled with Pole when he found the cause of all the ills of the time in tyranny, though we may be sure he would not have thought it proper to say so. [110] But he would hardly have agreed with Pole when he said that it "is in mannys powar, to electe and chose hym that ys both wyse and just, and make hym a prynce, and hym that ys a tyranne so to depose." [111] That is one of the most distinctive contributions of Starkey's Pole to the discussion of the commonwealth of the time.

Again, it is not easy to tell how much of this discussion should be attributed to the men who are named as participants in the dialogue, and how much to the author. But in either case it is surely not too fanciful to see in the personal experience of both men reasons for the reflections on tyranny. The remedy, the deposition of the tyrant was at hand in the traditional scholastic discussion of the subject. [112] And the better hope, though, as we have seen, Pole was not sanguine enough to think they stood any chance of getting the sort of heads which Plato described, was clearly influenced by Plato's suggestion.[113] For Pole rejected the accepted principle of succession and declared in favor of the election of the prince as among the Romans and the Lacedemonians.[114] Pole expressly said that he was not suggesting that the principle of succession, established as it was, was not the better at the present time for the prevention of discord and confusion, but he made it quite clear that that was not the best thing in principle.[115] And he returned so often to the theme that election was the best way to secure the kind of prince who would put the good of the realm before everything else [116] that there is no mistaking his preference. From first to last Pole declares for the "myxte state" with the laws having the chief authority, and the authority of the prince "temperyd and brought to ordur," if not by the old device of the Constable of England, then by a council headed by the Constable to protect the liberty of the whole realm.[117]

While the great influence of *Utopia* was to become apparent in the next century, there is abundant evidence of its popularity in England very shortly after its composition. And this early influence is especially interesting because it affords such striking evidence of the essential character of the book for the liberal-minded intellectual. The work which affords the most interesting and the most varied illustration of this influence was probably composed before Raphe Robynson's English translation had appeared at all, when *Utopia* was still known to the reading public only in its Latin form. It is *A Discourse of the Common Weal of this Realm of England,* generally believed now to be the work of John Hales and to have been composed originally in 1549, though it does not appear to have been published until William Stafford offered it as his own in 1581.[118]

There are, to begin with, direct references to *Utopia* in the text. For instance, the Doctor points out that we cannot control the outside value of our money, "except we weare in suche a countrie as Eutopia was imagined to be, that had no traffique with anie other outwarde countrie." [119] And there are many verbal resemblances, as Miss Lamond, the nineteenth-century editor of the work notes, between it and the first book of *Utopia*.[120] But the most important relations are in general scope and technique and spirit. To begin with, the work takes the form of a dialogue, more significantly than in More's choice of figures to speak or be present, between five men highly representative of the life of the time, a Merchaunte, a Husbandman, a Capper (or craftsman), a Doctor, who, it has been suggested by Miss Lamond, may be Latimer,[121] and a Knight, generally taken to represent Hales himself. This distribution of characters at once gives a certain dramatic and practical tone to the work, and, it should be added, a homelier one than that of the chance-met travelers of More's Antwerp with their recollections of the household of Cardinal Morton and their tales of the strange new world. The fact that all the classes of society principally involved in the social disputes of the time are represented gives a certain functional seriousness to the work from the very start. But the very fact that it starts out as a discussion of the griefs of the time from the point of view of each class,[122] while it puts the whole work on a more immediately practical level than that of *Utopia,* still deprives Hales' book of the tight-clenched effectiveness of that discussion on the hanging of thieves that opens the earlier dialogue.

Indeed, Hales' book is essentially a discussion of what was wrong with the time rather than a philosophic speculation as to the bases of society. This is clear from the questions with which he opens his preface: "First, what thinge men are greived with, then what should be the occasion of the same. And that knowen, howe suche greifes may be taken awaye; and the estate of the common weale reformed agayne." [123] Not surprisingly in view of this approach, the remedies which he proposes prove to be limited practical reforms rather than the sweeping reversals of the world's ways suggested in the free-ranging speculations of *Utopia.* Part of this is due, of course, to the fact that the personal circumstances which the two writers face are, in spite of certain basic resemblances, so fundamentally different. Both are men of large affairs, involving the public interest. More has just been serving on an embassy, Hales on a royal commission for dealing with a pressing social problem. But the preoccupations of war and peace with which More has been dealing figure only incidentally in his book, while Hales deals directly and mainly with the problem of economic well-being with which he has been recently concerned. There is a corresponding difference in the temper and spirit of the two works. Hales writes with a sense of urgency which we know from other sources has a substantial personal basis. His commission had been blamed for stirring up trouble in disaffected quarters; so he is at considerable pains to establish the underlying causes of the restlessness with which he has been seeking to cope.[124] He is dealing with an emergency, and one feels that. Actually the preoccupations of More's treatise are profounder and the sensitivity to the world's ancient woe sharper, but the occasion is more general, and the approach to the problem more leisurely and disengaged. This is a key difference between the two dialogues.

On the other hand, there is very little in Hales of the sharp impersonal pity of More's treatise. The bitter cry of the poor almost never breaks through Hales' lively and dramatic but confident and competent lines. Yet his discussion has its own distinctive excellence, and that is the expression of the reactions of the various classes of society, especially of those less intellectual classes whose feelings, because of their very inarticulateness, are usually ascertainable only in the reflected assumptions of their not always too understanding intellectual mentors and leaders. Two examples are especially interesting in view of the part which religious controversy played in the history of the period. The first is a speech of the Capper, who may be taken to represent the substantial and prosperous and by no means uninfluential class of successful craftsmen of the time. The Doctor has just been expatiating on the actual shortcomings of the supposedly privileged status of the clergy. They have lost some of their sources of income, and, after all, they need support. Especially he insists that their labor is not to be underestimated by the layman, for the labor of the mind leaves the body feeble.[125] But the Capper is not to be put off so easily from the traditional suspicion of the man who works with his hands of the reality of the labors of the mind. He has his remedy ready for the debilitating effects of scholarship: "I would set youe to the plowghe and carte." [126] That is an ancient remedy not unknown to some of the medieval social reformers who held that all men would be better off if they worked with their hands.[127] But the Capper goes on to explain his specific in terms that would probably be possible only in an age of bitter religious strain in which a good many men who were prepared to be good citizens in the spiritual realm found themselves called upon to put all their more pressing personal interests to the jeopardy of debates which had little meaning to them. There must have been many an honest heathen among the professed Christians of the day to echo the Capper's taunt:

". . . the devell a whit the good doe ye with youre studies, but set men together by the eares. Some with this opinion and some with that, some holdinge this waye and some that waye, and some an other, and that so stiffly as thoughe the truthe must be as they saye that have the upper hande in contention. And this contention is not the least cause of theise uprors of the people; some holdinge of the one learninge and some holdinge of the other. In my mynde it made no mattier yf theare weare no learned men at all." [128]

Another example of the same man-in-the-street reaction is to be seen in the Knight's contribution to the subject of the sins of the clergy. The Doctor has just been doing what so many of his cloth seem to have done generously at that period, repenting at large of the sins of his profession and offering them up as the chief cause of the troubles of the time. But the Knight very sensibly cuts him short by pointing out that the clergy have had enough punishment for their delinquencies to satisfy anyone.[129] There is something in the Knight's brusque matter-of-factness that suggests that the self-conscious reformer may a little have exceeded the normal appetite for penance. The Doctor, however, is not discouraged but proceeds with excellent vigor and lucidity to elaborate on what one may call the administrative problems of the church of the time.[130]

In basic social philosophy, the dialogue of Hales is as far from that of More as might well be. The Knight whose opinion may to some extent represent that of the author quotes with approval an old saying that "that which is possessed of manie in common, is neclected of all." [131] And he gives a turn to the theory of the relations of the individual and the common weal that is very different from that of *Utopia* and that is going to have great consequences for the material development of the age when he quotes with approval the opinion that "everie man is a member of the common weale, and that that is proffitable to one maie be proffitable to another, yf he would exercise the same feat." [132] But the Doctor has more reservations on the theory of individual profit, qualifying his agreement that "that thinge which is proffitable to eche man by him selve, (so it be not prejudiciall to anie other,) is proffitable to the whole common weale, and not other wise; or els robbinge and stelinge, which percase is proffitable to some men, weare profitable to the whole common weale, which no man will admitt." [133] And when the Knight in the discussion of the methods of the landholders of the time asks, "Who can let them to make the most advauntage of that which is theire owne," the Doctor objects at once: "Yes, marie; men may not abuse theire owne thinges to the dammage of the common weale; yet for all this that I se, it is a thinge most necessarie to be provided for." [134]

Indeed, in general, the Doctor serves as a restraining influence on the aggressive spirit of secular enterprise, as represented by the spokesmen of the other classes. He is interested in the preservation of the theory of the matter as in the above discussion, but more especially he is concerned with the human elements involved in the rush for material development. When, for instance, the Capper as the representative of the craftsmen of the town objects to a scheme for the raising of the price of corn on the ground that every man has need of corn as he does not have of other things, the Doctor retorts: "Therfore the more necessarie that corne is, the more be the men to be cherished that rered it." [135] But in spite of all this the Doctor is as far from the communism of *Utopia* as the Knight himself. On the subject of the use of money, a topic which has often tempted the imaginations of the unworldly religious, the Doctor is cautious: "Thoughe it be commendable in some private man, for contemplacions sake, to set a side as muche as he maye well use of oure money, it is not necessarie for the common wealthe that all men should doe so, no more then [for

all men to be virgines], thoughe privately in some it is commendable." [136] This moderation of spirit is of a piece with the Doctor's
acceptance of the Knight's protest that not all enclosures are to
be condemned and the Doctor's restriction of his condemnation
to such landlords as turn arable fields into pasture and make
violent enclosures.[137]

This same moderation or caution extends to what the Doctor
has to say on religious topics, an important matter in view of the
proportion of the treatise that is devoted to them. It is true that,
like Latimer, he is sympathetic with the Reformation movement
so far as it has progressed in the official England of his time. There
is no question, for instance, that he looks to the civil power for
the correction of ecclesiastical abuses. But it is equally clear that
he already has very definite misgivings inspired by what has happened in the confiscation of monastic property: "I praye god send
oure magistrates temporall the mynde to reforme theise thinges
with their seculer powre, and to studie for the reformation of
theim, rather then for theire possessions." [138] Indeed, he is aware
that the opportunities of learned men for preferment, even for
necessary support, are worse than they were, and that the hazards
of his profession have been increased: "Marie, have youe not sene
how manie learned men have bene put to trouble of late, within
these xij or xvj yeares, and all for declaringe theire opinions in
thinges that have risen in controversie?" [139]

That might suggest that the Doctor had been alarmed by the
restrictions which the conservatism of the reign of Henry VIII
had imposed on the more advanced Protestants, but there is much
in the essay to suggest quite the contrary. Indeed, the resemblance
between the Doctor's position and that of Latimer is nowhere
stronger than at this point. For the Doctor complains that in the
science of divinity "everie boy that hathe not redde scripture past
halfe a yeare shalbe suffered not only to reason and inquire
thinges, (for that weare tollerable,) but to affirme new and straunge
interpretations uppon the same never heard of before. What end
of opinions can theare be while this is suffered?" [140] And eager as he
is to have the magistrates undertake the reform of ecclesiastical
administration, he is alarmed at the behavior of laymen who

finding the clergy not living up to their professions take upon themselves, "the judgement of spirituall thinges, to whome it dothe not appertayne." [141]

On the other hand, it should not be forgotten that the Doctor, for his part, plunged with gusto into the discussions of international trade and made his due share of practical suggestions.[142] That is, after all, in keeping with the spirit of the treatise with its emphasis on the practical solution of practical problems within the existing framework of church and state, with its emphasis on the necessity of doing justice to the various classes in society, and its general devotion to order and prosperity. Its judicious moderation has much in common with the spirit of More's dialogue, but its basic point of view is very different, and so are its objectives, literary and philosophical.

All this becomes more clearly apparent in the form in which, so far as we know, the work first enjoyed wide circulation in the sixteenth century. In 1581 a W. S., Gentleman, generally assumed to be William Stafford, brought out this work as his own under the title of *A Compendious or Briefe Examination of Certayne Ordinary Complaints, of Divers of Our Country Men in These Our Dayes.*[143] Though probably not unique for the time, this outright appropriation of another man's work is audacious enough in itself. But under the circumstances described in the dedicatory epistle which W. S. addressed to Queen Elizabeth he must have had a devotion to the cause of social complaint not common in his age, or a calculated impertinence that was even more remarkable. For W. S. would seem to have been already in trouble on suspicion of disturbing the peace, and to have got off rather better than he had any reason to hope for. So as a token of appreciation of the Queen's clemency, if we are to believe his dedicatory letter, he has undertaken to set forth the complaints of the time. The address takes a highly philosophic as well as unimpeachably loyal tone, especially in its beginning: "*Whereas there was never anye* thinge hearde of in any age past hetherunto, so perfectly wrought and framed, eyther by Arte or Nature, but that it hath at some time, for some forged and surmysed matter, sustayned the reprehension of some envious persons or other: I doe not much mervayle most mighty Pryncesse that in this your so noble and famous a government, (the Glory whereof is now longe sithence scattered and spread over the whole face of the Earth,) there are notwithstanding certayne evill disposed people, so blinded with malice, and subdued to their owne parciall Conceiptes: that as yet they can neyther spare indifferente judgements to conceyve, or reverent tongues to reporte a known truth, touching the perfection of the same." [144]

But though Stafford in his address professes to answer the criticisms,[145] he does not give much evidence of any desire to soften the effect of the specific complaints which he prints. Indeed, though to a critical eye some of them might seem a little out of date, they have the surface plausibility of the conventional social complaint, in which the resentment at a specific social abuse often survives its actual menace. He does make some rather incomplete gestures at bringing the complaints up to date, notably in the discussion of the coinage,[146] but on the whole Hales' complaints are left substantially as Stafford found them when he appropriated the work without troubling to give any account of its provenience. By and large the persistence of the same or similar complaints in the sermons of the time, as we shall see presently, would make it seem reasonable that this effort should pass relatively unchallenged. After all, the social critic like the preacher deals too much with the enduring elements in individual and social experience to be troubled by the problem of topical exactness and contemporaneity. It is not surprising, therefore, that Stafford's unacknowledged appropriation should have gone through at least three editions within the year of its first appearance.

Another work of the same period that in spite of its preoccupations with the question of government, yet gave a good deal of attention to the social structure of society, especially as it is involved in the relation of the individual effort to the common weal, is a treatise on vocations, published in 1578 under the English title, *Politique Discourses, treating of the Differences and Inequalities of Vocations, as well Publique, as Private.*[147] This was described as a translation from the French by the author, a lay gentleman, one Aegremont Ratcliffe, who addressed his work to Sir Francis Walsingham. The key to the enterprise is to be seen in what Ratcliffe has to say of his own time and the restlessness thereof:

"For, who ever sawe so many discontented persons: so many yrked with their owne degrees: so fewe contented with their owne calling: and such a number desirous and greedie of change, and novelties? Who ever heard tel of so many reformers, or rather deformers of estates, and Common weales: so many controllers of Princes, and their proceedinges: and so fewe imbracing obedience?" [148]

A passage like this has back of it, however, something more than a reaction to the restlessness of a period of rapid social change. One can see at work in it a reaction to the reforming spirit itself. This is, in part, perhaps due to weariness, but still more to a belief that the fecundity of the time in public changes is not sufficient, that some stabilizing effort is needed. There is a good deal in Ratcliffe's unknown French source to meet this need for stability. For the French author like so many of the English writers of the time is anxious to stem the tide of ambition that is characteristic of the new age and to encourage men in the lower ranks of society to take pride in the possibilities of satisfaction within their own degree, in other words, to be contented with their proper vocation. [149] The fact that this effort to secure social stability is joined to a fully-developed theory of a governing class, we may be sure, only commended it the more to the established England of the time.

Yet the French author, or his English translator, in several respects recalls the point of view of Sir Thomas More. Ratcliffe in his dedicatory letter draws alike upon Seneca and that "coelestiall Philosopher, and moste blessed Apostle Saint Paule" for the theory of vocation. [150] And so does his French original. Indeed, he takes what Plato has to say of his communal idea perhaps more seriously than any English writer of the time after More. Far from elaborating a defensive disclaimer, he uses Plato for the springboard of what is practically his culminating appeal:

"And this union, and mutuall commerce of men, saith *Plato*, is so allowed of, as that it is impossible to devise or imagine a more assured

Commonweale, and neerer approaching to the immortalitie of the Gods, then the same wherein there is a Commonaltie, and union, not onely of all goodes, but also of each thing that nature hath appropriated to ech one: as of the eyes, eares, and handes: to the ende that whosoever shoulde heare, or doe any thing, shoulde employ the whole to the Common use, and profite . . . And *Plato* sticketh not to say, that the verie Commonaltie of women and children, was necessarie in a Common weale, and Citie well instituted, not in respect of any other communication, or societie, as it is most likely, then of mutuall love, and well ordeined charitie, minding to shewe, that there is nothing that ought to be so deare and precious, whiche by common affection shoulde not be common among us. For even as in the bodies of beastes, the partes of them live, be nourished, and take the spirite of life, by the bonde they have one with an other: So likewise the societie of men, joyned and fast linked together, with the chaine of this common affection, and respecte to the common weale, is by common foresight conserved, and increased.

"And truely this societie is the end whereunto each vocation ought to be directed: but yet for all that, not grounded upon I knowe not what peace, tranquillitie, and humane glorie, wherein the wisest and most renoumed among the Philosophers be falen on sleep: but referred to the place whence the same proceedeth, that is to say, to heaven, the honour and glorie of the Almightie. For as long as particular affection of glorie dwelleth and abideth in us, it is impossible that the true union which we seeke, should be in the societie of men. This being a most certeine and assured thing, that all glorie is accompanied by a particularitie, cheefe enimie, and adversarie to Commonaltie, the daughter of Charitie, who is meeke, humble, curteous, and patient, not seeking her owne commoditie: which is so high a point, that undoubtedly it forceth and streineth our nature, yea, all humane Philosophie. For there is nothing harder and more greevous to mans eares, inclined naturally to his owne profite, then to heare that he must renounce the love and good will he beareth to him selfe, wholy to abandon him selfe, to procure an other mans profite: yea, to quite his owne right: to leave the same to his neighbour. But therein do we not also with the Philosophers, followe nature as our guide, but the spirite of God, who warneth us in the scriptures, that the giftes and graces received of him, be by him freely imparted unto us, to be againe by us liberally imployed to common profite, and that therefore the right use of the good liberalitie bestowed upon us, consisteth in a liberall communication to other. That which the members of our owne body teache us sufficiently, no one of them being, which doth not imploy him selfe more to the commoditie of the whole body in generall, then to his owne particular." [151]

In other words, the highly theoretic character of the speculation is revealed by the ease with which the author slides from the communism of Plato to the Christian fellowship of the New Testament. In a certain sense one may say that the spirit of reconciliation is complete here. It is not that the desire for order and serenity has made the author ride rough-shod over some of the most controverted of the issues involved. It is rather that he seems quite unaware of those tensions beneath the social surface the awareness of which gives such a haunting relevancy to the fantasy of the author of *Utopia*.

In this, of course, he is only moving in the general direction of all the England of his time. Indeed, the urgency of the social problem tends to be quite lost sight of in the prevailing concern for order. A good example is to be seen in Thomas Floyd's *The Picture of a Perfit Common Wealth*, of 1600,[152] the title of which suggests the large promises of *Utopia*, but the subtitle of which immediately narrows the area of consideration significantly, "describing aswell the offices of Princes and inferiour Magistrates over their subjects, as also the duties of subjects towards their Governours." [153] For Floyd the restlessness of the masses is no challenge to a consideration of their grievances but an evidence of their incapacity for rule.[154] The very grounds on which he commends monarchy are significant of his whole social orientation: "There is no estate so highly established, or so perfectly ordered and managed, to be compared to the royall scepter of a Monarchie guarded with good and wholesome lawes." [155]

His highest flight on this theme occurs in "A Conclusion to the magistrates," in which he invokes the ideal example of

"the great king of Muscovy, (who was thought to controll all the Monarches of the world, having gotten such authority over his owne subjects, as well ecclesiasticall as secular, to whome it was lawful to dispose, as it were, at his pleasure, of their lives and goods: no man being willing to gainesay him, they also confessing publikly and openly his imperiall regiment, alledging withall, that the will of their Prince was the will of God, and all what soever he did, they acknowledging it to bee done by divine providence. Hee is (said they) The porter of Paradise, The chamberlain of God, and the executor of his will. By which meanes he grewe so mighty within a litle while, that all his neighbours, which were the Tartarians, Suevians, yea and the Turks themselves, canoniz'd him. Where such love and obedience is wrought in subjects towardes their soveraigne, and of the soveraigne towards his subjects, there shall vertue enjoy her freedome, and possesse her priviledge by the rights of law, and all the people shall flourish with equity: Justice shall maintaine peace, peace shall procure security, security shall nourish wealth, wealth felicity." [156]

These general tendencies of the more philosophical works are confirmed in one or two of the less theoretical and more practical treatises of the opening of the new century. Of these clearly the most interesting and the most timely are the work of a representative of that class that next to the landowner had given most concern to the socially-reforming preachers of earlier days, the merchant. By 1601 the merchant had eminently made good his place as a responsible member of society. In that year one Gerrard De Malynes, describing himself as "Merchant" on the title-pages, published two treatises, one of which, *A Treatise of the Canker of Englands Common Wealth,* he dedicated to Sir Robert Cecil, "Her Majesties Principall Secretarie," [157] the other, *Saint George for England,* to the "Right Honorable Sir Thomas Egerton, Knight, Lord Keeper Of the Great Seale of England," etc.[158] The second is, as one might suppose, the more theoretical of the two with more emphasis on moral exhortation, while the first is distinctly more practical with much more attention paid to the problems raised by fluctuations in prices and in the value of money, and much more stress laid on monetary reform. Social restlessness is the main preoccupation of the first treatise and prosperity of the second, but the underlying social philosophy of the two treatises is the same.

The general point of view is suggested vividly if not entirely coherently in what the author has to say on the classic theme of covetousness in the preface to the reader before the second treatise. He arraigns the dragon of covetousness on the ground that

"he overthroweth the harmonie of the strings of the good government of a common-wealth, by too much enriching some, and by oppressing and impoverishing some others, bringing the instrument out of tune: when as every member of the same should live contented in his vocation and execute his charge according to his profession. For albeit, that equalitie wold be the cause that every man should have enough, which made some of opinion that goods ought to be common: yet forasmuch as the same was never used or established in any age, reason requireth, that according to the course of humane affaires, all things should be governed in the best and most assuredst maner that can be devised, and as it were, seeking a certaintie, even in uncertainties, which is tearmed Pollicie. For all worldly and transitorie things being mutable, maketh the world properly to consist of strife, warre, discord, envie, rankor, burning, sacking, wasting, spoyling and destroying: a very uncertaine ground to build upon." [159]

Here it is interesting to see how the old trumpet call of social indictment, covetousness, now sounds for social stabilization, not for the redistribution of goods but for the confinement of every man to the proper sphere of his vocation. The memory of the communistic dreams of the past still lingers in the author's mind as is shown in the first treatise, but they have become a highly academic matter:

"Plato the Philosopher perceiving that equality would be the cause that every man should have enough, was of ·opinion and willed all things in a common wealth to be common, whom sir *Thomas Moore* in his Utopian common weale seemeth to imitate, to the end that an infinite number of lawes already made, and the making of so many new lawes as daily are made, might be abolished. . . . But this equality cannot be established, neither was there any such ever used in any age, or commaunded by the word of God, but that possessing these worldly goods, we should so use them with charity towards others, as though we did not possesse them at all." [160]

In other words, Malynes is still interested enough in the theory of equality of goods, a threat to which any merchant would probably be sensitive in any age however remote the threat might actually be, to take the trouble to point out that it has never been practically applicable. As for those religious radicals that are still using the word of God to support their dreams, he categorically denies their basic contention without troubling to go into the matter of texts himself. He has also paid glib and passing homage to the stewardship theory of wealth. In other words he has made clear that he is a sober and enlightened member of the Christian commonwealth. Then he plunges into what he is really interested in, which is not communism, or charity to the poor, or the scriptural basis of society but the national and international financial problems of the time. Monetary reform is what he cares about, for that seems to him the only practical way of remedying the ills of society.[161] Plenty of corn and plenty of money are in his judgment the "two pillars and props for the maintenance of a commonwealth, even as sinceritie of religion, and the love of the people are the two especial props or pillars of the state of a Prince." [162]

What is significant is the point of view which the practical man not especially interested in religion takes for granted, an orderly society in which each man sticks to his vocation, and in which wealth is used as a trust, and religion is regarded as with patriotism the main support of authority. He is aware of other points of view, but he is not really interested in them or really afraid of them. What he is afraid of is social restlessness and disorder, partly because he believes that they are always dangerous, and partly because he is aware of them in the world about him. It is characteristic of the Elizabethan social thinker that even when he is most convinced that restlessness is a bad thing or an ungrateful thing or an unnecessary thing, he does not allow his complacency to blind him to its existence. Part of this is, of course, sheer realism, but noticing how often restlessness is dwelt upon by people who have some cause to advance, practical or spiritual, one comes to suspect that it was a very good excuse for getting a hearing, a fact of which the propagandists of the time were not slow to take advantage.

As a whole, the Commonwealth tradition, unlike the Piers Plowman tradition, maintained its social objectives. It affords almost no evidence of that substitution of a new religious order for a new social order that is the striking feature of the later Piers Plowman tradition. Indeed, something of a quite contrary tendency is to be discerned, a tendency to a growing secular materialism of mood. True, the Christian commitments are still there, at times disturbing to the conscience and haunting to the imagination, but though taken for granted, they are clearly not in the foreground of the writer's or the reader's consciousness. That is held by very different considerations, considerations of governmental technique, of economic policy, considerations of an immediately practical nature.

When one compares these later works with More's *Utopia*, one is conscious of both a narrowing and a hardening of mind. One misses the wide range of More's mind, the flexibility of his imagination. These later works are more concerned with the world that is than the world that might be. The tendencies to social radicalism of More have been swallowed up in the prevailing concern for social order and stability. Plato and More are not forgotten, but the speculative discussion of revolutionary change has been relegated to the academy. The men who are carrying on the discussion of the commonwealth are as committed to the existing order as we shall presently find the preachers. Here again the humanist has given way to the practical man. And as always he has caught, perhaps without being aware of it, the main current of the time and is riding it with quite unselfconscious assurance.

CHAPTER III

THE REFORMERS AND THE WEALTH
OF THE CHURCH

In our study of the Piers Plowman literature we have seen how
a vigorous tradition of social-religious criticism came out of the
Middle Ages into the sixteenth century. It is not surprising that
to churchmen, probably in the main the spokesmen for this
tradition, the issue of religious reform should have seemed the
more urgent, but it is likely that to the masses of the people, the
hope of the social betterment to be won from religious change was
of at least equal interest and perhaps of even greater immediate
attractiveness. Certainly, at the beginning of the sixteenth century
the appeal to and for the poor was still being made by religious
reformers with great vigor and slight evidence of misgiving.

Two works may be taken as examples of the directions which
that appeal was taking. The first represents the more conservative,
the more traditional, type of social-religious criticism current in
the first quarter of the sixteenth century. Significantly, it is the
older. It is that famous treatise of the Carmelite, Henry Parker,
Dives and Pauper, the printing of which Richarde Pynson completed on the fifth day of July, 1493 and which Thomas Berthelet
was still printing in 1536. This is an interesting work in many
ways. It reveals, to begin with, a lively awareness of how men
feel as well as how they think. It is searching in its analysis of the
processes of the human mind, say in dreams,[1] and it is very practical and even homely in its approach to many of the problems of
the time. Above all, the choice of Pauper for the obvious mouth-
piece of the author's favorite ideas suggests that Parker's sense
of human values was very much like Langland's.

The book begins centrally enough with a declaration of the

equality of rich and poor, classically expressed in a citation from a revered authority, in this case Bede's interpretation of the twenty-second chapter of Proverbs: "A riche man is nat to be worshipped for this cause only that he is riche, ne a pore man is to be dispysed, bicause of his povertye, but the werk of god is to be worshippyd in them bothe, for they bothe been made to the ymage, and to the lyknesse of god." [2] That is a classically impersonal and general and sound enough opening, which few Christians of any age would probably dare to contradict, at least in theory. But Pauper soon brings the classic generality down to earth, with a cry of personal complaint as direct and sharp as anything in the Piers Plowman tradition: "I that am a pore caytyf symple and lytel set by, biholdynge the prosperite of them that been riche, and the disese that I suffre and other pore men like unto me am many a tyme steryd to grutche, and to be wery of my lyf." [3]

The root of the trouble is, as one would expect, covetousness.[4] The evil is not in the riches themselves. They are a hindrance to virtue for bad men, but a help to good. On the other hand, poverty will not bring a man to sin if he have patience.[5] But the rich man who denies help to the poor man who needs it, is, if the latter die, guilty of his death. If it does not come to that extremity but the poor man still wants for something of necessity, then the rich man is guilty of theft. "For al that the richeman hath passynge his nedful lyvyng, after the state of his dispensacion, it is the pore mannes." [6] That is fairly strong doctrine. For at the bottom is the basic notion that "by wey of kynde alle men ben evyn in lordeshippe and richesses, but by wychednesse of false covetise in the people men ben uneven in riches." [7]

So far Parker says nothing with which Langland would not have cordially agreed. But when he comes to apply this theory to the conditions of his own day, then one is reminded rather of Wyclif and his followers. For Parker concentrates his attention on the goods of the religious. And this he does deliberately, for he is at considerable pains to give his reasons. In so doing he shows that he has worked out the theory of the matter on the basis of both fundamental principle and history, as that history was apparently rather widely understood in his day:

"For the godes of religiouse shulde be more common than other mennes godis: to helpe the lond and the pore peple. And therfore sayth the law: that comon lyf is nedeful to al men, and namely to them that wyl folowe the lif of cristes desiples. . . . And therfore they that have most nede: have moste riȝt to godes of there religiouse[.] And the lordship is no more aproprid to the religiouse than to the seculeris. For bothe seculers and regulers shulde be holpen therby[.] But dispensinge governaunce: And kepynge of the goodys of holy churche: is approprid to the religeouse and to other men of holy churche. And therfore saythe holy writt that in the begynyng of holy church al thinges were comon to the multitude of al cristen people nat only to the apostlys: but to al cristen people . . . And therfore if religiouse mispende the godes that be taken to them, and help not the nedy peple: they do cristen peple grete wronge[.] For they withhold them her riȝt: and make propre to them that owthe be comon to al." [8]

Then he goes on to give an instance of the abuse of the principle of community property:

"It is a shame and an over great abusion: that a man of religion shal ride with his tenth summe or with his twenty summe on an hors of ten pounde in a sadel al gold bigon[.] And for povertye that be byndeth him to in his profession as they saye he maye not ȝeve an half-peny for goddys sone ne helpe his fader and moder at nede withouten axyng leeve of hys sovereyn." [9]

The first thing that is striking in this passage is that this is the old problem of individual property and community wealth that so vexed the founder of the Franciscan order for one, and against which he strove so unsuccessfully to protect his sons. The other and significant element in this complaint is that it bears out the objection that we have already met in the Piers Plowman literature, that the religious orders had raised to proud estate men who if they had followed in their fathers' footsteps would not have gone nearly so bravely.[10] One wonders how much the feeling of the monks' relatives that they should have a share in the prosperity of their more fortunate kin motivated the endless complaints about monastic wealth. At any rate, Pauper pronounced the whole business hypocrisy, charging that "under the color of poverte they maynteyn ther pride and ther avarice: and occupye gretter lordshipys than do many dukes eerlis and barons to greate hindrynge of the londe and gret disease of the pore people." [11]

But vigorous as Parker is in his arraignment of the wealth of the church, and sympathetic as he is in his expression of the complaint of the poor, he still shows a concern for the maintenance of the poor preacher that is not unlike the concern which Latimer is going to express later when he contemplates the wreck of the disestablishment:

"And therfore ye shal releve al the pore and nedy as ye may, but principaly them that be nedy and pore for goddes sake and by wey of vertue. . . . Therfore seint austyn saith thus. Thou shalt nat do to the pore prechoure of goddes worde, as thou dost to the begger passing by the wey. To the begger thou ʒevest, for Crist biddith the that thou ʒeve to eche that axith the. Butt to the pore prechoure thou owyst to ʒeve thouʒ he axe the nat. And therfore loke that the pore prechour goddes kniʒt nede nat to axe the[.] For if he nede to axe for thy defaute, and thy defaute and thy lacchesse, he shewithe the dampnable or he axe." [12]

This solicitude for the support of the preaching clergy is a manifestation of a certain practical spirit in Parker that is also reflected in his careful discriminations between the different classes of poor and the order of our obligations to them.[13]

Another element in Parker's social thought that forecasts Latimer and some of the later preachers is to be seen in what he has to say on the subject of submission. For his Pauper is very clear in his insistence on the recognition of the degrees of society so far as authority and government are concerned—"for drede of god worship thou thyn eldre and for drede of god worship thou thy king and thy sovereyn and all that be in hygher degre than thou art. For syth god hath put them in degre of worshyp: thou moste for drede of god worship them." [14] Indeed, Pauper goes farther: "Be ye sugettis for goddes sake: not only to gode lordis and welreuled: but also to shrewys and tyrauntis. . . . For thanne is man and woman worthy thanke of god, whanne for consciens and goddes sake he suffereth paciently diese wyth oute gylt." [15]

But it would be a mistake to think of Parker as in the end simply preoccupied with social order. The poetry of the tradition of social and religious criticism that flowered in the conception of Piers Plowman is also to be found in the pages of Parker. What he has to say of the unworthy poor is worthy of the charity of Piers himself, if it does not exceed it. In a characteristically medieval analysis he puts last in his list of the poor, deserving and undeserving, such as

"been pore only by synne, and for the love of syn as they that wast their gode in lechery and glutonye, in pride and pletyng, and in mysuse at the dyce in ryot and in vanite. Suche pore folke been laste in the ordre of almesse doynge, but their nede be the more[.] And nathlesse if they have pacience with their poverte they shal have mede for their pacience, if they repente theym, for their mysdedys." [16]

And for those who relieve the unworthy in their due order of claim upon the responsible steward-possessors of the world's wealth, "God shal shewe at the dome grete pite and moche mercy, whanne thing that is done for his sake to his enemyes and to his leest servantes, most unworthy, he shal accept it and rewarde it as it were done to his owne persone, and say I thank you[.] For that ye did to the leest of myne, ye dyd it to me." [17]

There is in Parker a certain combination of reasonableness and imagination, characteristic of the English humanists. This temper is shown dramatically in two passages. The first is that part of the dialogue in which Dives, who has been lamenting that the English are strong on external worship rather than true devotion,[18] suggests that it would be better to give the money spent on ornamenting churches to the poor.[19] That suggestion does not appeal to Pauper at all, for he insists that "every man pore and riche after his power is bounde to worship goddes house." [20] But he goes on to suggest that in times of peace and plenty when the poor are easily looked out for, then the main effort may be directed to the improvement of the service of God, but in times of war and want the main effort of Christian benevolence should go to the relief of the poor.[21] In general, that is typical of his position, practical in its adaptability to circumstance rather than iconoclastic.

The heights of which this spirit is capable are best to be seen in Parker's description of the heaven which he offers in rebuke to the tyrants and in comfort to their victims. After the conventional details of light and joy Parker goes on to develop the spiritual implications:

"In this cite alle men and wymen ben fre[.] The king of this cite axith no presauntes, ne ʒiftes of man ne of womun, but their hertis and their love and that thei fare wele[.] He puttith no man, ne woman there to travayle, butt he wole that alle be in rest in peas and in ease . . . ʒeve thy self to this blysse, and thou shalte have this blisse. Other pryce axith he none. For this blisse may nat be bouʒte, butt with love, and charite[.] In this cyte shalle every man and woman have so grete lordship that al they shalle have place ynouʒ with outen envye, and all be kinges and quenes, of asmoche as they desire. Ther shalbe no pleetyng for no lordship, for no londe[.] There shalbe none envye butt every man and woman glade of others welfare." [22]

That positive quality of spiritual vision that redeems the despair of Langland over the shortcomings of the Christian world is something still to be found in Henry Parker's work, and it should be noted that it springs out of the very tradition that has in his judgment been so often and so grievously violated. For though we know Parker suffered imprisonment at the hands of the Bishop of London for circulating a very vehement attack upon the spiritual shortcomings of the secular clergy and bishops which he had preached at Paul's Cross in 1464,[23] there is nothing in his treatise to suggest that he was not in his basic doctrinal positions orthodox. And there is no reason to believe that he had any more thought of overthrowing the order which he was trying to reform than Langland or most of the preachers whom Mr. Owst quotes in his study.

There is no need of such caution in speaking of the second of our two illustrations of the social-religious criticism current at the beginning of the sixteenth century. For there is no mistaking the revolutionary intention of Simon Fish's *The Supplication of Beggers,* first published in 1524.[24] It is quite clear now, and it was quite clear then. So dangerous did Fish's book seem to Thomas More that he went to the trouble of writing an answer to it.[25] It was too much even for Henry VIII, for according to Foxe he put it at the top of his list of forbidden books.[26] And when

Foxe himself came to gather up the story of the triumph of the Protestant Reformation in England, he reprinted it entire in his encyclopedic martyrology.[27]

The disingenuousness of Fish's appeal on behalf of the poor was challenged by his enemies in his own day, and his wisdom by the event. But that appeal must have made a deep impression on both the poor and their sympathizers. For Fish's thesis is very simple. The alms of the kingdom belong by right to the poor. If all the alms of the kingdom were given to their rightful recipients, there would not be half enough for the needy, and yet these sturdy beggars of monks and priests appropriate what there is.[28] The thing to do is to put these, the real sturdy beggars, to work, and then the wealth of the church can be used for the relief of those who need relief, and the wealth of the realm will be increased by the just labors of these idlers.[29] There will be no unemployment, and the social problem will be settled. That was a seductive program which Simon Fish offered in 1524, seductive because of its appeal to the most unfailing of human instincts, and because of its absolute simplicity. Here was the one thing needful to be done, and all would be well.

There was, as we have seen, nothing new in this attack on the monasteries. The Middle Ages had been just as free and thoroughgoing in their criticism of those institutions. But the sixteenth-century contribution to that continuing body of criticism is different from that of the past. On the whole, it is more concentrated. Except for monastic immorality, monastic wealth now pretty much takes up the field. And the attack is not only more concentrated, but also more thoroughgoing. Its basic premise is that conception of the purpose of monasteries which will be expressed with characteristic succinctness in a sentence in one of Latimer's sermons: "Abbeis were ordeyned for the comforte of the pore." [30] It is not easy to be sure whether Latimer was aware that they were ordained for other purposes as well, for instance, for the promotion of a more perfect Christian life, and for the carrying on of certain activities of prayer and worship that were deemed by their founders pleasing to God and beneficial to their fellowmen. That the monasteries often fell short of the hopes of their founders is a point on which all observers were agreed. Langland had some very sharp things to say of that, but he also said that life in the cloister properly lived could be heaven on earth.[31] And of that finest flower of the monastic way of life, contemplation, he had as we have seen, a very lively appreciation.[32] Even Wyclif, who quite completely repudiated the monastic system, still enjoined contemplation upon all priests.[33]

It was different in the sixteenth century. By and large the contemplative ideal had lost its prestige in the religious world. The temper of the sixteenth century is here as elsewhere activist. Religious effort is more and more spent on exegesis and controversy, perhaps inevitably so in an age of religious transition and redefinition. Certainly the vogue of the conference and the sermon points to a controlling impulse very different from that of the contemplative.

It is not surprising, then, that to men bent on overturning the old order the pretensions to contemplation of the monasteries should seem but a salve for cowardice and a pretext for idleness. Nor that with the uneducated, suspicious of the pretensions of intellectual labor, anyway, it was not difficult to convince many of them that the life of the monasteries was but a conspiracy for fattening the paunches of its lazy beneficiaries. Indeed, there is a good deal of evidence such as Foxe's comments on the state of Cambridge University in Cranmer's youth,[34] to suggest that it was not difficult to convince the average layman that the life of the universities was futility and idleness, too. Under these circumstances, it is not surprising that the one standard applied to the monasteries came to be that of ministry to the needs of the poor. With such a concentration of values, it was not difficult to prove that the monasteries were falling far short of the expectations of their critics. Indeed, when the ideal of devoting all the resources of the monasteries to the relief of the poor was set beside the actual fragmentary devotion, the prospect held before the needy must have been pretty nearly irresistible.

These hopes were challenged at the time, and the event more than justified the worst fears of the opponents of Fish.[35] The relief of the poor is the profession of most revolutions and the accomplishment of few. But it is very hard for the leaders of any aggressive movement on an established order not to expect the redress of all their complaints from the achievement of their immediate objectives. This was eminently true of the sixteenth-century supporters of the expropriation of the monasteries. Henry Brinkelow, a former Gray Friar, and a persistently optimistic supporter of the expropriation of church property, voiced the hopes of many when he reminded the king with unusual plainness that the confiscated property gave him an opportunity, not to be let slip:

"Now wold I wish a thing wonderous neadefull to the comune wealth, yet by the waye of peticion (although the kinges grace be bound in conscience so to do) that in as moche as his grace is come to great riches, by rentes in maner innumerable of the abbeylandes deposed (which was ryghtfully done) for which cause I say his grace is bound to study some waye, that part of the yokes of hys subjectes may be eased." [36]

Brinkelow made some very interesting suggestions, of which the first was that all judges and lawyers be granted a royal stipend and the poor charged nothing for the administration of justice.[37]

Some of the writers of the time were, it is true, a little more moderate in their expectations. A letter which Starkey wrote to Henry VIII probably in or around 1537 is an early example of such a cautious approach to the problem.[38] Starkey makes it quite clear that he is in complete sympathy with what has been done, but he is obviously concerned as to what is going to become of the monastic properties. He is very discreet in his procedure. He reminds the king that there are two sorts of men who deserve to be nourished of princes for the service of the realm, "men of letturys and lernyng, and men exercysyd in featys of armys and chyvalrye." [39] In the cherishing of these he hopes that the superfluous riches that in spiritual hands nourished only idleness and vice may now be turned "to the increase of al vertue and honestye." [40] All this sounds very general, but actually Starkey makes some very practical suggestions, notably for the leasing of the monastic lands at a low rent to younger brothers living unprofitably in service, and to men of even lower social position.[41] What Starkey desires is the breaking-up of the monastic estates into small holdings with the increase in population that would follow such a change. And what he and, clearly, a great many others are trying to avert is the leasing and the giving of the monastic lands to lords and gentlemen who are already furnished with vast possessions.[42] Starkey's letter probably never went any further than the king and a few of his advisers, but it shows how men were thinking at the time.

That they continued so to think is to be seen in a disclaimer in a sermon of Thomas Lever of 1550 which presents this more practical view of the matter. He is very carefully explaining that his complaints over certain elements in the existing situation are not to be understood as implying any lack of faith in the idea of the disestablishment itself:

"For in suppressinge of Abbeyes, Cloysters, Colleges, and Chauntries, the entente of the kinges majestie that dead is, was and of this our kynge now, is verye godlye, and the purpose, or els the pretence of other, wonderouse goodlye: that therby suche abundaunce of goodes as was supersticiously spente upon vayne ceremonies, or voluptuously upon idle bellies, myght come to the kinges handes to beare his great charges, necessarilie bestowed in the comen wealthe, or partly unto other mennes handes, for the better releve of the pore, the maintenaunce of learning, and the settinge forth of goddes worde." [43]

This is a more diversified program than that of Simon Fish, for instance, and a much more practical one in view of the actual situation. The poor were not to get all of the wealth of the monasteries, but a large share. The rest would go to the good of the state in replenishing the king's exchequer. Such a proposal was less in the spirit of the primitive church than of Fish, but it was more in harmony with the realities of the contemporary situation. Nevertheless, even this more moderate and reasonable expectation was doomed to disappointment.

It was easy enough to get the wealth of the monasteries into the hands of the king. The difficulty was in the next step. After all, the preachers can hardly have been the only people in the kingdom with ideas as to how the newly confiscated spiritual wealth might be spent to the enrichment of secular life. There survives from the reign of Élizabeth a document, drawn up apparently at the request of someone in authority, which gives a diagnosis of the ills of the commonwealth and a series of suggestions for their remedy from the point of view of a man who had been a Privy Councillor under Edward VI, Armigail Waad.[44] The whole approach to the social problems of the day of this writer is very different from that of the men to whom we have been listening, as we may see from the fact that of seven main causes of distress to the commonwealth, the first is the poverty of the queen, the second the poverty of noblemen, the third the wealth of the lower classes.[45] For the remedy of the second of these diseases, the author proposes that the temporal lands and houses of the bishops be seized, and that the bishops be provided with incomes out of the spiritualities of the shires where they reside and all their temporalities be given to noblemen who are in need of such relief.[46] It is quite probable that similar proposals were often advanced in the behind-the-scenes discussions of the time. At any rate most of the new wealth speedily found its way into the hands of a new set of what Robert Crowley was shortly to arraign so effectively under the old name of "possessioners." [47]

Lever well summed up the outcome of this long-hoped for redistribution of wealth in the famous half-taunt, half-challenge to the recipients of the monastic booty: "If ye hadde anye eyes ye shoulde se and be ashamed that in the great abboundance of landes and goods taken from Abbeies, Colleges and Chauntryes for to serve the kyng in all necessaryes, and charges, especially in provision of relyefe for the pore, and for maytenaunce of learnynge the kynge is so dysapoynted, that bothe the pore be spoyled, all mayntenance of learnyng decayed, and youonly enryched." [48]

Of course, Lever does not venture to blame the king for this disappointment; rather he invokes the old medieval scapegoat, the royal officer. "Howe beit covetouse officers have so used thys matter that even those goodes whyche dyd serve to the releve of the poore, the mayntenaunce of learnyng, and to comfortable necessary hospitalitie in the comen wealth, be now turned to mainteine worldly, wycked, covetouse ambicion." [49]

But whosesoever the fault for the way things had gone, there was no question that they had not gone as the reformers had intended. Indeed, too late, Lever and Fish and all their sympathizers discovered that however short of their standards the relief given by the old order had been, it was still much more than anything in sight from the new holders of the monastic lands. On this they were all agreed.

Fish who had so long complained with such bitterness of the wrongs of the poor for once can have hardly exaggerated when he described the disappointment of those who had been encouraged to hope for "theyr due portion" when the king turned out the "sturdy beggars," the monks:

"But alas thei failed of theyr expectation and are now in more penurye than ever they were. For, although the sturdy beggers gat all the devotion of the good charitable people from them yet had the pore impotent creatures some relefe of theyr scrappes, where as nowe they have nothyng. Then had they hospitals, and almeshouses to be lodged in, but nowe they lye and storve in the stretes." [50]

Thomas Becon is even more positive in his witness to the superiority of the old possessors of the monastic lands in this respect at least when in *The Jewel of Joy*, first published in 1553, he puts into the mouth of the main speaker in his dialogue, Philemon, the following arraignment of the rich worldlings who have come into possession of the monastic properties:

"Do not these ryche worldlynges defraude the pore man of his bread, wherby is understand al things necessary for a mans lyfe, which through their insaciable covetousnes set al things at so hie price, and suffer townes so to decay that the pore hath not what to eate nor yet where to dwell? What other are they than but very manslears? They abhorre the names of Monkes, Friers, Chanons, Nonnes etc. but their goods they gredely gripe. And yet where the cloysters kept hospitality let out their fermes at a reasonable pryce, noryshed scholes, brought up youth in good letters, they did none of all these things." [51]

Even Henry Brinkelow, who had, as we shall see in a moment, so steadfast a hatred of the old order, yet remembered in his exile the hospitality which the monks had kept in the much-condemned monastic benefices in contrast to the neglect of their successors. For in the fourteenth chapter of *The Complaint of Roderyck Mors,* in his arraignment "Of lordes that are parsons and vicars," [52] he admitted that the men that the monks had put into their benefices were better for the poor than their successors;

"And thogh they were not lerned yet they kepte hospytalyté and helped theyr pore frends. . . . And as touching the almesse that they dealt and the hospytalyté that they kept, every man knoweth that many thowsandes were well receaved of them, and myght have bene better; If they had not had so many greate mennes horses to fede, and had not bene over charged with such ydle gentylmen, as were never out of the abbays. . . . But nowe that all the abbeys with their landes, goods and impropred personages, be in temporall mennes handes, I do not hearetell that one halpeny worth of almes, or anye other profight, cometh unto the people of those parysshes." [53]

It would look as if there must have been a good many noblemen who were of the opinion of the Duke of Norfolk, who in 1537 wrote to Cromwell of the swarming of vagabonds in Yorkshire, "And the almes that they have in religious houses is the great occasion thereof, and also the slackeness of the Justice of pease, for not doyng ther dewties." [54]

But the fault of the new landlords was not simply one of neglect. Their predecessors had been blamed often enough for laziness and inertia. That was not precisely the charge against their successors. Rather it was an active greed that could be satisfied only at the cost of the poor. For if we are to believe the reforming preachers, once the spirit of expropriation had been let loose, it cut a wide swath through the rich fields of centuries-old benevolence and piety. Even some of the local grammar schools had been seized, and their supporting funds appropriated.[55] Indeed, in the indiscriminate seizure of religious and pious goods, apparently resources purely and primarily eleemosynary in character had been laid hold upon, like the flocks of cows that had been kept in certain towns to relieve the poor and which in the confusion of redistribution had been sold with the resulting funds appropriated by the new owners.[56]

But even this was not enough. For the easily-won wealth of the old religious order had whetted the appetites of the newly-rich landlords until now the spirit of acquisition had turned to active and positive oppression. It is that spirit for which Lever, who had lost none of his old contempt for the monks, taunts their successors:

"For yf ye were not starke blynd ye would se and be ashamed that where as fyfty tunne belyed Monckes geven to glotonye fylled theyr pawnches, kept up theyr house and relyved the whol country round about them, ther one of your gredye guttes devowringe the whole house and makyng great pyllage throughouce [sic] the countrye, cannot be satisfyed." [57]

The forms which that pillage took were, of course, many and various, and, needless to say, they were not, by any means, peculiar to the new landowners. The literature of the middle of the century is full of complaints about landlords in general. They were raising the rents of their tenants and confiscating the lands for which the tenants could not meet their dues, and, in general increasing their holdings at the expense of the poor of the countryside.[58] Landlords as a class were the prime object of the hatred of the suffering people and of the indignation of the preachers.

Especially did the new landlords come in for their share of the odium of the enclosures, that long-drawn-out, not yet by any means climactic business, of which so many of the writers of the time complained, and which they probably overemphasized to the neglect of other, at least temporarily, more potent economic factors, like money. The new landlords certainly did not begin the business of enclosure. Mr. Tawney has shown that from the middle of the fourteenth century on, the old open-field system of the medieval manor had been undergoing a gradual dissolution.[59] The peasants themselves had been redividing and exchanging their lands, hedging and ditching their little holdings and nibbling away at the waste.[60] This was a thoroughly spontaneous, not to say unconscious, movement from below.[61] It had been most advanced in those sections of the country most exposed to the influence of trade and a money economy. Although this movement had served to break up the rough equality of the old village community into large copyholders and small, it had so far as we can tell, evoked no protest.[62] And it is significant that when the Elizabethan government tried to put a check on landlords' enclosures, it made no effort to interfere with these enclosures from below; indeed, it seems rather to have given them its sanction.[63] What did awaken protest was a different type of enclosure, what one may describe as enclosure from above. This, too, goes back to a time before the disestablishment. Its root is in the success of the Tudor monarchy in breaking the power of the feudal nobility. The military requirements of the old feudal lord had made a host of tenants and retainers a necessity. When the need for tenant-soldiers and retainers was taken away, numerous tenants ceased to be an asset. Now it was to the interest of the landlord to get the maximum economic return from his land. Changing social standards made the magnificent country house set in a spacious park the symbol of dignity rather than the hall full of retainers.[64]

At the same time the growth of the demand for wool in our period showed the landlord a ready way to raise the wherewithal for this new way of life.[65] The transformation from the old farming into pasture-farming was not a new thing. Again, it had been going on for a century.[66] If the sixteenth-century landlord had been hesitant to fall in with the new ways of agricultural life, by the middle of the century the fall in the value of money was pressing upon him severely enough to make him look to the more profitable exploitation of the lands he held and to their possible extension.[67] The demesne land was enclosed and converted into pasture with the result that fewer tenants were needed for labor on it. Then if the landlord enclosed the commons, the tenants lost indispensable subsidiary sources of income and, above all, the means of keeping the horses and oxen necessary to the cultivation of the arable land.[68] That was disastrous enough for the small tenants, but worse was in store. For the landlord was driven by the rising prices of the time to make the most of his land by amalgamating the small holdings of the tenants into large lease-hold farms which could be used effectively for pasture. He had no choice but to get rid of the small tenants. This was easy in the case of the tenants at will or short-term lessees. It was harder with the copyholders. Here he had to induce them to accept leases, or if they would not, then raise the fines for admission.[69] The result was great, if not ruinous, hardship for many small copyholders and tenants. For the progress of the time had done nothing to relieve the small cultivator of the legal rightlessness which was his inheritance from the Middle Ages while the disturbances of customary rights, characteristic of a period of rapid economic change, had swept away the practical security which he had derived from medieval custom.[70]

Such an account of this is, of course, only a diagram of a very complicated and extended process of evolution. There seems to be little doubt that the process was accelerated by the great land speculation of the decade between 1540 and 1550. The abbey lands had come into the market after 1536, and the lands of the gilds and chantries in 1547.[71] If they did not create the agrarian problems of the time, they unquestionably intensified problems already beginning to be evident. Particularly they were accelerating factors in two social phenomena that began to receive a good deal of attention in the middle of the century. The first is the emergence of the large-scale, speculative, exploiting capitalist farmer.[72] The second is the increase in vagrancy from the forcing of tenants off the land, either by direct or indirect eviction, that was so much to engage the attention of all sixteenth-century thinkers on social problems.[73]

Even with all his resources the modern scholar like Mr. Tawney is very cautious when it comes to defining the extent or specific incidence of such changes. It is the main movement, rather, current of tendencies, that he seeks to define. The case was the exact opposite with the sixteenth-century preacher. Of such things as movements or even tendencies of an impersonal economic character he had, of course, very little idea. He was accustomed to measure happenings in terms of particular and individual responsibility. What he saw was the individual case, the particular situation, and from it he did not hesitate to draw quite sweeping and even drastic conclusions as to the personal responsibility involved. Consequently, of what was from his point of view, the central fact, he had no doubt whatever. The landlords were making their profit of the situation, and the poor were paying the price. For instance, Thomas Becon in *The Jewel of Joy* in 1553 through the preacher Philemon laments the decay of the old agricultural order:

"Where many men had good lyvynges, and maynteined hospitality, able at al times to helpe the king in his warres, and to susteyne other charges, able also to helpe their pore neighboures, and vertuously to bring up theyr children in Godly letters and good scyences, nowe sheepe and conies devoure altogether no man inhabiting the aforesayed places." [74]

However, more was probably never said on that great theme than was said in 1549 by Latimer in two famous sentences: "Then these grasiers, and inclosers, renterearers, are hindrers of the kings honour. For wher as have bene a great meany of house-holders and inhabitaunce, ther is nowe but a shepherd and hys dogge." [75]

As for those small landholders who did survive the process of enclosure, their lot was far from enviable. Here the responsibility of the new landlords would seem clearer. At least the preachers of the time thought so. Latimer, in particular, has a passionate indictment of the landlords who took advantage of the changes of ownership of the time to raise rents:

"You lande lordes, you rentreisers, I maye saye you step lordes, you unnatural lordes, you have for your possessions yerely to much. For that herebefore went for .xx. or .xl. pound bi yere, which is an honest porcion to be had gratis in one Lordeshyp, of a nother mannes sweat and laboure: now is it let for .l. or .C. pound by yere." [76]

There speaks the son of the old yeoman whose life work Latimer was so proudly and so wistfully to sum up in one of the most moving and dramatic passages he ever wrote, simple and clear with the bright lucidity of a vanished world:

"My father was a yeoman, and had no landes of his owne, onlye he had a farme of .iii. or .iiii. pound by yere at the utter most, and here upon, he tilled so much as kepte halfe a dosen men. He had walke for a hundred shepe, and my mother mylked .xxx. kyne. He was able and dyd fynde the kynge with hymselfe, and hys horsse, whyle he came to the place that he should receyve the kynges wages. I can remember that I buckeld hys harness, when he went unto Blacke heath felde. He kept me to schole, or elles I had not bene able to have preached before the kings majestie nowe. He married my systers with v. pounde or .xx. nobles a pece, so that he broughte them up in godlines, and feare of God. He kept hospitaliti for his pore neighbours. And sum almesse he gave to the poore, and all thys did he of the sayd farme. Wher he that now hath it, paieth .xvi. pounde by yere or more, and is not able to do any thing for his Prynce, for himselfe, nor for his children, or geve a cup of drincke to the pore." [77]

Passages such as these bear all the familiar marks of the misery that is likely to beset some sections of any land in a period of accelerated economic and social change. But to men who had hoped so much from the elimination of certain known evils and the achievement of certain promised advantages, the disappointment was bitter. And it was the bitterer, because it was not the habit of that age to think in terms of impersonal economic and social forces, but only in terms of individual human beings and their purposes and passions.

So widespread and so bitter is the outcry against the rent-raising and other exactions of the new landlords that Brinkelow is driven to what is for a man of his point of view a very remarkable admission with regard to the monastic lands and their former owners, namely, that

"but for the faiths sake I saye (for the whiche they were justly suppressed) it had been more profitable no doubte for the common welth that they had remayned styll in theyr handes. For they did not raise rents nor take such cruel fines as our temporall tyrauntes." [78]

The tradition of the disappointment over the new masters that succeeded the old was to linger long among men that would feel no tenderness for the old order as such. As late as 1636 Robert Powell of New Inn in his treatise, *Depopulation, Arraigned, Convicted, and Condemned, by the Lawes of God and Man*, after an arraignment of the landlords of his time that in its main lines does not much differ from Latimer's—destruction or neglect of houses, rack-renting, turning tillage into pasture, and so on—turns to a comparison of the old owners of the monastic properties and the new. He has no illusions about the character of some of the old owners. He cites a certain Abbot of Osney as a famous monastic "depopulator"; yet even such depopulators as he were in Powell's eyes preferable to their successors, for "as they made poore, they did in some competencie maintaine and releeve them; but these doe not only make many poore, but starve those that are poore." [79]

Yet sincere as the disappointment of the preachers was, especially on the score of the poor, it was not entirely vicarious. They had had their hopes, too, and they had been no less grievously disappointed. There had doubtless been some envy of the wealth of the abbeys and nunneries among the poorly paid lower ranks of the secular clergy.

And there had been widespread criticism of the system of monastic benefices, which had too often redounded to the benefit of monastic budgets rather than of the religious life of the parishes. But now as the fever of speculation in the monastic lands spread, the benefices and the parish-livings also went into the maw of land-grabbing. One of the most interesting descriptions of this development is to be seen in a passage from one of Lever's sermons. Quite obviously Lever had much more confidence in the city than his medieval predecessors had had, for he was very careful to contrast the creditable past of the rich merchant he was arraigning with his disreputable land-seeking present.

"As for example of ryche men, loke at the merchauntes of London, and ye shal se, when as by their honest vocacion, and trade of marchandise god hath endowed them with great abundaunce of ryches, then can thei not be content with the prosperous welth of that vocacion to satisfye themselves, and to helpe other, but their riches must abrode in the contrey to bie farmes out of the handes of worshypfull gentlemen, honeste yeomen, and poore laboringe husbandes, Yea nowe also to bye personages, and benefices, where as they do not onlye bye landes and goodes, but also lyves and soules of men, from God and the comen wealth, unto the devyll and them selves." [80]

Lever is indignant enough, but there is an even sharper note in the protest of Simon Fish. For Fish had been loud in his condemnation of all the arrangements whereby monasteries had corraled the alms of the kingdom to their profit.[81] But now those benefices that used to be under the control of men who, whatever their faults, might be presumed to have some interest in the maintenance of religion, had come into the hands of laymen and speculators. "What reason is it," he complains bitterly in 1546 in *A Supplication of the Poore Commons*, "that a surveyer of buildinges or landes, an alckmist, or a goldsmith, shoulde be rewarded with benefice upon benefice, which of very reason oughte to be committed to none other but such as through godly lerninge and conversation were able and would apply them selves to walke amydes theyr flocke in al godly example and puritie of lyfe." [82]

Lever and Fish's disappointment was shared by many other supporters of the new religious order. Theirs was a different disappointment from that of the poor who had looked for the opening-up of new sources of relief. Rather it was the disappointment of the revolutionary leader who had hoped to see some at least of the resources of the old order converted to the promotion of the new. The apparently widely held theory that lay-ownership was the readiest way to the purification of the supporting treasure of superstition could hardly be expected to satisfy the expectations of such men.

Thomas Rogers had put their point of view in a nutshell in the treatise on riches which he had taken out of the writings of Nicholas Hemingius. Upon the destruction of the old system, the question had arisen as to what should be done with the endowments which had been made formerly for the saying of Masses for the repose of the donor's soul. In some cases the lay heirs had laid claim to these bequests on the ground that now that Masses had been prohibited as superstitious, the purpose of the bequest could no longer be realized. But this the religious authorities successfully contested, as Rogers put it, on the following ground: "According therefore to the mynde of the Testatour, whiche was good, and devoute, the gooddes should bee transferred to the true service of GOD, whiche afore were given to the celebration of the Masse." [83]

Whatever concessions Lever and Latimer were prepared to make to the obvious needs and demands of the new monarchy, this was clearly their hope. The provision of a properly trained and active parish clergy had been one of the most constant objectives of the various schools of reformers for centuries. Now it was a matter of more than religious idealism. It was a matter of the sheerest necessity, if the changes which had been made in the religious establishment were to be maintained. As we shall see presently, the leaders of the reform, whatever claims for all but universal support they might make in the heat of controversy or the exhilaration of triumph, had few illusions as to the attachment of a very considerable portion, if not an actual majority of their flocks, to the old order. It was one thing to persuade the king and the leaders of the great world of the desirability of a fresh distribution of power and wealth. It was, as they were very shortly to find, quite a different matter to upset the centuries-old community life of the people. In other words, their victory was still to be won in the parishes.

They knew it could be won only by the provision of what they considered the proper clergy for these parishes. It was not just a matter of securing decent and literate priests to administer the sacraments to simple men whose universe was as yet undisturbed. It was rather the problem of putting into strategic posts of popular education and propaganda men who were imbued with the new principles and zealous for the promotion of the new order. This was, as we have seen, a matter to which the new lay holders of the monastic benefices were too often indifferent. The character of these new patrons had affronted, as we have seen, the sense of fitness of Fish. Lever was no less emphatic in his condemnation of their unwillingness to make what he considered adequate provision for the lay people for whose religious education and comfort these benefices had originally been set up.[84] Indeed, the man who used the wealth of the church for his own ends remains a by-word throughout the century, as may be seen in one of the lines in which John Weever in *The Mirror of Martyrs* defines "the world": "Shee builds high roofes with ruines of the Church." [85]

But there was an even more basic difficulty than this. For the leaders of the reform were not only worried by the unwillingness of the new patrons to put proper men into the parishes, but they were even more troubled as to the possibility of finding those men. For the disestablishment had badly damaged the support of the universities to which the reformers looked for the training of the men they wanted. Latimer, who had always been ahead of most of his contemporaries in his appreciation of the universal importance of education, was especially concerned at the neglect of learning that had resulted from recent changes. One of the most famous passages in his sermons concerns the desperate state of students at Cambridge University in the post-monastic days.

"Ther be few do study divinitie, but so many as of necessiti must furnysh the Colledges. For their lyvynges be so small, and vytaylee so dere, that they tarry not ther, but go other where to seke lyvynges and so they go aboute. Nowe therebe a fewe gentylmen and they studye a little divinite. Alas, what is that? it will come to passe that we shal have nothynge but a lytle Englyshe divinite, that wyl brynge the Realme into a verye barbarousnes, and utter decaye of learnynge." [86]

When it is remembered how much store Latimer set by education for the training up of a new generation of preachers in the doctrines of the Reformation, his concern is abundantly justified. The remedy he suggests is typical of the hopes of the times that some of the old benevolences could be revived and the resources that had gone to works of piety in the old days be devoted to the support of the instruments of propaganda and education. For he begs his hearers to put what they used to spend on pilgrimages and other exercises of piety into the help of poor scholars. [87]

This concern of Latimer's was also shared by Lever. He quite agreed with Latimer as to the effects of the disestablishment on the universities, [88] but there was another aspect of the university situation that concerned him no less than the neglect of learning and the sufferings of scholars, and that was the fact that whatever support was available for the universities was derived from sources he considered just as much a menace to the success of the cause he had at heart as the neglect of learning itself, that is impropriations of the revenues of parishes and benefices:

"Seyng that improperacions beynge so evyll that no man can alowe them, be nowe so employed unto the universities, yea and unto the yerelie revenues of the kynges majestie, that fewe dare speake agaynst them, ye may se that some men, not onlye by the abuse of ryches and authoritie, but also by the abuse of wysedom and pollicie do much harme, and specially those, by whose meanes thys realme is nowe brought into such case that eyther learning in the universitie, and necessarie revenues belonginge to the moste hygh authoritie is lyke to decaye, or elles improperacions to be mainteined, whych bothe be so devillyshe and abhominable, that if eyther of them come to effecte, it wyll cause the vengeaunce of God utterly to destroy this realme." [89]

In other words the universities were being supported at the expense of the parishes, of the provision of that instructed and resident clergy to which he looked for the winning of the masses in the ideological struggles of this transitional period.

But concerned as the leaders of the new order were with the inadequacy of the resources at their disposal for so large an undertaking, they were still more alarmed by the danger that even what they had might be taken from them. For they were beginning to realize that it is much easier to unloose a whirlwind of confiscation and destruction than to stop or direct it. They had long preached the insatiableness of greed. They were beginning to learn the reality of their preaching. For the distribution of the monastic wealth had served, as we have seen, to stimulate more appetites for wealth than it could possibly satisfy. Age-old inhibitions had been removed. Those of the secular clergy who had watched unmoved, if they had not actively promoted the disestablishment of the monasteries, had clearly no idea that the process of spoliation might eventually reach their incomes and possessions, too. But as the tide of confiscation rolled on, they found themselves threatened on two fronts.

The first was on the old ground of the robbery of the poor. And significantly, at least in the case of its loudest exponent, it arose out of the familiar attack on monastic wealth. For Fish had been, as we have seen, one of the most vigorous advocates of the recovery of the wealth of the monks for the relief of the poor to whom it had properly belonged in the first place. That first confiscation had not realized Fish's hopes, and he had, as we have seen, given equally vigorous expression to his disappointment. But disillusioned as he was as to his first line of attack, it was not in the nature of Fish to turn back. A little more than twenty years after the *Supplication of Beggers* Fish is back in 1546 with a new drive on church wealth.[90] This time it is the tithe, the great mainstay of the secular clergy and of the parochial structure, that he is seeking.

For, he insinuates, the sturdy beggars of monks far from turning to honest labor have worked their way into benefices. So he will have the priests routed out in order that the poor may have restored to them the provision of the tithe which was appointed to them in the beginning.[91] Of course, he blames the bishops for the way things seem to be working against the new order. Indeed, he accuses them of trying to bring old times back,[92] and he reiterates his charge that the priests and bishops profited from the old order.[93] But this time the full weight of his wrath falls especially upon the royal chaplains who seem to have carried on notably the old system of joining benefice to benefice for the support of ecclesiastical dignity. "Turne them out," he urges "the most victorious prynce Henry" of his dedication,[94] "after theyr brethren the pyed purgatory patriarkes: and restore to the poore members of Christ, theyr due portion, which they trusted to have received when they sawe your highnes turne out the other sturdy beggers." [95]

Either Fish had a very stout faith in the possibility of getting church property into the hands of the poor, or he felt that the defense of the new order was in such jeopardy that every effort must be made to bolster it, no matter what the character of the promises held out, or the possible effect of those promises. It is not necessary to challenge Fish's sincerity as his enemies did. The capacity of men to believe that what they think should be will come to pass is one of the great unexplored depths of human nature. At any rate, the attack on the tithe was serious enough and persistent enough to warrant the attention of men usually disposed to second most attacks upon the wealth of the church. Even when the attack was an old one, upon the wealth of the ancient order, Foxe the martyrologist was wary. For instance, in his account of John Florence, a turner of Shelton in the diocese of Norwich, who recanted and did penance in 1424, he quotes from Florence's alleged opinions the thesis "that curates should not take the tithes of their parishners, but that such tithes shuld be divided amonges the pore parishners." Against this he sets the marginal warning: "He meneth they should not claim such tithes by any exaction," [96] a sad attentuation of a by no means unique medieval assault upon the tithe.

But this attack upon the tithe was not the only line of attack which faced the leaders of the new settlement in the middle years of the century when they were so anxiously striving for the consolidation of their victory. There was another type of attack which was opening up as the limitations of their reformation became apparent. What those precise limitations were to be was not, of course, clear for a long time. Indeed, the struggle over them continued pretty much through the century. However, by the middle of the century it was apparent that the new order that was coming into being had fallen into the hands of men who, whatever their final position on specific issues might be, were not going to go more than so far from the old order. But the forces of revolution had been unleashed in a good many fields, doctrinal, liturgical, devotional as well as political and economic. There were men who were ready to go much farther than any of the presently-established leaders promised to go. And though no one knew as yet where the changes of the new order would stop, perhaps least of all the men who found themselves in positions of leadership, it was clear both to the more conservative and to the more radical, that that point would fall far short of the designs of some of the most convinced and aggressive reformers of the time.

Therefore, the more the existing order succeeded in equipping itself with material resources, the harder it would be for the more radical reformers to move it in the direction they wanted it to go. On the other hand, the more the existing order found itself in possession of the field, the more likely it was to take a firm hand with agitators against its premises. Everything was still too insecure, too much in process of determination, for either patience or tolerance. We may be sure that without always understanding the situation, all sides were practically and instinctively aware of it. Now the attack on the wealth of the old order had proved singularly efficient in undermining its power. The monastic world had been swept away, and even the old hierarchical organization of the secular branches of the church profoundly shaken. It is not surprising, therefore, that the unsatisfied radical should be found still driving against what remained of the ancient possessions of the church.

The wealth of the bishops was perhaps the most tempting target. The position of the bishops had been already challenged on grounds both of Scripture and of history. That challenge was a very complicated business, for the most part outside of the limited undertakings of the present inquiry. But one aspect of it is relevant. The bishops constituted with their various instruments of investigation and discipline a very considerable bulwark against the advance of doctrinal and liturgical innovation. It is not surprising that power exerted often with harsh effectiveness should make the office obnoxious to the proponents of change. Nor that an attack on the wealth of the bishops should make a very considerable appeal in certain quarters, combining as it did, the advantages of the appeal to the poor and to the rebel against ecclesiastical authority.

That is the beauty of Brinkelow's *The Complaint of Roderyck Mors . . . unto the Parlament house of Ingland,* of about 1548.[97] A former Gray Friar, he had, like a good many of his profession, welcomed the changes that destroyed the old order, but, again like many of the early supporters of the Reformation, he had clearly, to judge from his complaints about the way in which authority opposed godly preaching, pressed beyond the point which the church as a whole had reached by the middle of the century.[98]

Indeed, Brinkelow was one of those who saw in the order of the church of his time a conspiracy to preserve as much as possible of the old corruptions,[99] and he found the bishops the mainstay of that conspiracy.

Now in his address to the parliament of his native country he includes in a series of complaints about the existing social and ecclesiastical conditions of England, a very elaborate scheme of proposals for the alleviation of the lot of the poor, to be financed out of the present revenues of the bishops. The proposals in themselves are exceedingly interesting ones, ranging from a scheme for free medical service for the poor [100] to a provision for setting up needy couples in housekeeping.[101] In themselves they might be sure of a wide range of appeal to both self-interest and public spirit. But it is quite clear that not the least of the charms of these proposals from the author's point of view is that they would put the present misapplied wealth of the bishops to some good social use.

Indeed, Brinkelow is so eager to get rid of the bishops that he finally makes a frank and bare-faced appeal to self-interest, to be understood in the light not only of the humanitarian proposals suggested above, but also of his reminder that the portion of the bishops' temporalities to be granted to the king would lighten the burden of subsidies for the commons: [102]

"Now therfore I exhorte the higher powers in the name of the everlyving God, that if they will not loke uppon the spirituall extorcioners (I say bishoppes canons and chaunterers) for the Zeale which they ought to beare to the congregation of God, neyther for the love of God that they ought to have to the comen welthe and to the poore; yet let them remembre it for their owne welthes sake." [103]

Men who took the position of Lever and Latimer faced, therefore, a double threat, a threat from the greed and religious indifference of those "worldlings" whose appetites had been whetted but in no way appeased by the monastic wealth they had already acquired, and a threat from their fellow-clerics, which may be described as a two-pronged threat, involving, on the one hand, the old claim of the wealth of the church for the poor, and, on the other, to some degree at least, the determination to avert a premature consolidation of an incomplete revolution by depriving it of the material foundations of power. Lever and Latimer, as we have seen, were alarmed but in no way intimidated by these threats to the new order. They met them boldly, as we have seen, by insisting that benefices be administered for the instruction of the people, and that the old habits of charitable and pious support of the universities be continued for the education of the clergy that should establish the new order. That was a program that does credit to their singleness of religious purpose, and doubtless, if that were all they could have mustered, there would have been a good many of the new possessing classes who would have had enough active religious sensibility and attachment to the new, order to give them the support they asked for.

But there were more potent reënforcements at hand. The key to them is to be found in a tract of Robert Crowley's published in 1550, *The Way to Wealth,* with the title-page explanation, "wherein is plainly taught a most present remedy for Sedicion." [104] For there is a threatening note in his challenge to the greedy lay appropriators of the benefices that indicates the recognition of a new factor in the situation:

"Be warned betime, least ye repente to late leave of your gredie desire to pul away the liveynge from the cleargy, and seke diligentlye to set suche ministers in the churche as be able and wyl enstruct the people in al pointes of theyr dutie, that you with them and they with you may escape the wrath of God that hangeth presently over you both." [105]

That last sentence is a far cry from Simon Fish. The problem of the support of the reformed clergy is not to be solved by the confiscation of church resources. Crowley has no sympathy with those wives of the clergy who are anxious to cut a figure in the world,[106] but he does recognize that the seizure of benefices by lay patrons is doing the parishes no good.[107] To maintain a clergy who will preach the duty of submission to the king and patience with their lot is a wise way of spending money for social stability. It is hard to see how the ruling classes of Crowley's day could overlook his argument.

CHAPTER IV

SOCIAL RADICALISM AND RELIGIOUS REFORM

IN OTHER words, Crowley recognizes the presence of another factor in the campaign against ecclesiastical wealth that both the church-robbers and the church-reformers were too preoccupied with their own objectives to assess at its due value. It is not an isolated element to be settled by itself, but a part of a larger movement, of which the groundswell is to be felt in all the social agitation of the first half of the century, and that is the age-old protest of the have-not's against the have's. And the reason why Crowley recognizes it so clearly at this point and turns it so effectively to account in his appeal to the new possessing classes is that it is no new thing to him. For he has done in the immediate past as much as any man of his profession to feed it and encourage it, and even now as he takes measures to meet its peculiar dangers, he reiterates his sympathy with it, and his support of its essential justice.

This is clearly to be seen in a tract which he had published just two years before this, *An Informacion and Peticion agaynst the Oppressours of the Pore Commons of this Realme*,[1] which shows very plainly what sort of man he was. He was just as passionately against the old religious order and just as passionately in favor of consummating its destruction as Fish, but his view of the situation was much broader than Fish's and his analysis much less simple. When it is remembered that his appeal was to Parliament, then the text which he chose from Isaiah for his title-page becomes much more significant: "When you suffre none oppression to bee amongest you, and leave of your idle talke: then shal you cal upon the Lord and he shal hear you, you shal crie, and he shal say, Behold I am at hand." [2]

110

He does give the precedence to the clergy in the introduction of his thesis:

"Amonge the manyfold and moste weyghty mattiers (moste worthy counsaylours) to be debated and communed of in this present parliament, and by the advise, assent and consent therof, spedily to be redressed: I thynke ther is no one thynge more nedfull to be spoken of, then the great oppression of the pore communes, by the possessioners as wel of Clergie as of the Laitie." [3]

But the use of that word "possessioners" in that context is significant of a larger class orientation than that of Fish. And his application of it to the problems of the England of the hour is more sweeping than anything Fish had envisaged.

For he is afraid that the oppression of the poor will be passed over in silence unless God now works in the hearts of the possessioners of the realm "as he dyd in the primitive church, when the possessioners wer contented and very wyllynge, to sell theyr possessions and geve the price therof to be commune to al the faythful belevers." [4] This was the great age of the appeal to the example of the primitive church, but of all the aspects of the primitive church this must have been pretty nearly the rarest to be invoked. Apparently Crowley felt that he was running a grave risk, for he hastens to add a disclaimer and a qualification which is interesting on two counts. The first is that he should have been afraid that somebody would think he was advocating the making of all goods common; the second is the ground on which he cleared himself, namely that he would not have anybody supported without labor, a principle that carried to its logical extreme might have equally disastrous results to certain classes of possessioners:

"Take me not here that I shoulde go about by these wordes to perswade men to make all thynges commune: for if you do you mistake me. For I take God to wytnes I meane no such thynge[.] But with all myne herte I woulde wysh that no man were suffered to eate, but such as woulde laboure in theyr vocacion and callyng, accordynge to the rule that Paule gave to the Thessalonians." [5]

That is a classic position, already familiar to the reader of Langland or of the medieval sermon-writers, indeed to the whole Christian tradition, which has always had a low opinion of idleness. But however reassuring to his hearers, his anxiety to avoid misunderstanding does not turn him from his objectives:

"But yet I woulde wysh that the possessioners woulde consyder whoe gave them theyr possessions, and howe they ought to bestowe them. And then (I doubt not) it shoulde not nede to have all thynges made commune. . . . If the possessioners woulde consyder themselves to be but stuardes, and not Lordes over theyr possessions: thys oppression woulde sone be redressed. But so longe as thys perswasion styketh in theyr myndes. It is myne owne. Whoe shall warne me to do wyth myne owne as me selfe lysteth? it shall not bee possible to have any redresse at all." [6]

This is a direct attack upon the whole notion of property. But still more is to come.

"By nature . . . you can claime no thinge but that whiche you shall gette with the swet of your faces. That you are Lordes and governoures therfore, commeth not by nature but by the ordinaunce and appoyntment of God. Knowe then that he hath not cauled you to the welthe and glorie of this worlde: but hath charged you wyth the great and rede multitude.

"And if any of them perishe thorow your defaute, knowe then for certentye, that the bloude of them shalbe required at your handes. If the impotent creatures perish for lacke of necessaries: you are the murderers, for you have theyr enheritaunce and do not minister unto them. If the sturdy fall to stealeyng, robbyng and reveynge: then are you the causers therof, for you dygge in, enclose, and wytholde from them the earth out of the whych they should dygge and plowe theyr lyveynge. . . .

"The whole earth therfor (by byrth ryght) belongeth to the chyldren of men. They are all inheritours therof indifferently by nature.

"But because the sturdy shoulde not oppresse the weake and impotent: God hath apoynted you stuards to geve meate unto his housholde in due seasone." [7]

So much for the ground theory of possession. But for the Christian there is more than the notion of stewardship; there is also the notion of brotherhood and of fellowship. Crowley made the usual protest of his time and party against the tithes and fees of the clergy.[8] But he does not limit the devotion of spirit which he exacts of the clergy to them alone. He calls the attention of layman and cleric alike to Christ's giving his life for men:

"Accordynge to this exemple ought our frendshyp to be such, that we wyll not spare to spende our lyfe for the welth of our brothers. . . . Some perchaunce wyll thynke that this frendshyp is to be understande onely of the pastors and shepherdes towarde theyr flocke, because Christ sayth that a good shepherde geveth his lyfe for his shepe. . . . But for asmuch as the Laie and private persons, ar as well of the flocke of Christe as the other: thys frendeshyp parteineth unto them nolesse then to the other." [9]

Here Crowley is preaching doctrine doubtless much less congenial to the new possessors of abbey lands than the injunction of Simon Fish to take the tithe for the poor. Crowley does not fear to drive his lesson home. Indeed, he addresses Parliament in terms that forecast a thousand attacks since on the relations of the representatives of the people to society at large. He has just been reviewing the woes of the tenants of the day, when he turns suddenly to Parliament itself:

"Yea even you (moste christian counsaylours) whych are here assembled, to debate the weightie mattiers of thys realme: are not all so free from this kynde of oppression, but that you coulde be well contented to wyncke at it. And therfor, for asmuche as the inordinate love of men towarde them selves is such, that eyther they can not se theyr owne fauts, or else if they do se them, or be tolde of them they take them not to be so great as they are in dede: I thinke it no mervayle, though such of you (most worthy counsaylours) as have any profite by this oppression, do wythin them selves deride and laugh to scorne my fole hardines and rashe enterpryse herein, knoweynge that it is not the use of them that bee assembled to the intent to establish such thynges as shall be for the welth of a whole realme: to condescende and agree to those thynges whych shall be disprofitable unto the chief membres of the same." [10]

This admission might at first seem one of despair, but Robert Crowley is a man of resource. He has three lines of argument to jolt the possessioners, even those entrenched in Parliament, out of their complacency. The first is the religious one, the threat of the judgment of God.

"For even the same spirit that sayd unto Esaie, crye and sease not, declare unto my people theyr wychednes: cryeth also in my conscience, bydyng me not spare to tell the possessioners of this realme, that unlesse they repente the oppression wherewyth they vexe the pore commons, and shew themselves through love to be brothers of one father and membres of one body wyth them: they shal not at the laste daye enherite wyth them the kyngdom of Christe the eldest sonne of God the father, whych hath by his worde begotten hym many brothers and coheritours is [sic] his kyngdom." [11]

But it is not just a matter of waiting for the Last Judgment. Even here on earth there is judgment. In two directions Crowley threatens the oppressors, or rather with two types of argument he tries to convince them of the folly of their actions. The first is a very interesting argument from history, in which he cuts a fairly large swath. What he is saying is that the dominion of the oppressors does not stand very long before the vengeance of God. It is not easy here to be sure that Crowley's idea of time is any different from that easy contemporaneity characteristic of the usual attitude toward history of his time. If it is, then he is able to take a very large view of history, indeed, probably so large as not very much to impress his contemporaries:

"Consyder Pharao with his great armie, whom the Lord overwhelmed in the red sea for oppresseyng and persecuteyng his people. Yea consider all the nobilitie that have possessed the erth even from the begynyng: and then saye howe you bee theyr successours, and by what title you may cleyme that which was theyrs.

"Many hundred yeres sence, the noble Romains helde all Europa and parte of Affrike and Asia, in quiete possession: and where are they that succeade them in theyr impier? The brutishe Gothes invaded and vanquished the impier of Rome: and wher are theyr successours?

"What shoulde I stande in the rehersale of the great possessioners that have heretofore possessed the erth, whose lynial descent can not be founde?" [12]

But Crowley did not remain content with the memory of history and the threat of the last judgment. It was with something more immediate that he made his third appeal, speaking this time again to the possessioners in Parliament:

"Once remembre, that as the body wyth out the inferiour partes is but lame and as a blocke unweldy, and muste, if it wyll remove frome place to place, creepe upon the handes: even so you, if ye had not the pore membres of this realme to tyll the grounde and doe your other droudgery: no remedy you must nedes do it your selves.

"Use them therfore as the necessarie membres of the mistical body of this most noble realme, and be not in this poynt mor unnatural then the heathen Philosophers were." [13]

This is a pretty sweeping indictment not of the past order but of the present, not of the old regime but of the new, not just of the church but of all society, especially lay society. It reads much like a sermon of one of the great reforming friars of the Middle Ages such as Owst describes.[14] There is nothing said of a possible revolt, but neither is there anything said of the patience of the poor. And there is in it more than a suggestion of what things would be like if in some unspecified fashion the usual dependences of civilized life were removed. Furthermore, indictment of the possessioners is developed and, as it were, documented, with a precision not suggested in the passages above, perhaps, but nonetheless actual and impressive. It was certainly not Robert Crowley's fault if Parliament did not look to its ways. Not penned in any sense as a sermon, it is yet in the most substantial sense of the word a sermon, the type of sermon of which Parliament was to have all too few and need all too many in the years to come.

This essay of Crowley's was published about 1548. His preoccupation at that time was clear, the fear that the rich and the prosperous in their concern with other matters would forget, or find it convenient to forget the sufferings of the poor. Two years later something very different was in the forefront of his consciousness. The title of the work he published in 1550 makes it clear with his characteristic directness, *The Way to Wealth,* with the additional title-page description, "wherein is plainly taught a most present remedy for Sedicion." [15] Like, as we shall presently see, most of his colleagues of a reforming cast of mind, Crowley had been frightened. The social preaching of his own party and generation, indeed, the social preaching of generations of popular preachers had borne fruit in the riots and the uprisings of the last two years, especially those of 1549.

It would be dangerous to define too precisely the causes of the rebellions of 1549, for human motives at best are involved enough, and in times of great perplexity and confusion, they often become inextricably complicated. The century and a half between 1500 and 1650 is, as Mr. Tawney reminds us, the great age of the peasant uprisings in western Europe.[16] It is also the age of the Reformation, and, as Mr. Tawney again reminds us, that is to be viewed as a social as well as a religious revolution.[17] In any particular situation, therefore, there is always the possibility of a very considerable complication of forces at work. The years between the death of Henry and the accession of Elizabeth were years of great religious strain, and they were, also, years of acute agrarian suffering.[18] We may be sure, therefore, that in the widespread agitation of the year 1549–50 both social and religious motives played their part.

It would seem that social unrest had the larger part in the origins of the rebellion in Norfolk; certainly, religious unrest had the major role in the rebellions of Exeter and Cornwall.[19] Attachment to the old religion played its part in the fomenting of the rising in the north and in the expression of its purposes, as witness the banner of the Five Wounds with the plow above.[20] And though the social question had been in some respects less acute in the west, still there had been an epidemic of uprisings against the enclosures, which had been suppressed just before the rebellions of 1549 in Devon and Cornwall.[21] Certainly, there had been some traces of social unrest in the religious demands of the western rebels of 1549.[22] And the fact that the government tried the ringleaders of both rebellions together in Westminster doubtless had its share in identifying the two movements in the public mind.[23]

We can well understand the worry of the preachers of the religious revolution over this. They were anxious that violence should not disgrace a cause of which they approved, but they were still more anxious that it should not defeat that cause. It is probable that if they had thought at all about the relations of social and of religious revolution, they had thought of the one as helping the other. That the cry for relief from the existing social order should impede religious revolution was certainly not what they had contemplated, probably something they had never even dreamed of. Now these men were face to face with the problems of a movement which had been very zealously promoted by idealists who had not always gauged the relations between their hopes and the probabilities of the consequences of their actions with any more precision than idealists usually do, and who had found that they had pretty much lost control of that movement. The elements in the situation were of course many, and one may be quite sure that not all of them were apparent to the contemporary mind any more than all of them are recoverable by the mind of the present; and even of those that were apparent, it may, also, be taken for granted that they appeared often in a different light and with different emphasis from what they would today. But some elements occur so widely in the literature of the time that they may safely be taken as at least significant of what appeared important to the contemporary mind.

Of these elements two stand out in the writings of the preachers, at least, with special sharpness. The first is the presence in a good many places and in a good deal of force of what were then regarded as extremist social views, of what would, perhaps, in any age be regarded as extreme views. And it should be added, views held not as a matter of abstract speculation but as a pattern for immediate action. Mr. Tawney probably gave the best description of this radicalism in his phrase, "the spontaneous doctrineless communism of the open field village." [24]

Needless to say, the character and the extent of this radical agitation were not underestimated by the rich and the privileged who were frightened enough by the actual resort to violence to believe anything of the instigators of such outrages. Crowley in his post mortem on the rebellions describes the state of mind of the frightened "possessioners" with his customary liveliness and acumen; and with what seems from all the evidence to be a fair degree of fidelity:

"Nowe if I should demaund of the gredie cormerauntes what thei thinke shuld be the cause of Sedition: they would saie, the paisant knaves be to welthy, provender pricketh them. They knowe not themselves, they knowe no obedience, they regard no lawes, thei would have no gentlemen, thei wold have al men like them selves, they would have al thinges commune. Thei would not have us maisters of that which is our owne." [25]

The interesting thing about this passage is that it puts in a nutshell the three objectives usually attributed at this time to the social revolutionaries, especially the Anabaptists. They would abolish all magistrates and authority of law, they would level all social distinctions between the different classes of men, and they would have all property common. In other words, these are the traditional charges of social revolution, anarchy, social leveling, communism.

It is not easy to say how much of the anxiety expressed in such a passage is justified by fact, and how much is the product of imagination operating on fear. Most modern students of the matter would probably agree with Mr. Tawney that the initiative in the agrarian disturbances had been taken by the landlords who made the enclosures and not by the peasants who had seen their immemorial rights taken from them.[26] In that sense it is hard to see how anybody could disagree with his description of the agrarian revolts between the years 1530 and 1560 as essentially conservative. The peasants rose only to keep or recover what they had always had.[27]

Even so, there seems no doubt that in certain places under certain circumstances the time-worn leveling cries of medieval insurrection were heard. Lever makes allusion to the same phenomenon in a sermon of 1550:

"And the chiefest cause that maketh them to imagine this abhominable errour, that there shuld be no ryche menne or rulers, commeth because some ryche men and rulers (marke that I saye some, for all bee not suche) but I saye some ryche men and rulers by the abuse of their ryches and authoritie, dothe more harme then good unto the comen wealth, and more griefe then confort unto the people." [28]

Of course, there are certain leveling cries, that one may call the classics of rebellion, heard in any age when desperate men rebel against intolerable burdens. They are heard again with surprisingly little change from Crowley's report in the pages of a sermon of more than a half century later.[29] Again a preacher is talking of "the late Rebellion," this time in Northampton. It is the year 1607 and Robert Wilkinson is preaching what is substantially a post mortem before the Commissioners who had been sent down to settle the grim business.

His report is, of course, to be read in the light of those official presences; so perhaps the most one can say is that it represents what the official understanding of the circumstances was. He is tracing the course of the revolt:

"First they professe nothing, but to throwe downe enclosures, though that were indeed no part of common powre; but afterward they will reckon for other matters, They will accompt with Clergie men, and counsell is given to kill up Gentleman, and they will levell all states as they levelled bankes and ditches: and some of them boasted, that now they hoped to worke no more; the sword and the gallows making them true Prophets, and some of them in plaine termes, they thought that now the law was downe, as in times of common uproare, both civill and divine law and all goe downe: and what then shall wee thinke must have beene the ende of this?" [30]

This passage is interesting for two reasons. First of all, it demonstrates again the continuity of social restlessness, and, secondly, it shows a very good understanding of the snowball fashion in which revolt develops.

Between the dates represented by these two passages, one may be sure that at least a memory of the leveling agitations of earlier periods survived in the general mind. Probably that memory was under normal circumstances not much more precise or immediate than that suggested by a very unsympathetic but lively play of the last decade of the century on the theme of Jack Straw. One of the speeches of Parson Ball represents in a doggerel condensation the traditional slogans of the fourteenth-century social rebels:

"England is growne to such a passe of late,
That rich men triumph to see the poore beg at their gate.
But I am able by good scripture before you to prove,
That God doth not this dealing allow nor love,
But when Adam delved, and Eve span,
Who was then a Gentleman,
Brethren, brethren, it were better to have this Communitie,
Then to have this diffrence in degrees,

        *   *   *   *   *   *   *

But follow the counsel of John Ball,
I promise you I love yee al,
and make devision equally,
Of each mans goods indiffrently,
and rightly may you follow armes,
To rid you from these civil harmes." [31]

All this is, of course, highly dramatic. The whole treatment of the rebels and of the issues involved makes it clear that the author and his audience considered these ideas extreme and absurd, but in spite of that one feels in these bad verses something rather more than just a dramatist's man of straw.

As for more definite indications, we find a good many, both direct and indirect, in the writers of the middle of the century on, that ideas of a more specifically communistic and even anarchic character were in the air. But it is not possible to say just how much of any particular indictment is to be regarded as the product of the fantasies of fear, and how much is fact.

There is some fairly definite evidence on the subject. In a sermon of 1549 Latimer, in his discussion of the heretics who will have no magistrates or judges on earth, cites what he "hearde of late by the relation of a credible person, and a worshypful man, of a towne in thys realme of Englande, that hathe above .v.C. heritykes of thys erroniouse opinion in it." [32] To Latimer this is, of course, evidence of the devil's resolution to hinder the spread of the gospel by discrediting it. The number is probably like all the alarm figures of the Elizabethan preachers, somewhat high, but there is a good deal of evidence in the reports of radical Protestant activities in a town like Colchester, to suggest that he is undoubtedly correct as to the existence of considerable numbers of the more extreme Anabaptists in England at the time. For instance, William Wilkinson in a book against the Family of Love published in 1579 gives a very graphic account of the more extremist directions which the conversation sometimes took in the night meetings of the faithful in the inns of that town, which seems to have been a rallying-place for Protestants in the time of Queen Mary.[33] Indeed, according to the deposition of one Henry Crinell of Willingham, which Wilkinson quotes, the mysterious English propagandist of Familism, Christopher Vitels the Joiner, was there spreading his doctrines at an inn some time about the year 1555.[34]

But perhaps even more imposing evidence as to the presence of a noticeable radical opinion among the masses is to be found in a passage of *The Defence of John Hales ayenst Certeyn Sclaundres and False Reaportes made of Hym,* imposing because of the highly practical and even factual habit of the author's mind, and because of the fact that his service on one of the King's Highness' Commissions touching enclosures had put him in an unusually good position to inform himself of the facts concerning what he was talking about. He is endeavoring to account for the insurrections of 1548, which his critics have laid to the charge of his commission:

"And I cannot but moche merveyle, whie any man shulde suspecte me to be author of all these seditions, when as I have herde, it is for thre sondrye causes that they make these Insurrections. Some be papystes, and wold have ayen ther olde poperye. Somme be Anabaptists and lybertynes, and wolde have all thinges commen. And the thyrde be certen poore men that seeke to have ageyne ther revenues that have byn by power taken from them, and to be relyved of the great dearthe and pryces of vittell." [35]

Hales' disclaimer of sympathy with the Anabaptists and Libertines is the classic one of his time: "Anabaptistes and libertynes I have and do most abhorre, as sectes cleane contrary to goddes worde, nature and civyle pollicie." [36]

Such a disclaimer as this of Hales' is not by any means unique in the social literature of the time, but one seldom finds a man of his position in life defending himself from a suspicion of sympathy with the Anabaptists. Only the fact that his commission had been accused of fomenting the disturbances which he tries to account for on other grounds [37] can explain his troubling to exculpate himself from a suspicion more likely to attach itself to men of a humbler position in life and more ardent disposition.

Whatever the actual strength of the Anabaptists in England, there is no question that they were the objects of an odium that exceeded even that in which "Papists" were held by the sound Protestants of the time. For while like most such stories, that of Münster was not by any means a simple one, the tales of the excesses committed there had gone over Europe and had laid the whole left-wing movement of the Reformation open to suspicion.

Indeed, the Anabaptists were held by more conservative reformers to have brought discredit upon all Protestantism. For once Calvin grossly understated the facts when he said of the Anabaptists in the words of his English translator:

"Towching these pore phantasticals, which so myghtly vaunte them selves to have the worde of God for theym the dede sheweth howe it is. It is longe sence we have continually traveiled, that thys holy word might be set up: and to bryng thys to passe we sustaine a fight against al the world. They, what declaration have thei made, or wherin have they holpen this. But rather contrariwise, thei have hyndered and disturbed us." [38]

Certainly the Anabaptists had struck the social and political susceptibilities of the time at their most sensitive point, the fear of anarchy. When Poynet, by no means a defender of political absolutism, wanted to define the known extreme of lack of respect for civil authority, he cited the Anabaptists as the supreme example of those who would have all "politike power" done away with.[39] But this was an extreme of anarchy to which it would be very hard to get even any extremist of the time, in England at least, to plead guilty. For the existence of such a point of view we must rely on insinuation and inference, probably at best none too fair.

There is more reason to take seriously the charges of a deliberate attack on privilege that every so often crop up in the sermons of the time. Becon puts into the mouth of his Philemon in *The Jewel of Joy* a sentence that goes to the heart of the matter in an age when the distinctions of rank of feudal days had been accentuated rather than diminished: "Seyng than that as touching our corporal creacion there is no difference no prerogative, what nobilitye or worthynes of bloud, can there be more in the noble personage than in the base slave?" And from there he proceeds to a very eloquent attack on all pride of birth and family.[40]

When it comes to the definition of classes, it is doubtful if Latimer was as conscious of the issue as either Crowley or Lever, though as usual he has a single sentence that goes to the heart of the matter, this time in a form probably reminiscent of Langland and the ensuing Piers tradition: "The poorest ploughman is in Christ equall wyth the gretest prynce that is." [41]

On one issue, however, he does show a very lively sense of the problem of the relations of the different groups in society, and that is on the classic issue of hospitality. All those who lamented the good old times, and there is on several issues more than a trace of this nostalgia in Latimer himself, lamented especially the decline in that easy-going dispensing of shelter and entertainment and food that had been a feature of the somewhat patriarchal life of the countryside in the later Middle Ages. That and a modest alms-giving had been features of his father's life upon which, it will be remembered, Latimer had looked back with not a little pride.[42] In contrast to this, Lever is more keenly aware of the social importance of this function of the old order. For when he discusses the conditions of holding a benefice, he couples "honeste hospitalitie" with the duty of feeding the flock spiritually.[43] And when he examines into the causes of social distrust, he finds the chief "cause why the commens doo not love, trust, nor obey the gentlemen and officers, is, because the gentlemen and officers buylde many fayre houses, and kepe fewe good houses," [44] an aspect of the magnificent Tudor building not always appreciated.

But in general the preachers of the sixteenth century do not seem to have had so much to say of this aspect of the leveling program, and that for a good reason, namely, their preoccupation with the character and needs of their particular congregations. The preachers to the Court were naturally disposed to take the social distinctions of the time for granted, and preachers to the middle classes were properly more concerned with the pretensions of wealth than of birth, because these were the temptations to which from the nature of the case their parishioners were more exposed. Perhaps, too, some of them at least had begun to see that this aspect of the world's immemorial folly was better taken care of in literature by the gibes of the satirist and in life by the conquests of the middle-class merchant.

But if the anti-rank aspects of the leveling program did not much bother the preachers, what may be roughly described as its communistic tendencies did. It is easy to understand their concern. Their own attacks on the oppression of the poor had been more than enough to fire the resentment of the victims. Indeed, it is hard to see how anything more than what they had themselves said of the wickedness of the rich oppressors could be advanced even by the firebrands of revolution. The preachers may well, therefore, have felt some responsibility for that aspect of the rebellions. Furthermore, in their promotion of the confiscation of the riches of the monasteries, they had fostered what might well be taken as a precedent for relief by the victims of the unequal distribution of goods of the society of the time. Above all, in the accomplishment of the confiscation of the riches of the monasteries, the poor had seen what they had seldom seen before, the translation of preaching into action. The result may well have been profoundly inciting to optimistic imaginations.

Of course, the preachers had never meant that matters should go so far. They were used to fulminating and to having but a fraction of their fulminations taken seriously. And they were thoroughly aware of the discrepancies between the ideal and the actuality of a Christian or any other society, and quite prepared to be tolerant of an inevitable slowness in the approximation of the two systems. But they might well ask themselves whether in the fervor of criticism and denunciation, they had always made their qualifications and their limitations clear.

Moreover, the relations between communism and Christianity were not any easier then than now. Communism delivered certain challenges that Christianity could not lightly disregard. It professed a goal of brotherhood and equality to which no Christian could turn a wholly deaf ear, least of all the preachers. Langland, always concerned about the motives to action, might put the injunction to preach communism on the authority of Plato and Seneca into the mouth of Envy,[45] but he could not forget that there had been a holy commune on high in heaven before Lucifer fell.[46] Christianity had to reckon with even more than that. As Henry Parker had put it in *Dives and Pauper,* "saythe holy writt that in the begynyng of holy church al thinges were comon to the multitude of al cristen people nat only to the apostlys: but to al cristen people."[47] And even for his own day Parker would still insist: "And therefore sayth the law: that comon lyf is nedeful to al men, and namely to them that wyl folowe the lif of cristes desiples."[48] This was a familiar tradition coming out of the wrestlings of the fourteenth and fifteenth centuries with the problem of goods and religion. When the Anabaptists agitated these ideas, Poynet might retort on behalf of the sixteenth-century Christian what the practical mind of earlier times had clearly acted on, that this was sheer perfectionism in defiance of man's very nature. The Anabaptists, he taunted, "ymage man to be of that puritie that he was before the fall, that is, cleane without sinne, or that (if he will) he maie so be: and that as whan ther was no sinne, all thinges were common, so they ought now to be."[49] Calvin, himself, who took the doctrinal and political "phantasies"[50] of the Anabaptists so seriously that he wrote against them at length, might dismiss their alleged communism as an absurdity which they themselves had begun to discard:

"Touchynge that some amonge them have holden opinion that all goodes shoulde be commune, also that a man maye have manye wyves, so that they have compelled some whiche were contente wyth one, to take moe, and a thousande other absurdites: I wyll speake nothynge at al. For they them selves beyng confused in ther selves have for the most part by littel and littel withdrawen them selves." [51]

Yet the challenge remained.

Even when with the passing of years the Anabaptists had come to seem much less of a practical menace, their alleged addiction to communism remained a by-word, matter for jesting even among serious-minded men as may be seen in a passage in Henrie Smith's *The Poore Mans Teares* of 1592. It is in an account of the beggars who on Gads Hill and Shooters Hill seize horses by the head and bid men deliver their purses that he lightly concludes that "these fellowes are of the opinion of the Anabaptists, that everie mans goods must be common to them, or else they will force them to part it." [52]

For the preachers of the mid-century, however, communism was no jesting matter. They had to reckon with the agitation of actual rebels against the property arrangements of the day. That they did so is to be seen in their constant disclaimers of any intention to support communism. And still more is it to be seen in their attempts to refute communism by systematic attack on its premises. One of the most painstaking of these efforts is a sermon of one of the greatest of the preachers of social reform. It is the sermon which Lever preached in the "Shroudes" at Saint Paul's in London on the second of February, 1550,[53] a sermon to which we shall have occasion to refer more than once, because of the fullness and vigor with which he arraigned the social iniquities of the time. In the course of his argument Lever had occasion to define what he considered the Christian theory of goods, and this he did very pithily as follows: "For so is it mete, that christen mens goodes shuld be comen unto everi mans nede, and private to no mans luste." [54]

But this principle, he sees instantly, may be taken to involve dangerous concessions to the theory of common possession of the goods of society. So he goes on to refute this theory:

"For they that Imagine, covet, or wishe to have all thinges comune, in suche sorte that everye man myght take what hym luste, wolde have all thinges comen and open unto everie mans luste, and nothynge reserved or kept for any mans nede. And they that wolde have like quantitie of every thing to be geven to everye man, entending therby to make all alyke, do utterly destroy the congregacion, the misticall bodie of Christ, wher as there must nedes be divers members in diverse places, havinge diverse dueties. . . . And thus to have al thinges comen, doth derogate or take away nothynge from the authoritie of rulers. But to wyll to have all thynges comen, in suche sorte that idle lubbers (as I sayde) myghte take and waste the geines of laborers without restraint of authoritie, or to have lyke quantitie of everye thynge to be geven to every man, is under a pretence to mende al, purposely to marre all. . . ." [55]

In other words, Lever is afraid that the establishment of a thoroughgoing communism would destroy the diversified structure of a more advanced society, and that the right of access to all the goods of society might be abused by the lazy. This was an ancient fear, but one may be sure that it was accentuated by the sixteenth-century emphasis on industry and application to one's job.

The extremes to which the rebels had carried the social complaint of the preachers was, then, a cause of distress and anxiety to them. But there was more even than this in the mid-century insurrections to worry the reformed clergy. The sixteenth century took very literally the scriptural saying, "By their fruits ye shall know them." The preachers of reform had made very large promises of the good to be won by the adoption of their program. Now much of that good had failed of materialization, and there had been a great deal of strife and turbulence. Indeed, as we have seen, some of the reformers themselves had conceded that the poor were worse off than before.[56] It is hardly to be wondered at, therefore, that a good many people who did not care much about the issues of the time but did, like easy-going human beings in any age, value their peace, should have wondered if the bother were worth it, should have been ready, indeed, to listen to arguments that a return to the old order would dispose of these difficulties. The preachers knew this and were troubled about it. "Oh mercifull father of heaven, I can never lament inough, to heare the

Gospell thus blasphemed, to be named a thing causing sedicion, whan it is the only cause of concord and peace, in conscience unto the faithful," lamented Brinkelow.[57]

In other words, Brinkelow like the other reformers insisted that even though the religious changes had not produced the social results they were supposed to, they were worthwhile in themselves. Such men were too firmly convinced of the rightness of their cause to let their confidence waver or to think even for a little of turning back. Rather they met the charges of their enemies head-on and, where possible, turned them back upon them. One way of meeting what was probably the most widespread and irritating charge of all, namely, that in the old days things were quiet whereas now there was nothing but trouble is to be seen in the ingenious comfort which Thomas Becon offers to the Princess Elizabeth in his dedication to her of *The Jewel of Joy:*

"But as we have an urgent cause to rejoyce for the restorynge of the true light of Christes Gospell unto us, seynge by it we receyve so manye commodities and singular profyts for the health of our soulles so lykewyse have we no meane cause to lamente, that wyth thys precious wheate the fode of our inwarde man, wholsome tares and noysome cockell riseth and springeth up through the envye of Satan our enemye, wherby we maye learne howe studious and diligente the devyl that olde adversary of mankynd is to molest, disquyet and trouble the congregation of Christ, and to take away from us the most comfortable food of our soulles. What wicked and ungodly opinions ar ther sowen now a dayes of the Anabaptistes, Davidians, Libertines, and such other pestilente sectes in the hertes of the people unto the greate disquietnes of christes churche, movinge rather unto sedicion than unto pure religion, unto heresy then unto thynges godly?" [58]

In other words, a man like Becon saw in the very disorder that had been flung in the reformers' teeth evidence of the activity of the Old Enemy of mankind, sure to stir whenever he saw any good work forward that might cheat him of his hoped-for prey.

Yet adequate as this explanation might be thought, it was not the habit of the sixteenth century for all its faith to rest content with the exclusively supernatural any more than the impersonal explanation. The devil might be busy, but he had his agents and his aids. And both Lever and Crowley knew where to look for them. Crowley in particular has some very pointed things to say on this subject. And what he has to say is all the more interesting because if we can judge from certain episodes in his own career, he is himself hardly to be taken for a model of non-resistance, certainly in matters ecclesiastical. In fact, he seems to have had the reputation with his superiors at least of being something of a firebrand.[59] Of course, it may well be that to so convinced a Puritan idolatry seemed the one thing that justified resistance, but it is more probable that the authority of a bishop had no such force for him as the authority of the king. So we cannot judge his general practice by his behavior in the hands of Archbishop Parker. What is more probable is that Crowley, knowing the psychology of the clerical non-conformist from the inside, was quick to recognize the work of the agitator wherever he encountered it, and nonetheless readily when he found it on the opposite side from his own. Certainly there is no mistaking his reaction to the social agitators in the following address to the rebels:

"The false prophetes shoulde never have perswaded the that thou myghtest revenge thyne owne wronge. The false prophetes shoulde never have caused the to beleve that thou shouldeste prevaile againste them with the swerde, under whose governaunce God hath apointed the to be. He would have told the that to revenge wronges, is in a subject to take and usurpe the office of a kinge and consequently the office of God. For the king is goddes minister to revenge the wronges done unto the innocent." [60]

Of course, the clergy should have made this clear to their parishioners. But Crowley had no illusions on this score. What he thought of the parochial clergy of his day is quite clear from a passage of commiseration for the poor parishioner that is strikingly prophetic of what Milton will later have to say of the clergy of his day:

"But thy shepherde hathe bene negligent as (alas the while) all shepeherdes be at this daie, and hath not enstructed the aright. He espied not the wolfe before he had woried the, or happlye he knewe him not from a shepe. But it is mostelike he was but an hirelinge, and cared for no more but to be fedde with the milcke and fatlinges and cladde with the woule, as the greateste number of them that beare the name of shepeherde in Englande be at this daie." [61]

Lever was clearly of the same opinion when in a sermon preached before the king in 1550 he asked with regard to the parochial clergy, how many of them could be found who were not either "supersticious papystes" or "carnal gospellers." [62] There were clearly a good many of the clergy in England, who had no use for the religious changes in themselves. And there were probably still more of the laity who had no desire to see their religious habits disturbed. And still more who, if they were fairly indifferent in matters of religion, certainly would not wish to see their material condition altered for the worse for religious changes in which they were not especially interested. There must, therefore, have been a good many people besides the actual rebels who would have been murmuring that all this trouble was what might be expected from changing the old faith and that it would be much better if things could be as they had been. Here was a field very fertile for either the priest completely devoted to the old religious order or for the social reformer exasperated by the disappointments of the last years.

But sometimes the role of the disaffected clergy was more active. We must not forget Langland's complaint of the curates who misled their flocks with the wrong kind of advice. [63] Apparently, we are in the presence here of a continuing social and religious phenomenon, this of the parish priest who moved by dissatisfaction of his own, or pity for the hardships of his parishioners, or both, encourages discontent, if not worse. This becomes quite clear when Crowley turns his attention to the pluralists, those men who had absorbed the incomes of several parishes, leaving the duties of the benefices to be executed by usually ill-paid curates:

"For a great numbre of youre unworthye curates have bene the stirrars up of the simple people in the late tumultes that have bene, where as if you had not robbed them of that which thei paye yearely to have a learned and Godly teachar, they had bene better enstructed, as appeared by the quietnes that was emonge them that had such shepeherdes." [64]

Such a passage in the light of certain others in the essay suggests that among the lower ranks of the clergy there were various approaches to the problems of the time not apparently always under easy control by authority.

But it suggests another conclusion that will for the future be even more important, and that is that whereas there were curates who stirred up their flocks to rebellion, there were other curates, "learned and Godly" who kept their flocks quiet. Now one may be quite sure that Crowley would never apply those epithets to curates in sympathy with the old order. What he is trying to drive home for the benefit of people and government alike is that where the parish churches are left in the hands of the old clergy, there is either no effort to restrain the people from rebellion, or else they are encouraged to rebellion. But where the parishes are in the hands of the reformers, then all is quiet.

Lever takes a similar line with his rebuttal of the charge that the new religious doctrines are responsible for the popular rebellions:

"Now I heare some saye that thys errour is the fruite of the scripture in englyshe. No, neither thys, nor no other erroure commeth because the scripture is set forth in the englishe tonge, but because the rude people lackynge the counsell of learned menne to teache them the trewe meanynge when they reade it, or heare it, muste nedes folowe their owne Imaginacion in takynge of it." [65]

In other words, both Lever and Crowley take the argument of their enemies and turn it to the support of one of the main causes for which they had been arguing all along, the provision of an adequate parish clergy for the instruction of the people in the reformed religion. But in doing so they make a very definite and a very considerable claim as to the general social good to be gained from the provision of such a clergy. It is, in a word, that the reformed clergy can be counted on to teach a social doctrine that will restrain even a suffering and indignant people from resorting to rebellion.

CHAPTER V

SUBMISSION

IN THE preceding chapter we have seen how the traditional exuberance of the preachers on social themes was curbed by two factors, the extremes to which their preaching was carried by the leaders of the social rebellions, both lay and clerical, and the turning of the attack on the social order not as hitherto to the support of the religious reform but to the support of the religious tradition. On the first score, they could count on being followed by most of the substantial and influential elements in the society of the day. But on the second, they emphatically could not, and they knew it. In the face of the fundamental threat with which they were thus faced, it was only natural that they should make every appeal for the continuing support of the royal authority to which they were already bound by ties of gratitude, and, on the other hand, that they should bring to the support of the royal authority all their very considerable moral and spiritual influence. This was the easier because of their own convictions on church and state.

To begin with, there was much in the circumstances of the development of the Reformation in England to bind it to the new monarchy. The first of these is the sense of obligation of the reformed clergy to the royal power. Whatever the degree of their insistence on the ultimate providence and mercy of God, the reformers knew that without the support of Henry VIII, they would not have been able to shake the old order. The more critical of them must have been aware of the complexity of motives that won them his support, but the fact was overwhelming. And that they accepted with boundless gratitude. They knew, too, that any successful diminution of the royal power would mean the weakening of their basic support. Custom and tradition, those powerful supplements to established power, were not on their side, were, indeed, against them. That they knew perfectly well. They had done their best to undermine the weight of tradition and precedent by their psychology of "light out of darkness," of the release of the new age from the bondage and ignorance of the past. But that was in itself a new psychology in a world accustomed to relying on the authority of the established and the safety of the customs of one's fathers. It would take time to change that psychology, to turn it to the account of a new establishment of custom and loyalty. And the reformers were aware of this, too.

Moreover, they knew from their own experience that any existing power has its cross-currents of restlessness, of dissatisfaction, of ambition, to contend with. They would have explored that subterranean world more intimately than most men of their profession, and they would be instinctively and steadily aware of its potentialities. They would know that the most serious threat to the emerging order would come from the exploitation of such forces by religious zeal. Their own experience would have taught them that, however loath they might be to acknowledge it even to themselves. We have seen how quick Crowley was to recognize and identify and understand the role of the clerical agitator in the mid-century rebellions. Themselves the leaders of a successful rebellion, the reformers would know better than most clerical members of a long-established order, what the dangers of any disturbance of the supporting civil power would be at this point. They had everything at stake, and they knew it.

This was true of pretty much all parties in the reform movement. Those who felt that the process of change had gone far enough for the present, and were anxious to see the church put in order on the existing basis were quite aware of the consequences that might ensue if the succession of a less sympathetic ruler should remove the present restraints upon bishops and nobles sympathetic to the old regime, and the enhanced power of the new monarchy in things religious be turned against the reformers. Latimer, in particular, engaged in constant struggle with still formidable rivals in ecclesiastical affairs, and trying to reduce his own domain to order was well aware of what might be expected from the succession of Mary, and did his best to give warning.[1] This was to be expected. After all, there is no defender of the status quo more convinced than the rebel who has just successfully established his rebellion, and no one less sympathetic to other revolutionary prospects. It takes a certain degree of security and confidence to be tolerant of what in all probability would jeopardize both. Convinced as they were of the rightness of their position, the reformers by the mid-century had not achieved anything like the security that would have justified the relaxation of vigilance.

Many of them remembered the difficulties of the more advanced reformers in the divagations of Henry's later policy; indeed, some had suffered personally, but in the reign of Edward it was easy to blame these difficulties upon the bishops, and absolve the great champion of the reform, the good king Henry VIII. Moreover, the general policy of the government of Edward VI, though not at all points by any means satisfactory to all the reformed parties, was basically committed to the reform, and in the outlook for the future likely to advance the hopes of the more ardent reformers, rather than retreat.

Therefore, they would not want to risk any attack on the existing order, because they knew that the profit of any such disturbance would go to the strongest opposing force, and that was still the old order. The reign of Mary would confirm and justify their instinctive fears here. The result is that by the nature of their position the reformers were tied to the support of the existing power. Only when, as in the reign of Mary, it deserted them, would they even morally desert it. But at the period of which we are speaking, that difficulty is still in the future. And the problem they are facing as an actual fact is the popular insurrection against the established government.

All this is, of course, a very much simplified diagram of a very complicated situation. A complete picture would have to take account of a great many factors outside of the purpose of this very limited study. Especially it would have to consider the relation between civil and religious power in all of western Europe at the time. After all, what happened in England was not unrelated to the long struggle between civil and religious power of the preceding centuries. As Mr. J. W. Allen has said, "What we call the Reformation was, in one aspect, the definitive triumph of secular authority in a struggle with the Church already centuries old." [2]

In other words, the center of gravity in the world of power had shifted, and men of thought beset with all the perplexities and anxieties of an age of revolution, might be counted on to respond consciously and unconsciously to that most basic of all changes in their groping for support and some measure of security. The Erastianism of a man like Gardiner, who seems never to have dreamed of any undermining of the traditional structure of doctrine and rite, is an illuminating illustration of something fundamental in the thought and feeling of the time. "Since owing to causes which he could not or would not bring himself to judge, the authority of the Pope had passed away, the king's undisputed power was to be the corner-stone of the new social and religious fabric," [3] so a modern editor sums up his position.

A great many elements went into the making of this aspect of the Tudor monarchy, ranging all the way from the theocratic ideal of the Old Testament to the victory of the Lancastrian kings over the ancient feudal nobility of England. Especially should David and Gervase Mathew's suggestion that "the idea of kingship was linked with a deep religious tradition which varied between the fervent devotional practice of Henry VI and the more robust and mechanical piety of the early Lancastrians" be remembered when we try to understand the confidence which churchmen of high and low degree seem to have placed in the king. [4]

Certainly for Gardiner and his contemporaries the figure of the king held an impressiveness and a magnetism beyond that to be won by any theory. Rather it was the peculiar potency of power growing and consolidating itself before their eyes, filling their horizons with a majesty and a promise that are possible only when men see an ideal realizing itself in their everyday experience. Nor should it be forgotten that a good deal of this ideal element is due to the fact that this new definition of power was meeting a very deep need in the society of the day, that into it the currents of the recognized and the submerged life of the day alike were pouring. Those who went with it in England had the strength, then, of riding the tide of the future.

But this respect for royal authority was no mere matter of political prudence and expediency. Rather it was the very stuff of the conscience of the time. "It will probably be generally agreed," says Mr. Whitney with justified assurance "that, up to the middle of the century, nearly all men in England, whatever their particular shade of religious belief, were unanimous in feeling that disobedience to constituted authority was not only among the most heinous crimes which mortal man could commit but, so far as the well-being of the state was concerned, was even more disastrous than any other crime. That attitude was very nearly the most important single ingredient in Erastianism." [5]

The result is an attitude to the power of the ruler that may be summed up in one word which we shall hear often in Elizabethan and Jacobean sermons, and that is the word, "submission." Now the social preachers did not invent the word or the concept. Their contribution is to be found, rather, in the assimilation of the recognition of the new power to the Christian framework of ideas, to the rationalization of it in recognized religious terms, to the making it acceptable to the consciences of men, finally, to the winning for it of the support of the religious devotion of the patriotic Christian. In this, they but follow the example of the great pioneers of the Reformation movement. Luther, Melanchthon, Calvin, all agree on "an all but unqualified duty of obedience to any and every duly constituted authority." Of course, no Christian is ever permitted to obey commands which are clearly contrary to the law of God, but he is never justified in trying to avoid punishment by forcible resistance to lawfully constituted authority. On this they are all agreed.[6]

For England, the whole theory is to be found clearly worked out before any of the sermons we are studying were delivered in William Tyndale's *The Obedience of a Christen Man* of 1535.[7] Indeed, one may find in that chapter, "The obedience of Subjectes unto kynges princes and rulers" the ground plan of all the homilies on obedience to royal authority from *The Institution of a Christen man* of 1537 [8] to *An Homelie against Disobedience and*

Wylful Rebellion of 1571.[9] Tyndale bases his case upon scriptural injunction, the famous thirteenth chapter of Paul to the Romans, beginning, "Let every soule submit him selfe to the auctorite of the hyer powers." [10] Like the theorists of the natural law origins of society, Tyndale goes back to the beginning of society. But he does not find it where they do in the need for cooperation between men in their work for the glory of God and the securing of the material basis for their struggle for the salvation of their souls,[11] but in the fact that no man can be the judge in his own cause, being apt to be blinded by his appetites and lusts. Therefore God has given laws to govern the actions of men, and put kings and rulers "in his awne stede to rule the worlde thorow them." [12]

But it is not just this divine appointment of kings that gives their position such peculiar force. Rather it is the belief that the position of the king is outside the law—"the kinge is in this worlde without lawe and maye at his lust do right or wronge and shall geve acomptes, but to god only." [13] Now that is a very different conception of the king's position with regard to the law from that which Fortescue inculcated upon the young son of Henry VI and Queen Margaret in his famous essay.[14] Quite literally the king is the vicegerent of God, as Tyndale goes on to point out: "Heedes and governers ar ordened of god and ar even the gift of god, whether thei be good or bad. And whatsoever is done to us by them, that doeth god, be it good or bad." [15] The important thing is that they should rule. So great is the benefit of the king,[16] so important is it that this business of ruling should be accomplished, that it is better that a people should be under a tyrant than under a passive king who does not rule.[17] For a people who are allowed to do as they like are not free. To follow one's lusts is not freedom but bondage,[18] is the basic principle to which Tyndale appeals.

The duty of the subject, then, is obedience and submission. "Let us receave all thinges of god whether it be good or badde. . . . A christen man in respect of God is but a passive thinge, a thinge that suffereth only and doeth nought." [19] The duty of the Christian in this world, then, is one of obedience, giving to the king the obedience he owes to God. That obedience God will reward, the blessing of obedience being the life of this world, the curse of disobedience, the loss of it.[20] Christ set the example for us in the episode of the tribute to Caesar, showing us that the Christian should submit himself to the power of the ruler.[21] This submission should be given cheerfully, not out of fear, but because of the obligations of conscience.[22] Even where the subject feels that he has been wronged, he still has no alternative but obedience. For no inferior is ever allowed to avenge himself upon his superior.[23] Here Scripture has given us an example in the way David behaved to Saul. David had Saul in his power, but he forbore to take advantage of the opportunity so offered to him.[24]

In no case may we resist evil rulers, for to do so is to incur still greater misery.[25] The fact that we are given evil rulers is an indication "that God is angry and wrath with us." [26] They are a punishment for our disobedience to God.[27] Especially is England suffering now because the prelates are so wicked that if they find that one of their flock craves "true knowledge of Christe" they will kill him.[28] It is significant that at this point Tyndale does not waste any time inculcating submission to the prelates, but devotes his energy to the explanation of the reason for this affliction. And it is significant that his explanation has something of that circular character we have already encountered in Crowley's discussions of the rebellions of the time. For Tyndale explains the suffering of England from the prelates as "the hande of god to avenge the wekednes of them that have no love ner [sic] lust unto the trueth of god when it is preached: but rejoyce in unrighteousnes." [29] In other words, if only those who are resisting the new order will see the light, all will be well.

But even in the present state of misery Tyndale is not without comfort for the righteous man. For the righteous man may count on spiritual gains from persecution endured without rebellion. He will feel God's spirit within him, and he will be purged of his sins.[30] So the discussion ends on the high note of the spiritual advantages to be gained from Christian submission even to tyranny. The importance of this treatise of Tyndale's lies not in any originality of the ideas but in the fact that a brief and complete rationalization of the Christian's relation to the new order is laid out in a clear and persuasive fashion.

The same view of the matter is presented in *The Institution of a Christen Man* first published two years later. The purpose of this little book is to give the average literate Christian something of the same summary of the things needful for every Christian to know that used to be put in the beginning of the Prymer. It contains an exposition of the Apostles' Creed, of the seven sacraments, of the ten commandments, of the Pater Noster and the Ave, and "the articles of Justifycation," and "Purgatorie." [31] The interesting section of this book from our point of view is "The declaration of the .v. commaundement." [32] For the second point of the explanation makes it clear that this commandment applies not only to children and parents but to subjects and inferiors in their relations to heads and rulers.[33] This extension of application is developed in detail on the basis of the forty-ninth chapter of Isaiah: "For Scripture taketh princis to be, as it were, fathers and nouryces to their subjectes." [34] It is from this general function that the author deduces their specific duty to see that "the right religion" is maintained,[35] a very understandable point to emphasize in a book of public instruction in a time of religious transition.

Needless to say, subjects may not for any cause rebel.[36] But more than that, and of great importance in view of the inquisitorial methods of the regime in dealing with any matters suspected of connection with treason, it is the duty of any subject who hears of anything going forward that may cause damage or annoyance to the prince's person or estate, to disclose it to the prince or his council. "For it is the veraye lawe of nature, that every membre shall employe hym selfe to preserve and defend the heed." [37] And this is followed up by scriptural citations from the epistles of Saint Paul and Saint Peter, with especial emphasis on Romans, chapter 13: "Every man muste be obedient unto the hyghe powers: for the powers be of god." [38]

The warning against rebellion is likewise driven home by scriptural examples of the vengeance which God had in times past taken on rebels, notably those rebels who are to figure in so many comminatory passages of the next fifty years: Korah, Dathan, and Abiram.[39] On a lower level the discussion closes with a reminder to servants that the commandment also covers the duty which they owe to their masters, again a matter that is going to engage the attention of the preachers for a good many years to come.[40] The instruction naturally covers less ground, and, as would be expected from the elementary character of the whole undertaking, does not pretend to go as deeply into fundamental principles as does Tyndale's essay. The tone is, as one would expect from its official character, much more matter-of-fact and coolly expository than Tyndale's, but the point of view is basically the same.

Still more is this true of the tenth of *Certayne Sermons, or Homelies* which were published in 1547 by the king's appointment, to be read by all "persones, Vicares, or Curates" every Sunday in their churches.[41] This particular sermon is titled: "An exhortacion, concernyng good ordre and obedience, to rulers and magistrates." [42] It begins even more largely than Tyndale's essay by appealing to the hierarchical order of the created world as an argument for the necessity of men in their sphere keeping due order, some in high place, some in low. One is reminded of some of the preachers' hints at the presence of leveling ideas in the agitations of the time by this insistence on the differences of degree in the organization of the natural world. But the explanation of the origins of civil power is essentially Tyndale's, for it is pointed out that if kings and magistrates were taken away, there would be no safety for anybody,[43] a somewhat Hobbesian turn to Tyndale's account. Even the wicked ruler has his power from God, as is shown by Christ's answer to Pilate,[44] and by David's respect for Saul.[45] The latter example in particular is developed at length.

Therefore, submission is the duty of everyone. Indeed, on the authority of Saint Paul, the homily explains that everyone, not excepting priest or apostle, owes submission and subjection to the higher powers.[46] And this prescription is reënforced by the example of Christ's patience and suffering without any thought of resistance as the pattern for all Christians.[47] Both Christ and Saint Peter are cited for the teaching of obedience to kings as the chief and supreme rulers in this world, next under God.[48]

And this teaching is reënforced by the example of Mary, though with child, going to be enrolled, as an example of Christian obedience.[49] It should be added that this is a rather rare instance of appeal to Mary for authority of example in this, on the whole, quite un-Marian literature.

In general, then, a very complete notion of obedience is enjoined, but more by scriptural example than by such detailed analysis as Tyndale's. And this is again what might be expected of an official work, intended for the instruction of the great mass of the people. For in general the common man is more impressed by example than by casuistry. And, it should be noted further, that the main emphasis of the homily is positive, enjoining obedience rather than warning against rebellion.

This does not mean that there is no warning against rebellion. The sixteenth century understood too well the potentialities of terror to neglect the salutary warning. Especially must the question of the ruler who commands his subjects to do something contrary to the commandment of God be provided for. Although church authority cannot have had any fear that so godly a prince as Edward or his thoroughly Protestant administration would order anything contrary to God's commandment, still the possibility of the accession of Mary must have been strongly in their minds. At any rate, pretty complete provision was made even for this dreaded eventuality. For it was laid down as a principle that even in such a case where the righteous man cannot obviously do what is contrary to the commandment of God, he still must not resist or rebel, but must suffer all, referring the judgment of his cause only to God.[50]

As for the unrighteous man who does rebel against his ruler, he is warned by the familiar examples of the retribution which overtook Chore, Dathan and Abiron, who "grudged" against God's magistrates.[51] Indeed, the discontented are reminded that not even secret treason can expect to escape unpunished of the vengeance of God.[52] Altogether it is a firm but constructive handling of a large issue on the plane of universal and self-evident truth. There is little disposition to descend to argument. Rather it is a matter of explaining recognized duty. Already one is conscious of the quiet accent of an established tradition. Even the concluding note is an evidence of this confidence. For it is a prayer that the rulers may follow the examples of the good kings in the Bible, ruling justly, and one need hardly be told, assuring the "defence of the Catholique faith, conteined in holy scripture." [53]

So much for the theory in time of peace. If one wishes to see the theory in action in time of crisis, one has a chance in a sermon which Cranmer is said to have delivered between July 31 and August 27 of 1549.[54] It is styled *A Sermon concerning the Time of Rebellion*. Cranmer took the business of this sermon seriously, as we can tell from the preparatory notes that survive. These notes are especially valuable because they make clear in a rather sledge-hammer fashion just what were the points which Cranmer wished to drive home:

"Sentences of the Scripture against sedition . . .
How God hath plagued sedition in time past . . .
The sword by God's word pertaineth not to subjects, but only
      to magistrates." [55]

So with appropriate texts he proceeds on what are now central and recognized lines.

It has been suggested that he gave these notes to Peter Martyr to expand, and then revised the completed draft.[56] The manner of composition is not important for our purposes, because the personal elements in the sermon are much fewer than the institutional. There are one or two statesmanlike touches that may be taken as evidence of Cranmer's own hand. For instance, when Cranmer asks himself why England is being troubled with sedition in what should be these times of light and peace, he answers that the powers that be have been too lax, not punishing offenders against the peace, and now disorder has become a plague.[57] Another possible touch is his answer to the oft-heard popular charge that the misery of the poor is due to the oppression of the gentlemen, namely, that the gentlemen were never poorer themselves than they are now,[58] a disposition to defend the ruling classes perhaps more to be expected from the statesman than the preacher.

But Cranmer is both preacher and statesman when he finds the basic cause of the disturbances in the greed of all classes for wealth, poor as well as rich,[59] and tells them all that they are mad to put so much stress on riches.[60] And there is a certain impartiality in the way he threatens with damnation the greedy gentlemen who spend all their thought on joining house to house [61] and assures the poor that poverty however grievous is no excuse for rebellion.[62] Nor is sedition any remedy as they can well see from the results, for they are all poorer as a result of the destruction wrought in the recent disorders.[63]

But most of the time his approach is that of the preacher, occupying himself with the moral and religious wrong which the rebels have committed. To begin with, he asks them if they have forgotten that God is the distributor of the goods of this world.[64] Then he reminds them that God has given the sword to the prince and not to them.[65] And he reminds them, too, that no good man in Scripture ever took the sword against his prince or the nobility.[66] As for the instigators of these recent troubles, he has already called them the ruffians they are.[67] Now he accuses them of oppressing others in their turn whenever they get the chance,[68] and he asks dramatically what the state of the realm would be if God were so offended with their countrymen that he allowed them to be made governors over the realm.[69] So much for the secular character of the rebels. As for the spiritual elements involved, whatever the wrong the gentlemen have done, the rebels have been guilty of greater wrong in their mutiny.[70] The gentlemen have done wrong only to the commons, but the rebels have done wrong to the king ordained of God. That is their ultimate and basic crime.[71]

Cranmer is quite aware of the entanglement of religion and social agitation. Some of the rebels, he says, pretend to be Gospellers, but their actions belie their profession.[72] Rather he finds the root of the trouble in hatred for the Gospel and hypocrisy on the part of those who only pretend to receive the Gospel.[73] He solemnly warns these latter that the worst punishment is reserved for those who have received the word of God and failed to keep it. For example he cites the various punishments of the Jews in Scripture and from recent history the "chances of the Germans," a euphemism for the Peasant War.[74] And with the circular reasoning characteristic of the time, he concludes this section of his sermon by pointing out that the present difficulties in England with all their attendant unrest are the plague sent by God for rejecting or abusing the word of God which they have had preached to them.[75] Then he reënforces this salutary diagnosis by a glance at the plagues that, to judge from the example of past time, remain in store for those who stir up sedition.[76]

His remedy is repentance,[77] a reliable preacher's remedy. But unlike many preachers of the age, after all the threats he gives examples of sinners who repented in time, for the encouragement of his hearers. They are a classic list: Adam and Eve, David, Peter, Mary Magdalene.[78] In keeping with this theme he ends with a prayer for forgiveness for the sins of all the people.[79]

Such was the theory of submission as set forth by one of the men most influential in the definition of the reformed point of view, and applied to the crisis of 1549.

This politico-religious theory was not, however, confined to the ecclesiastical statesman. It was the theory of the practical man of affairs as well, as we may see from a treatise which Sir John Cheke published in the year 1549 under the revealing title: *The Hurt of Sedicion howe Greveous it is to a Commune Welth.*[80] The title, as we shall see presently, reveals a point of view in general different from that which we have just been studying. But the treatise springs quite obviously from the same general premises. That is clear from the frontispiece which not only portrays Absolom in contemporary costume being caught by the hair and speared in Scriptural fashion, but, that the lesson might not be lost on the densest of wit, is plainly labeled, "the rewarde of Absolom the Rebell." [81] With such a salutary warning at the beginning, it is hardly necessary for the "true subjecte" to remind even the rebel [82] that all subjects are bound to obey the king for conscience' sake like Christians.[83] Cheke is writing with an eye to the rebels for religion among the authors of current disorders. He reminds them that in their rebellion, they have, first of all, offended God, secondly, they have offended their sovereign lord, and, thirdly, they have disturbed the whole commonwealth.[84]

To their pleas of conscience he retorts that the magistrate is the ordinance of God [85] and concludes that "if ye would stande in the trueth, ye oughte to suffer like martiers." [86] And he tries to exorcise their doctrinal scruples by the direct challenge to what he clearly considers their presumption: "Dare ye commons, take upon you more learnynge, then the chosen Byshoppes and Clearkes of this realm have?" [87] Clearly he considered this an unanswerable challenge to the rebels for religion.

But his answer to the "other rable of Norfolke rebelles" with their killing and spoiling of gentlemen [88] is more diversified. The supposed claim to political equality is answered with the reminder that "every man may not beare lyke stroke, for everye man is not lyke wyse, and they that have sene moste, and beste habyll to beare it, and of just dealynge beside, be most fit to rule. It is another matter to understande a mans owne griefe, and to knowe the common welthes sore." [89] As for the economic argument, he seems at first sight disposed to be summary when he flatly tells the rebels that if it is the riches of their more fortunate enemies that offend them, then it is envy which drives them on.[90] But he proceeds to argue the matter at length. Almost his first point is an interesting reversal of Latimer's position on this issue so crucial to the advance of the middle class. For he tells the poor that if there should be established the equality of which they talk, "then ye take all hope away from youres, to come to anye better estate, then you nowe leve them." [91] In general, however, his argument follows more traditional lines. Riches are a matter of God's providence; [92] the Christian should be content with God's ordinance.[93]

Cheke comments very feelingly on the destruction and waste due to rebellion: "And what a griefe is it to an honest man, to labour truelye in youth, and to gaine paynfully by labour, wherewith to live honestli in age, and to have this gotten in longe time to be sodainlye raught awaye by the violence of sedition," and so on.[94] And then there is the social disturbance: "What say ye to the numbre of vagabondes and loitring beggers whiche after the overthrow of your campe and scatering of this seditious numbre wyl swarme in every corner of the realme." [95] This he finds inimical to the principle that the prosperity of the whole order must be maintained in every part of it.[96]

But it is not only the disaster at home that Cheke holds up for the remorse of the rebels. There is also the shame which they have brought upon their land in the eyes of other nations.[97] Indeed, he goes so far as to say that there had been good hope that the Scots would "have resonably condiscended to some good poynt of frendshyp, had not your busye and brainsicke heades come in to such a dusines of reason . . ."[98] Then there are those at home and abroad who seeing things go awry think that these troubles are deserved because of the religious changes: "Thei se not that where gods glorie is truliest set forth, there the devil is most busy for his parte."[99] This is perhaps his sharpest taunt to the rebels: "Thus have ye geven a large occasion, to stubburne papistes both to judge amis, and also to rejoyse in this wicked chaunce."[100]

Here in Cheke's treatise one sees a very practical application of the theories we have been studying to the issues of the moment in the religious, the social, and the political field. It was, as we have seen, the outgrowth of a long and sustained process of reflection and definition, the expression of what is an established tradition.

It is in the light of that tradition that the attitude of the social preachers, especially of Lever and Crowley, is to be understood. For they not only accept this whole theory of submission and preach it, but their acceptance is more than prudent conformity in time of stress. It bears every mark of sincere, even alarmed conviction. They commend submission to their audiences with an enthusiasm that often takes on the color and passion of their great denunciations of the social world of their day. Indeed, their insistence on submission is all the more impressive because of the sympathy with which they recognize the social wrongs which have driven the poor rebels to desperation.

This is particularly true of Crowley's approach to the problem of insurrection in *The Way to Wealth* with its illuminating subtitle, "wherein is plainly taught a most present remedy for Sedicion," of 1550.[101]

He puts an appeal for peace on his title-page, but he begins his essay by reminding his presumably disengaged reader that

"Sedition therfore beinge a daungerous disease in the bodie of a commen wealth: must be cured as the expert Phisicians do use to cure the daungerous diseases in a naturall bodie. And as the moste substanciall waye in curinge diseases, is by putting awaye the causes wherof they grewe: so it is in the pullinge up of·Sedition. For if the cause be once taken awaye, then muste the effecte nedes faile." [102]

This practical approach is followed up in Crowley's best manner by a swift summary of what the explanation of that cause would be if the poor man of the country should be asked his opinion. It is an amazingly inclusive indictment of the society of the day, but the most interesting thing about it is that it is an indictment of lay society. Robert Crowley like most men of his profession and his point of view was in all probability more interested in the clerical offenders than in the lay, but he had a sharp enough sense of the realities to know that ecclesiastical reform was not the first thought of the average layman in the year 1550, certainly not of those laymen who had so disastrously pinned their hope of social relief upon the restoration of the old religious order. Here he displays a degree of realism as well as a dramatic sense that is very unusual among his contemporaries of the cloth:

"If I shuld demaunde of the pore man of the contrey what thinge he thinketh to be the cause of Sedition: I know his answere. He woulde tel me that the great fermares, the grasiers, the riche buthares, the man of lawe, the merchauntes, the gentlemen, the knightes, the lordes, and I can not tel who, Men that have no name because they are doares in al thinges that ani gaine hangeth upon. Men without conscience. Men utterly voide of goddes feare. Yea men that live as thoughe there were no God at all. Men that would have all in their owne handes, men that would leave nothyng for others, men that would be alone on the earth, men that be never satisfied, Cormerauntes, gredye gulles, yea men that would eate up menne women and chyldren: are the causes of Sedition." [103]

Crowley has a good deal more of that sort of thing, and it is very effective. Here are the old villains of Piers Plowman, at least some of them, but here, also, are the men, not so easily identified, that almost invisibly seize power in an age of social transition. Robert Crowley is not entirely clear as to how he shall name them, but he has recognized their character and their activity, and he has accurately gauged the importance and the effectiveness of both.

He has caught, too, the mood of despair of the poor who have seen their world melting before their eyes, and who have blindly, as he thinks, thrust out their angry hands to save themselves: "No remedye therfore, we must nedes fight it out, or else be brought to the lyke slavery that the french men are in." [104] It is pathetic to see national pride thus fortifying desperation, and one wonders how old this variant of the feeling between France and England really is.[105] But the indictment, also, has a more modern ring, like all the specific cries of the race's distress:

"These idle beastes (?) will devour al that we shal get by our sore labour in our youth, and when we shal be old and impotent, then shal we be driven to begge and crave of them that wyl not geve us so muche as the crowmes that fall from their tables. Better it were therfore, for us to dye lyke men, then after so great misery in youth to dye more miserably in age." [106]

At that point Crowley can restrain his compassion no longer: "Alasse poore man, it pitieth me to se the myserable estate that thou arte in." [107]

That pity, however, is not for the material sufferings of the poor wretch who has so been driven to desperation. It is for his perilous spiritual state. He has chosen the wrong remedies. It is characteristic of Crowley's mastery of popular psychology that he arraigns the folly of the people not in terms of legal or theological analysis but in terms of threat and warning. He tells them what the consequences of their actions will be. And he tells them again not in general or abstract terms but in terms of examples, drawn from Scripture. Some of them are on the positive side, some on the negative. He stresses, for example, Christ's unwillingness to usurp authority not belonging to him, revealed in various familiar speeches of the New Testament, and he follows this up with a reference to a series of stories in the Old Testament that demonstrate with horrible warnings what has happened to people who usurped power not meant for them.[108] And he draws his conclusion drastically enough:

"If these examples . . . had ben diligently beaten into thine heade, thou wouldeste (no doubte) have quieted thy selfe, and have suffered thy selfe rather to have bene spoyled of al together yea and thy bodie toren in peces rather then thou wouldest have taken on the more then thou art called unto. For no cause can be so great to make it lawful for the to do againste goddes ordinaunce." [109]

Indeed, for Crowley the final count against the oppressors is that they have driven their victims to rebellion. And now they are expressing horror at the things which the rebels have done and proposing all manner of terrible punishments. Crowley does not protest any of this. He agrees with the landlords and the other members of the frightened upper classes who are counseling severity that the poor have deserved the worst the rich can devise,

"But yet if their offence were laied in an equall balaunce with yours (as no doubt thei are in the sight [of] God) doubt not but you should sone be ashamed of youre parte. For what can you laye unto their charge, but they have had examples of the same in you?" [110]

Certainly, this is a home-thrust of the theory of the governing class.

But Crowley goes even farther than that. He recapitulates the crimes of the rich oppressors with which we are already familiar, enclosing the commons from the use of the poor, levying greater fines than have been known before, depriving poor tenants of liberties held by custom, raising their rents, above all refusing to obey the king's orders to restore the commons they have enclosed.[111] And then he turns upon the rich oppressors and tells them that they who have done these things are really responsible for the crimes to which the ensuing despair of their victims has driven them:

"If he therfore that is the occasion of one mans fallyng unto any kynd of vyce, were better have a mylstone tied about hys necke and be cast into the depe sea wythall: what shalbe thought of you that have bene the occasion of so many mens fallyng into so detestable synne and trespasse agaynste God, as to disturbe the whole estate of their contrei with the great perill and daunger of their anointed Kyng in hys tender age, whose bloud (if he had perished) should have bene required at your handes as the bloud of al them that have perished shal?" [112]

Here Crowley speaks for practically all the sixteenth-century reformed preachers. For they are in no doubt as to the status of rebels. True, various men will go at the problem in different ways. Becon, for example, will rely chiefly on warning examples, but his conclusion is unmistakable as it is put into the mouth of the main speaker of *The Jewel of Joy*, the preacher Philemon: "How grevously thei have alwayes be punished that were sedicious and walked without any godly feare towarde the civille Magistrates, the historyes of Dathan and Abiron, of Zambry and Baasa of Bagathan and Thares, shewe manifestly." [113]

Characteristically, Lever is more analytical, more disposed to marshal the lines of his indictment systematically, for instance, in *A Fruitfull Sermon made in Poules Churche at London in the Shroudes*. It is the job of rulers to keep under subjection those stiff and stubborn rebels who cannot believe that their rulers mean to do them any good.[114] For, as Lever goes on to point out, good simple people trust their rulers.[115] Even the evil ruler must be obeyed:

"The man is sometymes evell, but the authoritie from God is always good, and God geveth good authoritie unto evyll men, to punyshe the sinnes of the evyll people. It is not therfore repining, rebelling, or resistinge gods ordinaunce, that wyl amend evyl rulers." [116]

Indeed, rebellion far from righting old wrongs, only creates new. And these are worse than the old. At this point Lever appeals to the experience of his listeners, to their own knowledge of the misery of which everyone is now complaining:

"And this dare I saye, takyng all you to beare record, that the soreste laws that ever any tiraunt made in any land, if they shuld continue many yeres could not cause such and so greate murther, myschief, and wretchednes as ye perceive and know that thys rebellion in England continuing but a fewe monethes hath caused: by the whych ye may learn that although lawers be comenly called most covetous, yet compare them wyth rebels, and as picking thefte is lesse then murthering robrie: so is the covetousnes of greedy lawers whych begyle craftely, far lesse then the covetousnes of rebels, whych spoyle cruellye." [117]

Whatever their wrongs the people may not rebel. What are they to do then? For we may be sure that the sixteenth century was no time to tell people that there was nothing they could do about a situation which the preachers themselves had denounced so passionately. Crowley answers for practically all:

"If thou wilt therfore that God shall deliver the or thy children from the tiraunie of them that oppresse the: lament thine olde sinnes, and endeavour emendment of life. And then he that caused King Cirus to send the Jewes home to Jerusalem againe: shall al so stirre up our yong king Edward to restore the to thy liberty againe, and to geve straight charge that non shalbe so bolde as once to vexe or trouble the. For the herte of a kinge is in goddes hand, and as he turneth the rivers of water, so turneth he it. Besure therfore, that if thou kepe thy selfe in obedience and suffer al this oppression patiently, not geving credite unto false prophecies that tel the of victori but to the worde of God that telleth the thy dutie: thou shalt at the time, and after the maner that God hath alredie pointed, be delivered." [118]

That is pretty absolute doctrine. And here, as before in his threats to the tyrannous and careless possessioners of two years earlier, Crowley brings up his heavy reënforcements of history, sacred and secular:

"There is not one storie of the Bible that serveth to declare how readi God is to take vengeaunce for thoppression of his people; but the same hath ben declared unto you to the uttermoste, beside the notable histories and cronicles of thys realme, wherin doeth most plainly appeare the justice of god in the revenging of his people, at such time as they have kept themselves in quiete obedience to their prince and rulers and their destruction when they have rebelled." [119]

So much for the comfort of the oppressed. But Crowley does not stop there. It is profoundly characteristic of his spirit that he presently takes the same argument that he has been using for this purpose and hurls it in warning against the oppressors. For Crowley has clearly seen that the oppressors may content themselves with the suppression of rebellion and look to see their preachers likewise content themselves with the counseling of the people to submission. So now he turns to them:

"Thincke not therfore, but if the people quiete them selves in theyr oppression and cal unto God for deliveraunce: he wyll by one meane or other geve them the spoile of their oppressours, He is as mighty nowe as he was in those dayes and is now as able to slea boeth you and youres in one night, as he was to slea al the firste borne of the Egiptyans: And then who shal have the spoile?" [120]

But that is, after all, only incidental. The main concern of these preachers is to restore order. And it is to restore order that the people may be about their proper spiritual business. For though these men had stood up manfully against the oppressors of the poor, and had voiced their wrongs with sympathy and with eloquence, it still remains true that there is very little in their work of that idealizing tendency to be seen, say, in Langland's handling of the plowman. They show no tendency to sentimentalize the figure of the common man. Lever, in particular, is very forthright in his attack on the spirit of the rebels, an attack that shows no disposition to make allowances for the common man but rather treats him as a morally independent and responsible human being, in every way as accountable as his social superiors.

This is still several centuries east of the new psychology, but the moral effects of repression seem to have been well known to Lever:

"There is as yet more styffe necked stubburnes, dievellysh disobedi- ence, and gredye covetousnes in one of you of the commune sorte that kepeth thys greate swellynge in the hearte, havyng no occasion to sette it furth in exercise, then is in ten of the worst of theim that beynge in office and aucthoritye, have manye occasions to open and shewe them selves what they be." [121]

Whatever they have to say to the oppressors of the poor, the main concern of these men is that the people should repent of their sins. But what are these sins? The answer to that question is one of the most revealing things in all this literature, for it is the key to a good deal of what comes after. True, Lever and Crowley will characteristically go at the matter differently, but they will come out at pretty much the same point.

Crowley begins on the old lines of Piers Plowman. Have they loved their neighbor rightly? He answers the question himself, no, a thoroughly safe answer in view of the known infirmities of Christians in all ages. But the direction which he next takes is interesting confirmation of the conjectures above as to the point of view and activities of the curates. For Crowley charges that instead of returning to the groundwork of Christian activity, they have given themselves up to the wrong religious practices, to, in fact, the accustomed religious observances of the old order. If they are to be saved, they must forsake their ancient iniquities and cease to stand in the way of truth. In other words, Crowley is trying to convince the people that the way to relief for their temporal ills is not through a return to the observances of the old order, that indeed such a return is bound to call down the wrath of God upon them afresh,[122] to heap higher the mountain of personal sin that is ultimately responsible for their woe.

Lever agrees with Crowley that what the people need to do above everything else is to repent of their sins, and he agrees as to what is the root cause of these sins. But his approach to the problem is, as is usual, different. It is almost syllogistic. He has just explained that God has ordained that England should be spoiled with greedy and covetous officers. He goes on to ask:

"What dyd make in theym suche gredy covetousnes? the indignacion of God. What kyndled goddes indignacion? the synnes of the people. What was the synne of the people? *Eloquium sancti Israell, blasphemaverunt.* They have blasphemed the holye woorde of GOD, callynge it newe learnynge and heretycall doctryne: *Ideo iratus est furor domini.* And therefore is the wrath of the Lorde kyndled."[123]

What they should do is obvious enough, as Lever goes on to explain to them in this sermon preached at Paul's cross: "Truelye the indignacion of God shal never be quenched, untyll that you wyth tender hartes, humble, obedyente, and thankefull myndes, receyve, embrace, and conforme your selves unto the holy worde of God set forth by the Kynges Magestye his gracious pro-cedynges." [124]

To the crowd thronging the pulpit at Paul's Cross this must have doubtless seemed reasonable and self-evident doctrine. To the rebels in the country, however, protesting the violation of ancient rights and hopes in the land and the derangement of old custom and habit in the village church, the reasoning must have seemed, if they thought of it at all, slightly circular. But there is no doubt that these preachers made this substitution of religious for social reformation in perfectly good faith. To them it seemed the essential thing.

Indeed, there is every evidence that they found it difficult to understand how any intelligent man of good will could fail to see what he would gain in forsaking the old order and embracing the new. Lever, especially, seems genuinely perplexed when he complains that the people bore patiently the darkness and privation of the old religious regime. Now that things have been remedied, they should be content, but instead of that they ungratefully stir up seditions and rebellion.[125] Becon was bothered by the same phenomenon. For through the mouth of Eusebius in *The Jewel of Joy* he expressed his distress that noblemen who had been so generous in supporting the old superstition should not be willing to spend something for the encouragement of true religion:

"There have bene, would God ther wer not now, whych have not spared to spende much ryches in noryshynge many ydle syngynge men to bleate in theyr chappeles thynckynge so to do God an hygh sacrifyce, and to pype downe theyr meate and their dryncke and to whistle them a sleape, but they have not spente any part of theyr substnunce [sic] to fynd a learned man in theyr houses to preach the word of God, to haste them to vertue and to dissuade them from vyce." [126]

By the middle of the century, then, the preachers of social reform who had assumed that religious and social reform ran together had discovered, first, in the disappointment of the dis-establishment of the monasteries and, second, in the uprisings of

1549 that in a good many parts of the country and in a good many groups they were running very far apart. What they were clearly trying to do was to rechannel them. Their main instrument was, as we have seen, the doctrine of submission. On the one hand, they urged it for their own cause upon the rebels who had been actively resenting the disappointment of their social hopes and the interference with their religious customs. And, on the other hand, they used it to persuade the government to a support of their religious program.

There is no reason to accuse them of sheer opportunism in this. Their faith in the authority of the prince had not yet been tested by the accession of an idolatrous prince. They, for the most part, can and do hold the doctrine of submission with completely assured fidelity. Therefore they do not hesitate to lay down the principle that it is the duty of the clergy to inculcate this social discipline with all the authority and the resources of religious conviction and religious organization. This submission is the will of God, and it is to be inculcated by the preachers of God's word, with all his authority. It is hard to see how even the most ambitious of magistracies could fail to be satisfied with the coöperation they proffered. Indeed, there can have been few times in the history of institutions when a new and growing institution like the sixteenth-century kingship was offered such substantial reënforcement with such generosity of conviction and of devotion.

Now in this development of the theory of submission, the preachers had always recognized the possibility that an idolatrous prince might command things forbidden of God, and for this they counseled non-resistance so far as physical action was concerned, and refusal at any cost to violate the ordinance of God. But it is one thing to think of such a matter in the abstract, and another to face the problem in a sudden and overwhelming emergency, and still another to envisage a continuation for an unknown period of the unfavorable situation.

The moral problem is obvious, but in the long run the intellectual problem is no less real. For there is likely to take place in the most sincere and convinced minds a shifting of attention and a shifting of emphasis, if not of basic position. It is, therefore, interesting to find that whereas the preachers whom we have been studying, in their insistence upon submission to the king as a matter of conscience to the Protestant had spent their main energy on the enforcement of obedience by Scripture authority and example; in the reign of Queen Mary a convinced Protestant, John Poynet, can be found devoting his *A Shorte Treatise of Politike Power, and of the True Obedience which Subjectes Owe to Kynges and Other Civille Governours* to a very definite and detailed discussion not of the extent of royal authority but of the limitations of it.[127] The earlier preachers would have quite agreed with Poynet that princes have no authority to dissolve or dispense with God's laws, but they would hardly have agreed with him when he said: "Than must it nedes folowe, that this absolute autoritie which they use, must be mayntened by mannes reason, or it must nedes be an usurpacion." [128] That is an approach to the nature of authority very different from that inculcated, say, by Crowley in his later sermons. The same temper is to be seen in what Poynet has to say of the relation of the prince to the laws of the land:

"Now if wher the people have geven their autoritie to their governour to make suche lawes, yet can he not breake or dispense with the positive lawes: how muche lesse maie suche governors, kinges, and princes to whom the people have not geven their autoritie (but they with the people, and the people with them make the lawes) breake them or dispense with them? If this were tolerable, than were it in vaine to make solemne assemblies of the hole state, long Parliamentes etc.?" [129]

Passages such as these are alien in spirit to the preachers and writers whom we have hitherto been considering in this chapter. Rather they are reminiscent of Fortescue,[130] and anticipatory of Sir Thomas Smyth's great sentence: "The most high and absolute power of the realme of Englande, consisteth in the Parliament." [131] So is Poynet's reminder of the ancient office of the High Constable of England, who could summon the king personally to appear before Parliament or some other high court for judgment. It is hard to imagine anyone persuading Henry VIII that it is God's will "that the magistrates doinges be called to accompt and reckoning, and their vices corrected and punished by the body of the hole congregacion or common wealthe." [132]

It is interesting, too, to notice Poynet's taste in scriptural example. David and Saul, David and Absolom, Korah, Dathan, and Abiram, those were the favorite examples of the early sixteenth-century preacher, with their admonitions to reverence for the king and their reminders of the horrible fates that have overtaken rebels against the authority appointed of God. But one of the many advantages of Scripture has always been the wide variety of example it offers to the discriminating and purposive reader. Poynet's taste is different from that of his predecessors. Ahab and Jezebel fascinate him, and he does not hesitate to underscore the moral of their fates: "Thus ye maie see thende of lustie lordes and ladies that will have their lustes a lawe, and their will to be folowed and obeied of their subjectes as a right in dede." [133] And still more enthusiastic is his account of the slaying of Queen Athaliah.[134] In other words, different examples come to men's minds in different seasons.

But Poynet drives the theme of the accountability of the ruler farther than even the plain-spoken Fortescue, when he discusses at length the question "whether it be laufull to depose an evil governour, and kill a tyranne." [135] This is a subject of debate that would have on the whole shocked the early sixteenth-century preachers. One is reminded of Starkey's dialogue, and of some of the speeches which he put in the mouth of Cardinal Pole.[136] And still more of a passage in the *Summa* which for various reasons Poynet could hardly be expected to cite at this time, in which St. Thomas rules that a tyrannical government cannot be considered just

"because it is directed, not to the common good, but to the private good of the ruler. . . . Consequently there is no sedition in disturbing a government of this kind, unless indeed the tyrant's rule is disturbed so inordinately, that his subjects suffer greater harm from the consequent disturbance than from the tyrant's government." [137]

On the whole, Poynet is more direct and resolved than Starkey's Pole, and more explicit than St. Thomas, when he declares that the killing of a tyrant is something "graffed in the heartes of men: not made by man, but ordained of God." [138] He proceeds to risk even the sixteenth-century English horror of extra-national interference by reminding his readers that in times past good kings counted it the highest honor to be called to the release of the oppressed.[139] And he makes the general observation that where the people and their rulers wink at each other's faults, then there will be general corruption. Where the people insist that their rulers behave, then the rulers will insist that the people behave, and all will be well,[140] a line of argument, so far as I am aware, original with Poynet. But then he distrusts the prince basically as much as most sixteenth-century moralists distrust the people. He advises rulers to tremble at a saying of the much-quoted Chrysostom that in general seems to have received little attention among English preachers to the king of this period: "I marvail that any governour can be saved." [141] And he advises the people to suspect princes' promises and "loke in tyme to thy selfe and to the state of thy naturall countraye. . . . Be thou Prometheus and not Epimetheus." [142]

As for the usual remedies which the preacher has suggested to the victims of oppression, it is significant that Poynet views them only as a matter of last resort:

"But if neither the hole state nor the minister of Goddes worde wolde doo their common duetie, nor any other laufull shifte before mencioned can be hade, nor dare be attempted: yet are not the poore people destitute all together of remedy: but God hathe lefte unto them twoo weapones, hable to conquere and destroie the greatest Tiranne that ever was: that is, *Penaunce* and *Praier*." [143]

Only at one point is he at one with the preachers whom we have been reading. He has been describing the terrible state of the England of his day, disobedience in right things, obedience in the wrong, and the persecution of the godly.[144] He cites some of the familiar scriptural examples of the mercy God has showed to the penitent in time past. And he promises his suffering countrymen that if they will give up idolatry and go back to the religious settlement of King Edward's time, and behave themselves as Christians should, all will be well. And there will be no persecution of godly men, or famine or sedition, or any other of the ills from which they are suffering or with which they are being threatened.[145]

Now it would be a mistake to regard Poynet as typical of his time. The Protestant leaders whom we have been studying kept to their principle of non-resistance and fled, or suffered, or kept quiet, or maintained their agitation in secret. But he does show the differing channels into which men's thoughts may run in differing circumstances. Poynet had some inkling of this fact himself, as he shows in his discussion of obedience. He has made the classic observation that a commonwealth is kept in good order by obedience, but he qualifies this observation by going on to a discrimination not usually made at this time, namely that either too much obedience or too little makes trouble. Of course, the Anabaptists are his example of those who would have all politic power taken away. Then he takes up the opposite extreme: "Others (as thenglishe papistes) racke and stretche out obedience to muche, and wil nedes have civile power obeied in all thinges and that what so ever it commaundeth, without respecte it ought and must be done." [146]

Now he is aware that that has not always been their position, for he complains that they think that no obedience should be given to a prince who tries to reform them because he is a heretic. But he charges that if the prince will only wink at their abominations then: "Suche a one (saie they) must be obeyed in all thinges, none maie speake against his procedinges, for he that resisteth the power, resisteth thordinaunce of God, and he that resisteth, purchaceth to him self damnacion." [147]

In other words Poynet throws into the teeth of the Catholics a point of view which had been the prevailing burden of the submission sermons of the Protestant preachers in past years, and was shortly upon their deliverance by the accession of Elizabeth to be their burden for years to come. Whatever the many faults to be laid to the charge of the English Catholics by Protestant preachers in the years to come, excessive obedience to any king was not to be one of them. One would have to go outside the limits of the present inquiry into a larger study of Catholic as well as Protestant political-religious theory to find for this century any contrasts as dramatic as this.

But though Poynet is hardly to be called typical of his party, he is far from unique. Even more resounding expression to not dissimilar views was given by John Knox, for one. Although Knox was a Scotchman and the most dramatic episodes in his career belong to the story of the Reformation in that country, it is nonetheless true that by virtue both of his ministry in England and his association with the Marian exiles in the English Congregation at Frankfort on the Maine he exerted a very considerable influence upon the thinking of the English leaders of the time. This is particularly true with regard to the events in England which led both Poynet and Goodman to reconsider the traditional theory of submission. The two main issues that Goodman handled in his treatise, the succession of a female ruler and the claims of the idolatrous ruler to obedience, also engaged his interest. And upon both of them he expressed himself with characteristic vigor.

It has been suggested that he was the "certain Scotchman" who submitted some questions on these points to Bullinger in 1554.[148] He may very well have been. The incident is important because it reveals the caution which the great divine of Zurich displayed on the ticklish issues of the relations of civil and religious power in those years of crisis for the reformed cause. Bullinger had no doubt that the law of God provided that woman was to be in subjection and not to rule, but he was clearly unwilling to deny that under certain customary conditions and with the safeguards of a husband and councilors, it might be possible for a woman ruler's position to be such that it would be hazardous for the godly to challenge it.[149] For the question of obedience to the idolatrous ruler, Bullinger was quite clear on the basic premise that the magistrate or ruler should not be obeyed when his commands were clearly contrary to "God and his lawful worship," but he was quite aware that the maintenance of right may be made a pretext for very different purposes, and he was clearly unwilling to commit himself on any specific case without knowing more of the circumstances.[150] Apparently it was much easier for the Swiss reformer to take a statesmanlike view of the matter than for those more immediately involved in the issues.

Knox had a double reason to think of the matter, the woman ruler of his native Scotland, and the woman ruler of his second home, England. The result of his prolonged and anguished meditations is one of the masterpieces of invective of that or any period, *The First Blast of the Trumpet against the Monstrous Regiment of Women,* published at Geneva in 1558. The book begins calmly and comprehensively enough:

"To promote a Woman to beare rule, superioritie, dominion, or empire above any Realme, Nation, or Citie, is repugnant to Nature; contumelie to God, a thing most contrarious to his revealed will and approved ordinance; and finallie, it is the subversion of good Order, of all equitie and justice." [151]

That admirably sums up the main development of Knox' case, but it gives no notion of the magnificent sweep of his indignant and contemptuous indictment of the sex. With ferocious thoroughness he scours the anti-feminist ranks of history, philosophers, poets, lawyers, church fathers, every authority from Scripture, history or legend that he can think of for his indictment of the crimes and the follies of woman. Quite the finest passage in this marshaling of condemnation, sacred and profane, is that from Tertullian's book on women's apparel with its devastatingly total arraignment:

"Dost thou not knowe (saith he) that thou art Heva? The sentence of God liveth and is effectuall against this kind; and in this worlde, of necessity it is, that the punishement also live. Thou art the porte and gate of the Devil."[152]

But there was more even than this to Knox's indictment, for he did not hesitate to include those who supported the rule of a woman, declaring that "in so mainteining that usurped power, they declare themselves enemies to God." [153]

This attack upon the supporters of "idolatry" is carried still further in *The Appellation of John Knoxe from the Cruell and Most Injust Sentence pronounced against Him by the False Bishoppes and Clergie of Scotland, with his Supplication and Exhortation to the Nobilitie, Estates, and Communaltie of the Same Realme,* printed in Geneva in the same year of 1558. He begins by ingeniously removing himself from the jurisdiction of the bishops who have accused him of heresy, on the ground that he had already accused them in his letters to the Queen Dowager of all crimes, and that as accused criminals they are incapable of delivering judgment until they have freed themselves of these accusations.[154] But though that contretemps clearly gave him pleasure, it is obvious that he knew it was nothing to rely upon. So he addressed himself to the serious business of justifying his appeal from ecclesiastical authority to civil.[155] He began classically with scriptural example, invoking the example of the prophet Jeremiah whom the princes and the people delivered when the priests still stood to their sentence of condemnation. From this he concluded that "the Civile sword hath power to represse the furie of the preests . . ."[156]

So with regard to the king. The nobles and magistrates are bound to aid the king in whatever he attempts for the glory of God and the welfare of his commonwealth. Likewise, he reminds them,

"by your gravities, counsel, and admonition, yee are bound to correct and represse whatsoever ye know him to attempt expressedly repugning to Goddes Word, honour, and glorie, or what ye shall espie him to do, be it by ignorance, or be it by malice, against his subjects great or small. Of which last part of your obedience, yf ye defraud your King, ye commit against him no lesse treason, then yf ye did extract from him your due and promised support, what time by his ennemies injustly he wer pursued."[157]

He reminds the nobles of Scotland of the miseries of the nobility of England under the regime of "wicked Jesabel," and he concludes:

"The same plages shall fall upon you, be you assured, if ye refuse the defence of his servantes that call for your support. My words are sharpe, but consider, my Lords, that they are not mine, but that they are the threatnynges of the Omnipotent, who assuredly will performe the voices of his Prophetes, how that ever carnall men despise his admonitions." [158]

Although he worked with the English Protestants both in England and on the Continent, the main objective of these treatises of Knox' is the Scottish situation. His ideas were brought to bear, however, on the English by his fellow-exile and colleague, Christopher Goodman, who advanced very similar arguments in a treatise printed also at Geneva by John Crispin in the same year as Knox' own *The First Blast of the Trumpet against the Monstrous Regiment of Women,* in 1558, under the discriminating title, *How Superior Powers Ought to be Obeyd of their Subjects: and wherin they may Lawfully by Gods Worde be Disobeyed and Resisted.* Like Knox Goodman was a very stout controversialist with the black-and-white vigor of the sixteenth-century classic, as is seen when early in his treatise he declares that "the papistes have not so muche as one worde or promesse to prove that they are (as they impudentlie bragge) the Church of God, but manie rather moste playnlie provinge them to be the verie Synagoge of Satan, and livelie members of Antichriste." [159] His position on the main controversies of the day may be guessed at when he goes on to say that the party now in power in England "beleve not onelie upon Christe crucified, and hanged upon the Crosse, but in the conjured Idoll, hanging by a corde over the alter." [160] No less vigorous is his attack upon saints' days.[161] Indeed, all his writing is vigorous, for he never forgets that he is writing in a time of great crisis, grim with the slaughter of "thousandes of martyrs," as he estimates, in England alone.[162] He is conscious, too, that he cannot claim a clear majority, for almost at the end of his book, he asks:

"But when the people them selves agree not, when they are devided amongest them selves, and the greatest parte of them perchance papistes, and will be maynteyners of such ungodly proceadings as are now broght in to Englande, how is it possible that by the weaker parte, Gods glory shulde be restored?" [163]

Goodman is not discussing ideas in academic detachment, then. He is trying to meet a definite crisis for his side, the regime of Mary, "wicked Jesabel: who for our synnes, contrarie to nature and the manyfeste worde of God, is suffred to raigne over us in Goddes furie." [164] In herself, she is most objectionable, a bastard,[165] a hypocrite and an idolatress,[166] a traitor to God and a promise-breaker to her best friends, who when they helped her to her unlawful reign, were promised the religion which had been preached under King Edward.[167] But in the very fact of her position she is contrary to nature:

"For God is not contrarie to him self, whiche at the begynninge appoynted the woman to be in subjection to her housbande, and the man to be head of the woman (as saithe the Apostle) who wil not permitte so muche to the woman, as to speake in the Assemblie of men, muchelesse to be Ruler of a Realme or nation. Yf women be not permitted by Civile policies to rule in inferior offices, to be Counsellours, Pears of a realme, Justices, Shireffs, Baylives and such like: I make your selves judges, whither it be mete for them to governe whole Realmes and nations?" [168]

If he never rises to the heights of Knox' general indictment, there is no question that Goodman surpasses it in the detail and particularity of his arraignment of the individual woman.

Whether in the nature of things the anointing of a woman as ruler was a crime against God and nature to which the Catholic was more disposed than the Protestant is a question which need not engage our attention now. What is certain is that three women rulers did stand in the way of the progress of the Protestant Reformation, Catherine of Guise, Mary of Scotland, and Mary of England. Calvin might take the long view and through Cecil seek to appease Elizabeth of England.[169] The immediate crisis was too overwhelming for Goodman as for Knox. He might call Elizabeth "that Godlie Lady, and meke Lambe, voyde of all Spanishe pride, and strange bloude," [170] but the principle stood in Goodman's book, and, it need hardly be added, in Queen Elizabeth's memory.[171]

But passionately as Goodman felt on this issue, it was not for this that his tract stood condemned in quarters that would have had no more tenderness for Queen Mary than he felt. It was rather for his direct and systematic attack upon the whole notion of obedience.

It is significant of the topical character of these treatises that for Knox it is the regiment of women that calls forth his largest range of consideration and discussion. On the second theme his scope is much more particular, even personal. For Goodman the case is the opposite. His handling of the regiment of women is much more restricted and more narrowly personal. On the second theme he not only takes a much wider range, but actually goes much farther in developing the course of action implied by Knox. That corresponds to the more advanced state of the general crisis with which he was confronted.

He went to the heart of the matter when he took up the famous text of Saint Paul, "It behoveth every soule to be subjecte to superior powers, because there is no power but of God," and declared that those who invoked that text to justify their obedience to Queen Mary in the teeth of their consciences and the word of God, plainly misunderstood Saint Paul.[172] For the proper interpretation of that text he invoked another which had not hitherto figured very largely in this discussion, the answer which Peter and John returned to the Council who sought to restrain them from preaching Christ, "Whether it be right in the sight of God to obey you rather then God, judge you." [173] In other words, princes and "all powers upon thee arth, are not to be compared unto God." [174]

As for the text of Paul that had so awed his generation, he explains it by appealing to the circumstances under which it was first delivered. Apparently, among the Roman converts there were many who thought that the office of the magistrate was not needed any more for those who professed Christ, much as did the Anabaptists and Libertines of Goodman's own day.[175] But no obedience is due to the magistrate but what is in keeping with God's law and so lawful.[176] In like fashion Goodman accounts for the oft-cited text of Saint Peter on the submission of subjects and servants, by pointing out that Peter meant that rough and forward masters were to be borne with, and not wicked and ungodly.[177] "Obedience is to heare God rather then man," always.[178]

But mere passive resistance is not enough. Goodman invokes an example not, so far as I am aware, remembered in any of the submission literature, the example of Mathathias in the second part of the first book of Maccabees, who slew not only the Jew who came to do sacrifice at the altar Modim but killed also the officer of the king Antiochus who had compelled him to do so and destroyed the altar,[179] and from the transaction Goodman drew the lesson:

"Then if Matathias herein did discharge his conscience before God and man, in resisting by temporal power the kinge, his commandements and officiers: it is not onely the office of Apostles and preachers, to resist, but the dewtie likewise of all others according to their estate and vocation." [180]

Of course, Goodman is quite aware that this book to which he appeals is not among the canonical books, but he meets any objection on that score by pointing out that "the facte of Matta-thias dependeth not upon the auctoritie of the boke, wherin it is conteyned: but upon the worde of God, wher upon it was grownded." [181]

Goodman has no patience with the common people who think that there is nothing they can do if their rulers are tyrants.[182] He reminds them that they ought not to suffer all power and liberty to be taken from them, that if they do, they are the occasion of their prince's becoming a tyrant.[183] And he taunts them with their stubborn resistance to King Edward. Here he does not hesitate to strike home on the score of the disturbances of that reign:

"To restore Antichrist agayne, whom ons God had banished to all your comfortes, you were not ashamed to terme it obedience, and to counte your selves therin no rebells, but lawful resisters: but to defende Christe and his comfortable Gospell (which then you had in possession) that are you persuaded to be open rebellion. To arme your selves agaynst your superiors, to defend your commons and earthly commodities with holden from you, by the greedy desier of new up-starte gentlemen, how willing and redie have you shewed your selves?

But to holde and reteyne your spiritual possession not promised onely, but geven in to your handes, you are moste slowe without all hope and courage." [184]

But in spite of his poor opinion of his countrymen's attachment to things spiritual Goodman persists in reminding them that if the magistrates betray the laws of God, the people subject to them will be condemned, too, if they do not maintain those laws against them.[185] He is aware that it may seem to many of his listeners that he is risking grave disorder when he urges the people to assume the task of punishing transgression, but he does not hesitate to proclaim that when the magistrates cease to do their duty it is then as if the people had no officers at all, "and then God geveth the sworde in to the peoples hande, and he him self is become immediatly their head." [186] Again Goodman is not discussing general principles but is thinking of specific applications to the England of his day. He is still addressing the common people of England:

"If you had required all Massemongers, and false Preachers to have bene punished with deathe (as is appoynted by Gods worde for such blasphemers and idolatrers, and if they to whom it apperteyned, had denyed, your selves would have seen it performed at all tymes, and in all places) then shuld you have shewed that zele of God, which was commended in Phinees, destroyinge the adulterers: and in the Israelites againste the Benjamites, as before is noted." [187]

But Goodman is not without some comfort for the good ruler. He has already given his ideal, which may be judged from the first requirement that "he be a man that hathe the feare of God before his eyes, and zeluslye with David and Josias, dothe studie to set forthe the same, hatinge unfaynedlie al papistrie and idolatrie." [188] To such a man Goodman can give the following hope, very much like what we have already heard Lever and Crowley promise:

"Therfore if thou be a Ruler and covete to have the people obedient to thee in Gods feare, this muste be thy first and principall studie to, procure that they may truely know God by the playne and diligent preaching of his worde, wherin if they be well instructed, there is no costume so longe continued, no idlenesse so longe used, no supersticion so deeply rooted, which they will not gladly and peaceably for go at thy commandement: yea, there is no thing which is evill, that they can for shame stande in: nor any good and lawfull demande, that they will deny thee." [189]

Although the author of so extreme a book as Goodman's found himself in much too delicate a position to join the press of homecoming exiles that followed the accession of Elizabeth,[190] still this last promise of his to the ruler who would take the right path was abundantly justified by the returned preachers. Just as the fear of the Marian experience had driven the earlier preachers into an enthusiastic support of the government in which their hopes rested, so the realization of their fears led them to welcome the deliverance of Elizabeth and, whatever their personal disappointments, to rally gratefully to her settlement. Perhaps not many will put it so plainly as did Stockewood when he reminded his readers, "howe joyfull was unto us the death of Queene Marie," [191] but the sentiment is constant in Elizabethan preaching of all shades of reformed opinion. It is no wonder that the grateful preachers repaid their rescuer with loyal support.

On the other hand, that support was needed and was asked for. The Elizabethan Church went back to the device for teaching and for propaganda that had proved so useful in the reign of Edward, the homily, which, prescribed for Sunday reading in the pulpits, carried the policy of the government into the parish churches. Indeed, the device had proved so practical that in Mary's reign Bonner issued a collection of homilies in 1555.[192] Of course, there was no homily on obedience in this collection. Indeed, the eighth homily was devoted to the more congenial theme "Of the Aucthoritie of the Churche," and the ninth and tenth to the theme "Of the Supremacy." [193] But the Elizabethan Church restored the *Homelies* of 1547, including the homily on obedience already discussed in the preceding chapter, in the *Certayne Sermons* of 1563.[194] And when six years later the Earls' Rebellion roused again the always latent fears of revolution, an even stronger treatment of the subject with the appropriate topical allusions was issued, the famous *An Homelie against Disobedience and Wylfull Rebellion* of 1571.[195] This may be taken as the epitome of all the literature on submission, for it gathers up in a striking fashion the ideas with which we are already familiar, reënforcing them and bringing them up to date with a good deal of adroitness. The very approach is apposite to the needs of the time, for the homily begins not with any abstract or general disquisition on the nature and origins of government, but goes straight to the heart of the problem by pointing out that rebellion is the fruit of the fall.[196] Then it gets under way in solid fashion by inculcating the basic principle that rulers are ordained of God.[197]

The second part of the homily presents the scriptural arguments from example for the reverence due to the authority and person of the ruler appointed of God, with which we are already familiar, notably David's sparing of Saul out of reverence for his kingship, however, dishonored,[198] and Mary's going to be enrolled though she was with child.[199] The third part presents some equally familiar examples of shameful and dreadful ends that have befallen traitors as evidence of the wickedness of all treason.[200] All these first three parts are highly traditional in character, but vigorous and graphic in style of presentation.

The fourth part is at once homelier and timelier in its combination of traditional and topical material. It begins with a firm insistence on the heavy wrath of God against such subjects as but inwardly "grudge" and mutter at the authority of their king.[201] It reminds those who have perhaps been trusting in furtive ways that Scripture shows that the very birds of the air will betray secret murmuring against the Prince.[202] But it takes up new ground when it turns to the pretexts and characters of rebels, for now it boldly comes out with what is clearly a reference to the late troubles. The redress of the commonwealth used to be the excuse of rebels. Now religion is used to give color to rebellion.[203] This is an interesting recognition of the general field of the relations between social and religious agitation, even if it is obviously unsympathetic to both. Even more up-to-date is the charge that it must be a "frantike" religion which needs rebellion for its support,[204] an interesting example of the Elizabethan tendency to label all dissenting zeal as frantic, very much in the way in which the seventeenth century was to stigmatize such zeal as "enthusiastic." This general charge is followed by a still more personal attack upon the character of the rebels in which the hearers of these homilies are invited to contrast the sober character of the men who make up the Queen's Council, the bulwark of the established order, with the obvious worthlessness of the leaders of the rebels.[205] This last, in particular, is a very good illustration of the general competence of the Elizabethan government in the field of popular propaganda.

Still more up-to-date so far as meeting the problems of the time is concerned, is the analysis of the causes of rebellion, ambition and ignorance. The definition of ambition, in particular, as we shall see presently, is strikingly in the spirit of the time. "By ambition, I meane the unlawful and restless desire in men to be of higher estate then God hath geven or appoynted unto them." [206] Then the hearer is again reminded that Christ and His Apostles not only were themselves obedient to the magistrates of their time but urged other Christians to follow their example.[207] Not surprisingly, in view of the religious involvements of the Earls' Rebellion, the homilist devotes a good deal of time to the claims of the pope,[208] with especial stress on the pope's alleged habit of stirring up rebellion against princes,[209] a thesis supported by characteristic illustrations ranging from the pope's treason to the emperor and to God in the iconoclastic controversy [210] to the pope's recent attempts "to breake downe the barres and hedges of the publique peace in Irelande, only upon confidence easyly to abuse the ignoraunce of the wylde Irishe men." [211] Even at the present moment, so the homily charges, the princes of Christendom are kept so busy with quarrels and rebellions fomented by Rome that they are not able to gather their forces to defend Christendom from the "Moores and Infidels." [212] Appropriately, the homily is followed by "A Thankes geving for the Suppression of the Last Rebellion." [213] In other words this is the tradition of submission brought up to date. But it is more than an official imposition. As we shall see, it is the formulation of a policy which the preachers as a whole and characteristically supported. And they supported it because it met the needs of the situation as they saw it.

To begin with, there was the fear of rebellion, not only on a large scale, which threatened rarely, but on the small scale of local disorders, a pretty constant threat throughout the period. And, it should be added, the possibility was not confined to the field of religious and political agitation; rather, there is evidence of endemic restlessness for social reasons. There was throughout the period widespread unemployment, and though men's ideas as to causes were often far from clear, the possible results of such enforced idleness were only too clear at least to men's fears. The author of *Tom Tell Troath* obviously had an ax to grind, but most men of his day, particularly of the comfortable classes, would have uncomfortably agreed with what he said, probably in 1591 (though the book seems not to have been published until some time later, well into the next century): "There are many thousands of your Majesties subjects, able, and proper fellowes, that lie languishing, ready to rebell, for want of imployment." [214] The remedy which Tom suggests is to send these potential rebels to the aid of the French Protestants and the glory of their nation. [215]

Sometimes the dreaded rebellion, at least on the scale of rioting over local grievances, did materialize. A very interesting example of such a disturbance, occurring shortly after the close of our period, is to be found in a sermon of 1607 to which allusion has already been made. [216] According to the title-page, Robert Wilkinson had preached this sermon the preceding June at Northampton before the Lord Lieutenant of the County and the rest of the Commissioners "there assembled upon occasion of the late *Rebellion and Riots in those parts committed.*" It falls a little outside of our period, but it sums up the prevailing attitude of the preachers of our period so well and shows it in action in application to a specific emergency so dramatically that it has seemed helpful to look at it here. And the more so because it affords some striking parallels to the sermons of Crowley on the same topic at an earlier time.

To begin with, Wilkinson resembles Crowley in his very real ability to enter into the plight of the rebels. There is no question of the shock with which he describes the conditions around Northampton which had precipitated the riots and disorders which had brought his Commission-auditors to his sermons, particularly when he declares that

"the image of God in one man is more worth then all the sheep in the world; and it is time, yea high time to speake of this, the text of it already being written in bloud; and no marvell if they which feele it, runne madde and wilde upon it, since wee which but see it are so much amazed at it; for a stranger which coasteth these countries, and findeth heere and there so many thousands and thousands of sheepe, *et nihil humani generis,* in so many miles not a thing like a Man, might take up a wonder, and say with himselfe; what? hath there bin some Sorceresse, or some *Circe* heere that hath transformed men into beasts?" [217]

So the cry against the sheep persists. And one is reminded, too, of the preachers of a half century before in what he has to say of the comparative iniquity of agricultural oppression and rebellion. For sympathetically as Wilkinson viewed the sufferings that had precipitated rebellion, he seems with equal sincerity and profundity to have felt that great as was the sin of the enclosers, it was yet nothing to compare with the sin of the rebels, of which he says:

"I think the sin of these men by many degrees to exceed the other, for Pasture-men indeed do horrible mischiefe, but they do it by degrees; first one breaks the law; and then another is bold to break it by example; now evils of such passage are more easily prevented; but that which growes by mutinies being sodaine and violent, is lesse resistible. Pasture-men indeed destroy a few townes, but mutiners by civill commotion depopulate whole kingdoms, and that partly by making way to forraine enemies, who usually increase their dominions by such advantage, but chiefly by sacking and harrying their owne country with their own hands." [218]

Sympathetic as Wilkinson was with the despair of the rebels, he is nonetheless emphatic as to the mistake they have made, indeed, as he points out, addressing the rebels directly, the opportunity they have thrown away:

"Therefore marke (good people) what honor God had offered to us, if patiently wee had borne the oppression which is put upon us, for by this reckoning depopulators are persecutors, and oppression is persecution, and we by oppression had come to martyrdome, if patiently we had borne it. But heaven and earth are witnesses how farre we are from bearing; yea bearing is come to bearding, and because of a little want, men have buried their patience as they buried hedges." [219]

This is certainly one of the most interesting examples of the martyr cult of the time.

And then one can imagine the preacher's turning to some of the local audience, doubtless sitting there sullen and terrified by the memory of those who had been hanged for their rebellion; and asking "what a fearefull thing were it for us to live in that sinne, which these poore wretches detested when they dyed?" [220] And then he goes on to make the usual plea for patience, a whole line of argument, one might add, not only slightly circular but also brutal. It must be remembered, however, that even for a humane and compassionate man like Robert Wilkinson, the most shocking thing about the whole transaction was the breach of the public order in the flouting of the reverence due to royal authority when the rebels insisted that the king answer certain demands:

"And as if brambles had bin annointed Kings, an inferiour Magistrate is now too meane, but the great King must come to compound himselfe. . . . A King of three great kingdomes must capitulate with a Tinker, whether by Proclamation or by privy Seale hee shall manifest his will and pleasure: and yet all this is called Reforming." [221]

This sermon is, however, exceptional in the urgency with which it discusses the problem, as in the urgency of the occasion. Usually the issue is discussed in less immediate and more general terms, with the result that the right attitude is taken for granted rather than insisted upon. The allusions to submission are more often incidental and in passing, brief rather than expanded. All this makes for a sense of security and confidence. But the approach to the matter is basically that of the homily and the tradition which it represents. And this is true regardless of the position of the preacher on other issues, whether it be the on the whole conformist Bishop Babington interpreting the scope of the Fifth Commandment to cover the reverence due to the place and calling of magistrates: "I say, their place and calling, that portion above others which the Lord hath given them of his authority, majesty, and excellency, prooveth unto us, that we must reverence them," [222] or the distinctly critical Henry Smith summing up the basic principles in a sentence: "Our first lesson, is *Feare God:* the next is, *Honour the King:* that is (as Paul interpreteth), *Wee must obey for conscience,* not against *conscience.*" [223]

In general, however the preachers may discourse on the nature of the royal authority, what they say amounts to little more than this. Occasionally, the influence of what may be called humanist ideas is to be discerned. A striking example is to be seen in *A Preparative to Contentation* which John Carpenter published in 1597 on the classic text of the seventeenth verse of the second chapter of the first epistle of Peter: *"Love brotherly fellowship. Feare God. Honour the Prince."* [224]

For Carpenter widens the field of discussion as to the foundation of the ideal commonwealth when he goes beyond the concentrated biblicism of so many of the reformers of the time with a broader appeal to experience. In many ways Carpenter's line of attack is an extension to the field of social reform of the line of reasoning which Hooker about the same time was applying to things religious.[225] In response to those who were challenging the basic principles of subjection to the scriptural demands of the reformers, Carpenter replies that we should try to make our social life conform "to that which not onely the written word, but also nature, reason, and the consent of all wise and learned men, have received and embraced, as things good and profitable," namely, that princes and magistrates are necessary for the welfare of the commonwealth.[226]

It is significant that Carpenter turns to the Greek poets for support as to the supreme evil of anarchy.[227] But though there is much in Carpenter's general handling of the bases of authority that reminds one of the law-of-nature approach of both Hooker, on the one hand, and St. Thomas, on the other, there is no suggestion in Carpenter of that recognition of the representative character of the person in authority to be found in St. Thomas' discussion "Of Respect of Persons," where in answer to the third article of the sixty-third question, "Whether Respect of Persons takes place in showing Honour and Respect?" St. Thomas replied:

"Now it is to be observed that a person may be honoured not only for his own virtue, but also for another's: thus princes and prelates, although they be wicked, are honoured as standing in God's place, and as representing the community over which they are placed, according to Prov. xxvi. 8." [228]

Nor is there, in general, in this literature.

Rather the emphasis is that of Calvin's summary in the 1561 edition of *The Institution of Christian Religion:*

"Finally we owe this affection of reverence yea and devotion to all our rulers, of what sort soever they be. Which I do therfore the oftener repete, that we may learne not to searche what the men themselves be, but take this for sufficiente, that by the will of the Lord they beare that personage, in which the Lord himself hath emprinted and engraved an inviolable majestie." [229]

But for all his humanism Carpenter himself comes home solidly to rest in his own tradition when he turns from his Greek poets to scriptural texts and draws the orthodox conclusion to the discussion: "Agaynst this power of the Prince, the Lorde forbiddeth anie man to rise, resist, or rebell, by this woorde in the Lawe (which *David* also remembreth) *Touch not mine annoynted, and doo my Prophets no harme.*" [230]

On this principle, then, there is solid agreement. Where there is difference, it is a matter rather of weight of emphasis. A very interesting example of this difference in emphasis is to be seen in two characteristic and representative passages from the work of Sandys, who for all his Puritan tendencies was in this field a thoroughly orthodox and representative Elizabethan bishop, and Perkins, almost certainly the greatest of the preachers and writers on the Puritan side. Both support without reservation the doctrine of submission, but there is an illuminating difference in emphasis in the way the two men handle the official doctrine at the point where it was bound to raise questions in the minds of thoughtful men, namely, the unjust or faithless ruler. Sandys in one of the sermons delivered at the seat of his episcopal authority, York, sums up the official teaching with admirable pith and point:

"First there is no power but of God. The powers that are bee ordeined of him. Be the magistrate Jewe or Gentile, Christian or Heathen, good or bad, hee hath his authoritie from God the magistrate of all magistrates. God hath placed him and ordeined him to bee thy governour, in respect whereof thou art bound for thy conscience sake towardes God for to obey him. Another reason why everie soule should live in subjection to the higher power is, because whosoever resisteth the ordinaunce of God provoketh the judgement of God against himselfe. If God for thy sinne set a wanton, an hypocrite, yea or an Infidell over thee, thou must obey that wanton, that hypocrite, and that Infidell, and not rebell against him." [231]

So Sandys moves with firm, somewhat peremptory steps over the field of difficulty, as one might expect the primate of England to do about the year 1585.

It is not possible for Perkins to get over the difficulty so easily, and probably he knew that some among his hearers would find it even less easy, for when almost at the beginning of *A Discourse of Conscience,* he takes up the basic text of submission, the second verse of the thirteenth chapter of Romans, he finds himself stopped by the question of limitation on subjection:

"Magistracie indeede is an ordinance of God to which we owe subjection, but how far subjection is due, there is the question. For body and goods and outward conversation, I graunt all: but a subjection of conscience to mens lawes, I deny.[232]

Of course, Perkins grants that in matters not contrary to the commandment of God there is an obligation of conscience. Indeed, in a moment he is going to deliver a very definite rule on the subject:

"Wholesome lawes of men, made of things indifferent, so farre-forth bind conscience by vertue of the generall commandement of God, which ordaineth the Magistrates authoritie: that whosoever shall wittingly, and willingly with a disloyall minde, either break or omit such lawes, is guiltie of sin before God." [233]

But it is clear throughout that he wants to keep the source of authority more firmly in mind than the representative of authority. Again, it is a matter of emphasis, but one can see at work in the mind of Perkins a ferment of speculation that is going to lead his followers eventually in a very different direction from that of the followers of Sandys.

But for the present, there is no doubt that Perkins is exerting his vast influence for the maintenance of peace and order. For in *The Whole Treatise of the Cases of Conscience,* the great encyclopedia of Puritan casuistry, he discusses the crucial theme of how a Christian should conduct himself in time of persecution, and in the course of that discussion he is most emphatic in his insistence on the doctrine of non-resistance even to tyrannous authority.[234] Though to a man who found so much unsatisfactory in the direction which religious affairs were taking in England as Perkins did, the possibility of having to face persecution for his principles seemed less remote than it did to one of the pillars of the established order like Sandys, still Perkins is as firm as Sandys in insisting on the necessity of maintaining the peace and order of the land. And quite in the spirit of the official homily in his *A Godly and Learned Exposition upon the Epistle of Jude,* he holds up the terrible end of Korah, Dathan and Abiram before those traitors, rebels, Jesuits, etc., who "gainsay the ordinance of God, and stand out in deniall or resistance of their lawfull and naturall Prince," and expresses his confidence that the same punishment will overtake them.[235]

But whatever the illuminating citations of authority or the persuasive examples, from the pulpits of the land this doctrine of submission was preached steadily. And it is hard to believe that this preaching was other than impressive. For this doctrine of submission was not something which the preacher delivered to his flock from a loftier height. He thought of himself as bearing the same relation to the superior power as they did, with the same obligation of obedience. Indeed, he thought of himself as more bound to such an obedience, if possible, because of the relation between church and state in which he had a double capacity.

But if the modern reader is tempted to see in this wholehearted propagation of the doctrine of submission only an abject surrender of the independence of the church, he is mistaken. For the relation between church and state which the preachers envisaged was a two-way relationship. As would be expected, Sandys goes to the heart of what might be called the official position of the church, when he defines the relations between the minister and the magistrate as follows: "They are Gods two hands, to build up withall the decayed wals of Jerusalem." [236] In other words, just as the church is bound to support the state, so the state is bound to support the church.

In the sermon from which the sentence above on the relation of the minister and the magistrate is taken, Sandys is preaching before the Parliament at Westminster. A large portion of what he has to say is devoted to the task of persuading Parliament to mend the civil ills of the kingdom. Here he moves cautiously. For instance, he makes a very explicit disclaimer of any intention to go outside of his realm:

> "It is commonly saide that the common wealth is sore diseased, and that everie member of that bodie seemeth to be grieved. Remedie would bee sought in time, least remedie come too late. But I am no Phisition for that bodie, and therefore is it not fit for me to minister any medicine to it. But I shall pray for the health therof, and set it over to such as have skill and can helpe." [237]

This is in general typical of his approach to this aspect of his work. For when he does take up the theme of the responsibility of magistrates elsewhere, in a sermon preached at an assize, he uses fairly impersonal and even classical terms to warn them: "You to whom the sword of justice and judgement is committed take heede unto it. Let it not spare mightie men: for their sinnes are mightie sinnes." [238]

In contrast he is much surer and freer when he takes up the second theme of the sermon before Parliament above, the duty of Parliament to ensure the maintenance of the religious establishment. This is illustrated very well by his handling of the delicate matter of compulsory church attendance. Apparently, Sandys anticipated at least some hesitation in certain quarters as to the propriety of compelling all the nation to come to the services of the Established Church. At least he thought it wise to meet such possible objections with a good deal of vigor:

"Although conscience cannot be forced; yet unto externall obedience, in lawful things, men may lawfully be compelled. . . . Seeing that the whole service in our Church is no other than Gods written worde: as there can be alleaged no just cause, why any man should withdrawe himselfe from this word; so appertaineth it unto princes that feare God, within their dominions to compel every subject to come and heare this worde: least the church by this evill example should be greatly offended." [289]

Most of Sandys' colleagues did not feel his delicacy about this matter. When Robert Pricke in *The Doctrine of Superioritie, and of Subjection, contained in the Fift Commandement of the Holy Law of Almightie God,* according to the title-page "a pretious memorial of the substance of manie godly sermons," drew up in catechetical dialogue form a summary of the prevailing teaching, he prescribed for the magistrates doing their duty by saying in round terms that "they are to enforce and compell the people: First of all, to resort to the ministrie of the worde of God; yea, to give eare thereunto with reverence and attention, and therewithall to performe all duties concerning the outward worship of God." [240]

But Babington on this point is even briefer. He does not trouble to enter into any detailed excuses or explanations, contenting himself in *A Profitable Exposition of the Lords Prayer,* at least, with a sentence of summary contempt in his discussion of the sixth petition:

"But men may not be compelled against theyr conscience. A prettie ground of all Libertinisme, and an high way to overthrow all estates under heaven." [241]

The conclusion of that warning brings in, however, another aspect of the matter, which Sandys in the sermon before Parliament above does not this time hesitate to set forth unmistakably, namely, that the maintenance of religious uniformity is quite as much in the civil interest as in the religious;

"This libertie, that men may openly profess diversitie of religion, must needs be dangerous to the common wealth. What stirs diversities of religion hath raised in nations and kingdoms, the histories are so many and so plaine, and our times in such sort have told you, that with further proofe I need not trouble your eares. One God, one king, one faith, one profession is fit for one monarchie, and common wealth." [242]

In such sermons as these it is easy to hear the official protagonists of the Established Church speaking. With all their hopes to see the religious order purified and strengthened, they obviously regarded the maintenance of the order they believed in as the best guarantee of the welfare of the nation, civic and religious, material and spiritual. They would have every ground for finding the basis of the continued social welfare of the realm in the sustained strength of the church. That is, naturally, the prevailing position of the supporters of the Establishment of their day. In no sense was this idea that the state was bound to further the reformation of the church peculiar to the English preachers. Luther had held it the duty of the secular magistrate to undertake the reformation of the church.[243] Calvin had gone farther, insisting that it was the duty of the government not only to maintain true doctrine and worship, but also, if necessary, to suppress heresy by force.[244]

Even those men who were not satisfied with the progress which the Church of England by law established had made in the direction of a true and complete reformation, looked no less insistently to the civil power for the realization of their hopes.

Laurence Chaderton obviously found much amiss in the church organization which permitted such a swarm of "idle, ignorant, and ungodly Curates and Readers" to infest the land,[245] as we shall presently find him complaining, and he makes no secret of the fact that he prays for the reform of the discipline of the church as administered by Chancellors, Commissaries, and Officials.[246] But the very terms in which he expresses his faith that his prayer will be answered make clear his adherence to the existing order as he promises that God "will stirre up and arme with power, wisdome and zeale, as well those Magistrates, which he in mercie hath alredie given us, as all those also, with whome in time to come, he shall vouchsafe to blesse us, to refourme these and all other the blemishes of his Church, according to his worde." [247]

Henry Smith is even more plain-spoken in his weariness of official compromise, but it is still a loyal prayer that he prays for rulers:

"Oh, woulde that Princely spirite woulde once come upon them to go before the people, which Moses appoynted for the Kings place, and not lagge after them like Herod which sayde, he would come after the wise men to Christ." [248]

These are the perfectly loyal and even prudent utterances of thoroughly responsible men, but their purport is unmistakable. Even more unmistakable is the utterance of a man who, however one admires his courage, must for the time be regarded as rash in hurling his challenges directly at the royal head in his famous sermon of 1569, Edward Dering.[249] The great difference between Dering's and Sandys' conceptions of the role of the minister is very well set forth in a sentence of the prefatory address, the work of an unidentified I.F., who seems thoroughly to have grasped the significance of Dering's position; and with full sympathy commended to the Christian reader his sermon "as it was not long sithens uttered zealously, and no doubt by the purpose of God him selfe (who openeth the mouthes of his Ministers to speake without feare)." [250]

In other words the function of the minister is that of the prophet, as Dering himself makes quite clear in a direct charge to the Queen herself:

"If you have prayed in tymes past unto God, to molify your enemies hartes, and to bring their cruell practises to nothing: now that you your selfe are set in safety, be not cruell unto Gods anoynted, and do hys Prophetes no harme." [251]

But it is not enough for the Queen to do the prophet no harm. It is her duty to listen to what he has to say:

"It is true that the Prince must defende the fatherles and wydow, relieve the oppressed, and have no respect of persons in judgement, seeke peace unto hys people, and gyrd hym selfe with righteousnes: But thys is also his deuty, and hys greatest dutye, to be carefull for religion: to mayntayne the Gospel: to teach the people knowledge, and builde hys whole governaunce wyth faythfulnes." [252]

In general, this prophetic note is more likely to emanate from preachers who were moving like Dering in a Puritan direction than from men who were fairly well satisfied with the general lines of advance of the church as a whole, if not of all of its individual members. It takes a Henry Smith to warn those who are overawed by the majesty of princes and rulers that "though they judge here, yet they shal be judged hereafter, and give account of their Stewardship howe they have governed, as straight as their subjects how they have obeyed." [253]

Still more for something really dramatic on this theme one must go to one of the recognized Puritan leaders like Laurence Chaderton. For instance, when Laurence Chaderton is discussing the always delicate matter of how the poor preacher shall deal with sinners in high place, he does not hesitate to include princes in the roster of all estates and degrees of callings which the prophets in Scripture have rebuked for their sins:

"It were to long, and in deede needelesse in so plaine a matter, to cite and alledge the witnesses of all the Prophets, who as they had great experience of both these kindes of men, in all estates and degrees of callings: as of Princes, Priestes and people: so they did with great aucthoritie and boldnesse discover their severall and particular sinnes, and threaten against them present destruction, and the fearefull Judgements of God." [254]

It must be recognized, however, that this prophetic criticism on the part of the pre-Puritan preachers was not by any means so general as some of these statements might suggest. After all, it is not usually the way of the prophet to leave the call to reform general. Nor did these prophets. One of their lines of specific attack will serve to show how considerable was the threat they offered to the peace of the proponents of the existing religious settlement. It is the old attack on the character of the clergy, which had proved so effective in an age when the confidence of men in the existing order had been shaken. And it was effective for the simple reason that in the nature of things, no body of imperfect human beings can ever hope to realize the ideals set for them either by the religious geniuses who usually define the basic patterns of the clergy or by what average humanity with no propensity for perfection in itself usually expects from its spiritual leaders. Effective, also, because the average man does not find it hard to believe that those whom in his better moments he hoped were better than himself are found to be faulty, too. And of course, there is always an element of special excitement and conviction in the revelation of clerical weakness when it is made by members of the clergy. The earlier years of the Reformation had abundantly illustrated the effectiveness of this technique as well as the peculiar danger of it, namely, that faith once shaken is not so easily recovered for hoped-for redirection.

But the attack on the character of the clergy was still a good weapon for those who wanted to see the existing order moved nearer to their ideal. An interesting example is to be found in a sermon which John Stockewood, Schoolmaster of Tunbridge, preached at Paul's Cross on the tenth of May in 1579.[255] His main theme is the widespread contempt of the time for the ministry, and his earnest desire is to see a proper concept of the dignity of the high calling of the clergy vindicated.[256] There is no question of his sincerity, but it is hard to imagine Sandys or Jewel describing even their less admired colleagues as wandering

"uppe and downe like maisterlesse houndes, being glad to serve, as the Lord threatneth to the posteritie of Elie, for a piece of silver, and a morsel of bread; but we have too few of faithfull and paynefull labourers: for if a perfect viewe were taken throughout the lande, I feare mee it woulde bee founde that in every Shiere and Countie, scarse the twentith parishe were provided of his able Teacher. No marvell therfore if there dwel in the people suche horrible and woonderful ignorance," etc.[257]

And while there is abundant evidence of the truth of Stockewood's complaint that all the nobility shunned the ministry and nearly all the gentry, too, so that only the "meaner and poorer sorte" were left for the recruiting of the clergy,[258] still the most careless of the new patrons can hardly have very often given even the small village cures to "their Faukener, their Huntesman, their Horsekeeper, or any other such like, so as he can reasonablie read englishe." [259] And when Stockewood begins to refer to a considerable body of his colleagues as "idle shepheardes, dumbe dogges," [260] then one is reminded of Laurence Chaderton's more restrained but no less devastating complaint of the "whole swarmes of idle, ignorant, and Ungodly Curates and Readers," whom he urged to take up some other calling within their capacity,[261] or Dering's attack upon the presentations of the time in the famous sermon before the Queen to which we have already alluded:

"Looke after thys upon your Patrones, and loe some are selling their benefices, some farming them, some keepe them for their Children, some geve them to Boyes, some to serving men, very fewe seake after learned Pastors. And yet you shall see more abominacions than these: Looke upon your Ministery, and ther are some of one occupation, some of another, some shake bucklers, some Ruffians, some Hawkers and Hunters, some Dicers and Carders, some blynde guides, and cannot see, some dum Dogs and wyll not barcke." [262]

In such passages one begins to recognize Stockewood's attack for what it is, the spearhead of that Puritan attack on the Prayer Book as the stronghold of the Elizabethan Settlement that was to have such dramatic consequences in the next century.

Men will seldom admit that their adversaries have any right to use the same type of argument that they have used, but they will instinctively recognize the impact of techniques which they have employed successfully themselves. The leaders of the English Church, having achieved with more difficulty than is always realized something of a religious equilibrium, were naturally in no mood to have it upset. Like the leaders of the state, just come through a period of violent stress and agitation with very real threats to security at home and abroad always in mind, they were above all interested in the maintenance of order. They believed sincerely in their order, and they found it very difficult to enter into the minds of men who did not. That is a capacity of the imagination that has very little chance to develop anyway in a period of fierce contest such as this which England, like most of the western world, had just come through. It seemed to them, therefore, that even those who on some particular issue were not satisfied with the existing order must see that it was better to sacrifice some fine points rather than have everything upset again. As a matter of fact, throughout the century a good many of these who were not satisfied were willing to be patient and trust to a slower and more peaceful achievement of their ends. Chaderton and Perkins are conspicuous examples. It was easy, therefore, for the defenders of the status quo, to feel that this maintenance of order was so important that all reasonable men would agree to it, to see in any threat to it not only a material danger but the manifestation of an irrational fanaticism.

One finds already in the sixteenth century the intensification of that psychology that in the seventeenth century was to stigmatize a warm promotion of any radical departure from the established order as "enthusiastic." In the stress of the religious changes of the century the leaders of all parties had done everything in their power to arouse the emotional energy of their followers as well as to consolidate their convictions. Religious passion so fanned had been one of their most powerful instruments. But the men who were trying to stabilize the religious situation discovered soon enough that however hard it is to fire religious enthusiasm, it is harder still to check and control it when it has once been let loose. It is always more exciting emotionally to press on to new positions than to settle down to the day-to-day grind of making good those already won.

Aside from all questions of whether the Church of England had been reformed according to the will of God, fighting "popery" was a good deal more exhilarating than fighting oneself on sound Protestant lines. And the Anglican leaders found the dragon-slaying, idol-breaking mood a very difficult one to exorcise even when they had no more use for it. In the sermon which he preached at his first coming to York, Sandys made the orthodox episcopal appeal for zeal in the service of God, but he felt obliged to qualify his appeal with the following caution:

"But everie zeale God doth not accept or like of. For as there is a zeale according to knowledge, so there is a blinde headie zeale voide of true knowledge, and therefore of true faith." [263]

The spirit of religious inquiry, of challenging and weighing and sifting one's old religious convictions and practices, had been one of the forces most useful to the reformers, but it, too, had its disadvantages for a period of stabilization. Later, men were to take up their stand permanently in the position of Seekers, but that position could hardly commend itself to men who were anxious above all to stabilize a situation that had been unquiet long enough. Jewel exhorted some of his hearers who, he feared, might be looking to greener pastures to stay where they were: "When you have tried and found out the truth, be constant and settled in it." [264]

Above all, the men who were trying to stabilize the religious situation in England were afraid of the spirit of perfectionism with its exacting discontent, its meddlesomeness, its restlessness. Bishop Babington was only expressing a common state of mind on the part of the supporters of the existing order when in his discussion of the third petition of the Lord's prayer he declared with characteristic brevity: "It is Anabaptisticall to dreame of a perfection here." [265]

This was no new discovery, this of the Anglican leaders. Calvin had long ago become aware of the difficulty and in his warning to good Protestants against the Anabaptists had dealt with it in characteristic fashion, pointing out that "when under the colour of a zeale of perfection, we can beare no imperfection, other in the body, or in the membres of the churche, it is the devyll whyche puffeth us up wyth pryde, and seduceth us wyth hypocrisie, to make us forsake Christes stocke." [266]

The very fact that the Anglican leaders were trying to stabilize an achieved order exposed them to the attacks of the perfectionists just as their predecessors had been exposed by their desire to maintain an established order. For men with something to defend are never so free as men with nothing but a hope of winning some advantage for their cause from the overthrow of the existing order.

The fruit of this psychological development is to be seen clearly in an unusually complete discussion of social stability and its spiritual bases, at which we have already had occasion to look, John Carpenter's, *A Preparative to Contentation*.[267] It is, in other words, a fairly systematic study of the causes of that restlessness of which so many of the observers of the time complain, and a suggestion of some remedies, mainly of a personal, spiritual nature.

The most interesting contribution which Carpenter makes to the subject of social restlessness and stability is his attack on the reforming spirit. It is not of course a disinterested attack. It is clear that Carpenter does not believe that the established order in church and state is in such drastic need of reform as do the critics whom he arraigns. That might be guessed. But the line which his attack takes is interesting, significant as it is, of the psychology of an established position now threatened by a state of mind which it has itself abandoned. Carpenter begins his attack by pointing out that there are some who claim

"that if their discipline were once practised in our Church, and their invented lawes provided for our Common-wealth, and al things ruled and ordred in points as they have devised, and could direct through the abundance of their spirit, then the Moone which is so oftentimes obscured, would shine in the night, yea, and also in the day, without the apperance of any cloud or blemish. . . . As if (forsooth) it were not onely lawfull for them to make, alter, and change lawes, and reforme al things at their owne pleasures: but also, that it were possible themselves could reforme all, and constrain every action of man to answer to right perfection in this world, wherein the very best things that be, do savor of imperfections. . . . They pretend with *Diogenes* to tread downe *Platoes* pride: but yet, with a more hawtie pride, then ever harboured in *Platoes* heart. . . . Howbeit, dreaming (neverthelesse) of *Platoes* Commonwealth, they waxe both extreame wise, and extreame just." [268]

This perfectionism is taxed with both pride and impracticality: "For they studie to utter rather loftie things, then meet things, and in the pride of their harts imagin themselves to be rather kings raigning with God in heaven, then men living among men on the earth." [269] It is not surprising that Carpenter goes on to arraign those who speak above their knowledge on great issues [270] and to raise the very basic question of who is entitled to dispute of religious matters,[271] a question fundamental to the disputes, social and religious, of the next century.

It is not always easy in Anglican apologetics of this period to be quite sure as to whether religion is being used to defend the power of the state, or the power of the state to defend the existing religious order. Probably in the thought of most supporters of the existing order in Carpenter's day the two were so inextricably intertwined that it was not easy for them to separate them. So Carpenter may not have meant any more than just what he said when he warned his readers against making divisions or sects against the power appointed by God in the name of religion, or dislike of magistrates or laws, or general desire of reforming things.[272] But it should not be forgotten that he had already inveighed severely against those who when they were punished for disturbing the peace, fancied themselves martyrs.[273]

Yet whatever the precise implications of any particular statement, there is no question of the central fact, that the maintenance of religion and the maintenance of the existing civil and social order were viewed as interdependent by the preachers, both those who were fairly well satisfied with the existing religious settlement and those who hoped to see it substantially changed. In other words, the doctrine of submission has become something more than a specific for rebellion and social restlessness. It has become the foundation of a basic orientation, both religious and social. And the keynote of that orientation is stability. Whatever the preachers may undertake to say, they dare not jeopardize the maintenance of the order to which they owe so much, in which they so sincerely believe.

CHAPTER VI

USURY

THE ELIZABETHAN preachers were still the defenders and promoters of a cause, but as compared with their predecessors whom we have been studying, they felt a much greater degree of security. The controversy with Rome was certainly a live one, and the Roman menace never far from their thoughts into the nineties, one may safely say. Those who most cordially supported the Establishment were, as we have seen, disturbed by the agitations of those who did not, and those who were being increasingly called Puritans were deeply concerned by what seemed to them the stagnation of a great movement. But the Church of England by law established was a fact, and a fact that with each passing year was gathering to itself the strength of prestige and supporting tradition. The preachers could therefore afford to take stock of their progress, to see how far things were going as they should, to admit disappointments, and to see what measures they could take to achieve their hopes. In this they were, we may be sure, stimulated not only by their own idealism but by the criticisms of their opponents.

Under the circumstances the remarkable thing is not that they preached patience to the poor but that they preached restraint and charity to the rich. Anxious as most of the preachers were not to disturb the status quo, sincerely as most of them believed that whatever the social ills of the time, they were not to be weighed against the religious blessings, it still remains true that within the limits we have suggested, the preachers tried to do their social duty. Tried to do it both out of allegiance to the Christian ideal of brotherhood and to the patriotic ideal of devotion to the commonwealth.

189

It was no small undertaking, this of giving moral guidance and control and correction and amelioration to a period of vast changes, some of which they sympathized with and promoted intentionally, some of which they helped more or less in spite of themselves and sometimes perhaps even against their intention, some of which they definitely distrusted and sought to stem with all the forces at their disposal. It was a very large and complicated field in which they operated, nothing less than the whole social order of their day. It is not, therefore, easy to give anything like a complete picture of their activity. But inasmuch as they were men of very definite purpose and very definite convictions, it is possible to discern certain main lines of thought and feeling on which they were operating in all their social preaching.

But to appreciate their undertaking we must take into account certain ways in which their approach to the problems of society would be very different from that, say, of the present day. The first is that a distinction commonly taken for granted today between personal and social or public morality did not obtain in that world where the distinction between social and personal life had not been drawn so sharply as it has been since, where, indeed, it had as yet made very little headway in a society still pretty much integrated on traditional lines. When, for instance, Perkins preached in the field at Sturbridge Fair some time around 1592,[1] he listed a number of matters of what would today be considered personal morality in his enumeration of the main sins of the England of his day, but he also included some that we should today consider more specifically social. The sins which engaged his attention are, first and obviously most inclusive, "ignorance of Gods will and worship," and *"Contempt of Christian Religion,"* a preacher's way of describing general neglect. Both of these, of course, cover a good deal of ground, being, indeed, the sources of the iniquities that follow. The fourth and fifth are *"Blasphemie"* and *"Prophanation of the Sabbath."* The fifth is what would in our day be recognized as more specifically social: *"unjust dealing in bargaining betwixt man and man."* [2] A little later in the same sermon, he gives a more inclusive and more summary list of the main sins of the day, beginning: *"Murthers, Adulteries, Usuries,*

Briberies, Extortions," a distinctly mixed bag from the point of view of today but not from that of Perkins' time.[3] Consequently, any selection we make to bridge the gap between the sixteenth century and the twentieth, such as is necessary for a study like ours, would seem to the sixteenth-century preachers both incomplete and arbitrary.

And that is not the only critical difference between their approach and ours. We are accustomed to thinking of impersonal tendencies and consequences. They were not. They thought in highly personal terms, in terms of personal motives and deeds and responsibility for consequences. For the sufferings of the poor they asked not what was responsible but who was responsible.

This is especially apparent in what is one of the most precise and complete lists of the sins of the time, the very graphic and ingenious summary of the failings to which the various professions and classes of men of his day were most liable, which Perkins gives in *A Treatise Of the Vocations.*[4] Perkins takes a large view of the social scene of his day, beginning at the top with emperors and princes. Like Thomas More, he stresses especially the greediness of princes who encroach on neighboring kingdoms.[5] The prize example he chooses for the imperialist is the Spanish ruler trying to make himself emperor of the west parts of the world.[6] While in general the late sixteenth-century preacher did not devote much attention to the shortcomings of princes, this particular example was certainly a safe one. From this he descends to the shortcomings of the professions, most of which are fairly traditional, easily to be paralleled in the *Vision of Piers the Plowman* and most of the social literature since, the injustice of the magistrate who takes bribes, and of the lawyer who takes larger fees than is legal or delays the settling of the suit to his own profit. More of the time is Perkins' complaint of the abuse of the ministry "when the word of God, the food of mens soules is with-held, as also when it is corrupted, partly by the poyson of mens errors, partly by the devises of mans braine," and one of Perkins' own hobbies, the physician who administers physic learned out of books without any experience.[7]

But it is in the ranks below these, doubtless comprising the majority of the audiences to which he was wont to preach, that Perkins finds, what is from our point of view, the most interesting lot of faults, and these he particularizes in considerable detail, doubtless to the immense interest of his audience, who had the satisfaction of seeing their neighbors if not themselves hit so neatly in the preacher's indictment. This list gives a very lively notion of how a great Puritan preacher, well in touch with the life of his time, would account for what he found wrong with the social scene:

"In the calling of the Merchant and trades-man, there is false weights, and false measures, divers weights and divers measures; ingrossing, mingling, changing, setting a glosse on wares by powdering, startching, blowing, darke shops, glozing, smoothing, lying, swearing, and all manner of bad dealing. In the patrone, there is presentation given, but with secret condition of having his owne tythes, or some other fleece out of the living. In the land-lord, there is racking of rents, taking immoderate fines, inclosing of grounds that have laien common time out of mind: and the cause is, want of sobriety and temperance in diet and apparel. In the husbandman and cornemonger, there is exceeding injustice, in hording up graine till the time of further advantage: and in taking whatsoever they can get for their own, though it be to the shedding of the blood of the poore. In the calling of the Printer, which should serve for the speciall good of the Church and Commonwealth, there is exceeding injustice done to both, by the publishing of libels, and hereticall bookes. . . . And in the calling of the Booke-seller there is like inustice [sic], in that they sel al bookes, good and bad, of truth and falshood, and that hand over head, without any regard, to every one that commeth." [8]

One thing more should be noted of this passage of Perkins', and that is that though there is no doubt of his compassion for the sufferings of the poor, it is expressed incidentally and by the way. Sharp and thoroughgoing as is his pity for the poor, their sufferings are not his main concern. What he is primarily concerned with is the calling of the sinner to repentance. The rebuking of sins, the enjoining of duty, the definition of ideals, the explication of ways and means, that is his business. That is, in general, true of the preachers of his time. When they approached the subject of alms, they did not as a modern preacher is apt to do, paint a moving picture of the sufferings to be relieved. Rather they attacked the hard-heartedness that made those capable of giving relief withhold it. They did not spend their main energy on the injustice of the social system of their day, but they preached to the covetous and the greedy. They did not elaborate schemes of redistribution of wealth or try to curb the making of fortunes. They went, rather, to the mainsprings of personal action, to the consideration of judgment and affection and will.

Now, of all the motives to sin in this region of man's relations to man, there is no question as to the one which the sixteenth-century preacher put first. It was greed, the greed for wealth. Of course, there is nothing new in the fact of this arraignment of greed. The medieval preachers had inveighed against it, and so had the reformers. The medieval preachers had not succeeded in eliminating it. And the reformers in the first upsurge of their faith in the possibility of remaking humanity had doubtless thought this failure, what might be expected of a corrupt and compromising religion, something that would be repaired in the new age of enlightenment and rekindling of faith.

Certainly, such an attitude is set forth in an anonymous tract of somewhere about 1560, perhaps to judge from the contents, a little earlier, *Robin Conscience and his Father,*[9] of which a considerable fragment has come down to us. The setting of the dialogue is of course a transitional one. The father is a Catholic, the son a Protestant. The father seems to be very much a man of the world, one of the advancing middle class of his day, who takes great pride in the thought that his son will enjoy a place in life that his grandfather never dreamed of having; but his son, enlightened by the new faith, knows that his father's wealth is ill-gotten and his ambitions mistaken. The war between the generations has always been good stuff for drama, and it is not surprising that the literary protagonists of the controversies of the day should be quick to exploit it to the advantage of their cause, especially when the circumstances of an age of transition must have afforded so many good examples. The effect is heightened when, as here, the father, however unregenerate from the author's standpoint, takes what was clearly the position of some of the most enterprising of his contemporaries and the son advances a view which, in its social aspects at least, belongs to an older tradition.

The opening of the first whole speech that survives puts this probably not entirely typical conflict of points of view very clearly and dramatically:

> "Father:
> 'What Robin, my thynke thou hast lytle wyt
> Doest thou thinke skorne, to come to promocion
> For to marye with gentilles, I trow it is fyt
> Havyng with them, of monye a good porcion
> What though it be gotten, by crafte or extorcion
> By the masse, it is all my delyght and pleasor
> To have here aboundaunce, of worldly treasor.
>
> "Robin:
> 'By extorcion father, mary God it forfende
> That any Cristen man, therin should delight
> Father geve me no stoolen goodes, my welth to amende
> Onles I do live, by the poore mans ryght
> As I feare that some doth, both Lord and knyght
> Wherefore good father, in time here repent
> And have a respecte, unto Christes testament.' " [10]

Indeed, Robin Conscience seems to be one of those who are beginning to look back to a past age that, however much buried in spiritual darkness, yet kept a better pattern of life for the poor at least. For he roundly reproaches his father with his neglect of the ancient hospitality in spite of his advance in worldly fortune:

> "You have ten tymes more grounde, and money in your hutch
> Then ever had my granfer, you wyll this alowe
> Yet he kepe a better house than, then ever dyd you
> Wher fore good father, amende and repent
> And have a respecte, unto Chrystes testament." [11]

That is, of course, thoroughly traditional social doctrine. And one can easily catch the voice of many of the more enterprising landholders of the time in his father's contemptuous rejoinder:

"Thou woldest have me, to live only by my londe
And to kepe open house, for every jacke lout." [12]

To this doubtless very common argument of the time the son opposes the stewardship theory of wealth, driving it home with the famous camel and the needle's eye text, in an access of unsuspected moderation adding, however, that this warning is not to all rich men but only to the "unsaciate." [13]

But even this concession does not mollify his father who rejoins with the immortal parental retort to the zealous young reformer:

"Mary syr, ye have gone to longe unto scoole
Agaynst my ryches, and welth to repyn
By the masse, yf thou to the scripture incline
Be sure that I wyll never, do the pleasor
Nor yet never helpe the, with none of my treasor." [14]

But as so often happens, the old man's bark is worse than his bite. In the end he owns that his heart is touched,[15] a gain from the author's point of view, not only for the young preacher but for the poor and, most of all, for the true faith. There is nothing especially fresh or original in the ideas here presented nor in the form in which they are presented. The important thing in this fragment of dialogue is the suggested line-up of values, the exploiting economic drive of the worldling bent on improving his material estate regardless of his duty to others, with the old religious order, and the stewardship theory of content with one's own and just respect for others' rights and one's duty of hospitality and charity to the poor with the new religious point of view, the whole underlined by the war of the generations, grasping age on one side and generous youth on the other. The allusion to the grandfather might suggest to one familiar with the tradition of social criticism that there was something wrong here, but it is doubtful if any such misgivings would occur to the minds of most of the simple readers for whom this dialogue was obviously intended.

But, as the reformers were to find, it is easier to change the average man's doctrinal allegiances than his moral predilections.

Whatever the changes in their manifestations, the old greeds persisted in the actions of those who were preached to, and the old charges persisted in the sermons of the preachers. It is probably true as Miss Lamond, the editor of Hales' tract, said, that by 1592 the problem of enclosures did not receive so much attention as earlier,[16] but that does not mean that under particular circumstances it might not become acute, or that individual preachers might not have it suddenly and dramatically brought home to them by the particular circumstances under which they found themselves, as we have seen happened to Robert Wilkinson in 1606.

Moreover, one need not always assume any such dramatic circumstances as confronted him in his assize sermon. For the preachers of the period, like the poets, it should be added, tend to run in fairly well-established grooves when it comes to social indictment, and one cannot always be sure that some of the particular items of their charge are entirely up-to-date. For instance, when in a sermon published in 1615 Richardson took up the classic theme of the oppressive landlord, he began his indictment with the enclosing of commons and rack-renting, and exacting excessive fines and voiding leases arbitrarily,[17] what had been the stock charges of landlord-worried preachers for nearly a century by now.

Closely allied to this charge of the poor against the rich, both logically and historically, is the protest against the tenacity and expansiveness of monopoly. So Robert Crowley's old view of the "possessioners" as the root of the world's maldistribution,[18] is revived with much wider connotations as becomes the larger context of a new age in a rhyme of the time:

> "Europe hath Owners in possession placed,
> Asia for her Subjects taketh care,
> Affrica her Inhabitants hath graced,
> America hath not a foote to spare,
>   And Indigence will not make thy Release,
>   Till some of these Possessioners decease." [19]

The notion of a world already filled up with inhabitants is a new and discouraging addition to the problem of the world's monopoly. But it seems a remote and academic thing, for all its vastness, when it is set beside the passionate indictment of monopoly in George Phillips' *The Life and Death of the Rich Man and Lazarus.* Here it becomes an immediate threat, swift and dire, in the author's charge that

"a fewe fat ones chop up all the wealth, and the most may goe beg, hange, or steale, or starve: and if they beg you cry a whip for them, if they steale a rope: but if they starve, you shall burne for it in the fire of hel; for you may keep most of them from begging, stealing, starving or hanging if you will, but so deep is your foundation laide in unmercifulnesse, that an earthquake cannot moove you." [20]

Still another of the ancient sources of wrong is found as in Piers Plowman's day in the cruelty of masters to servants, a cruelty that has its roots in the master's carelessness of the economic rights of the poor. Henry Arthington, for instance, notes the discharging of servants and apprentices as one cause of the poverty of the time.[21] George Phillips notes insufficient wages as another:

"There is also a sorte of poore that doe worke, but their labour is not sufficient to relieve them, eyther by reason of the hardnesse of mens heartes, who make them performe too much woorke for too little money, or else because life-stealing age, hath taken away the wonted nimblenesse of their fingers, and agillity of the bodye." [22]

And Richard Turnbull on the authority of Saint James cites the ways in which rich men defraud their hirelings, detaining their wages, or changing their wages, as one of the forms of wickedness produced by covetousness.[23] This last preacher particularly stresses the oppression of which landlords in their dealings with their tenants are guilty.

But whatever the sins of the landlord or the individual master. they are pushed into the background by the sins of the commercial classes. It is an ancient indictment that of *Tom Tell Troath:* "The Merchants, and Trades-Men: I, nor no man else can accuse of being sensible of any thing, but what toucheth their owne profit;" [24] yet it assumes fresh and critical importance in an age of great commercial expansion like the present. The result is that whenever in this period men ask themselves why the poor are suffering so much, commercial and mercantile delinquencies play, as they played in Perkins' indictment of the peculiar failings of each calling, a very large part. All the varieties of cheats receive their due as in the very full account of Perkins already cited, including those ancient villains, the engrossers and the regraters who abuse the trade and cheat the poor and make prices high.[25] "It is a lamentable thing," said Charles Richardson, "to see, what baggage stuffe *Apothecaries* and *Chandlers* sell to poore people, and make them pay as deare as if it were the best." [26]

But of all these mercantile and financial villains far the worst in the eyes of the preachers are the userers. Henry Arthington summed up the case against them when in his list of the ten grievous sins of the "poor-makers" he described the fourth as the "unconscionable extortion of all userers." [27] Dr. Thomas Wilson, whose view of society might be taken to be somewhat more diversified than that of the preachers, put usury next to idolatry and the renouncing of God and his magistrates on earth as the worst of the sins of the time.[28]

It would be safe to say that usury is the burden of more sermons and passages in sermons on social wrong of the time than any other single factor in contemporary life. The sermons of the second half of the sixteenth century quite literally abound in denunciations of what Henry Smith once called "the rich mans vice." [29] Such is the preachers' estimate of the prevalence of the sin. Thomas Rogers, who in 1578 published his translation of Philip Caesar's *A General Discourse against the Damnable Sect of Usurers* expressed the common pulpit opinion when he put on the title-page the commendatory addition: "necessarie for all tymes, but most profitable for these later daies, in which, Charitie being banished, Covetousnes hath gotten the upper hande." [30] And he still further underlined his concern when in the address to his patron, Sir Christopher Hatton, he explained why he had translated this treatise. Usury was in times past a vice so odious that to find a usurer in a city was a wonder. "But," exclaims Rogers with his customary fervor, "good Lorde, howe is the worlde chaunged? That whiche Infidels can not abyde, Gospellers allowe." [31] Rogers goes even farther in his explicit description of the situation:

> "Now, Usurie beeyng growen to suche a perfecte ripenes in *Eng-lande,* as almoste there is no man, but, if he have spare money, out it muste, whereby honeste men become beggers." [32]

Dr. Thomas Wilson, who had seen a good deal of the world, confirmed the opinion of the home-staying clergy of his time when he said that he did not know any place so given to usury as England in these last years.[33]

Indeed, so widespread was the addiction to usury and so confident the usurous in their iniquitous ways that for once the preachers seemed to have recognized that they were up against something pretty resistant to their best efforts. However limited and traditional their view, there were certain things they could not escape. At home they saw the countryside passing from the hands of the old nobility and gentry into the hands of the commercial middle classes with their habits of speculation and efficient exploitation of the means of profit.[34] And when they looked still further abroad, they were face to face with the mysteries of international finance which baffled their government's best efforts to understand, let alone control.[35]

The issue of the government's long struggle with the problem from the toleration of 1545 to the prohibition of 1552 to the compromise of 1571 [36] was such as to add to their troubles. For it confronted the preachers with the problem of legal tolerance in modern as well as ancient law. On the latter Nicholas Sander might contend that the "civil wisemen of Rome did not allow usurie but permitted it as they permitted fornication and divorce." [37] And on the former Smith could ingeniously retort to those who cited the Queen's statute and claimed that it allowed usury to the extent of ten in the hundred that "it doth not allow ten in the hundred, but punisheth that tirant which exacteth above ten in the hundred." [38]

Indeed, the government like the spiritual guides of the merchants still maintained the Christian ideal, but the pragmatic sensitiveness of the merchant was not deceived. Miles Mosse gave it as his opinion that the increase of usury was due to the fact that the authorities had not been active enough in suppressing it, and he appealed to Luther's advice that youth in the schools be taught the evil of the thing.[39]

But there was more to it than the tolerance of the government. The city merchant had not only fortified his customary imperviousness to considerations that would interfere with his profits with civil allowance, but he had discovered what he thought was a chink in the armor of the traditional religious forces arrayed against him. He had found what he was quick to believe was a new dispensation from the out-worn restrictions of the old regime. What he could not get from the doctors of the old order, he believed he had secured from the reformers of the new. Not from Luther, who in this area at least never departed from the basic orientation of the monk and the peasant,[40] but from Calvin. For Calvin came out of a more sophisticated economic world and had a larger experience of practical affairs and was more aware of the necessities of a commercial civilization.[41] Those he sought not to deny but to regulate in a Christian spirit. So lending at interest on condition that the rate was reasonable and loans were made to the poor without charge was allowed as not more objectionable in itself than the other indispensable techniques of economic life.[42] The allowance, however unwillingly Calvin made it, was sufficient, and the city merchant was free with a good conscience to follow his calling with little thought of the restrictions which Calvin had sought to impose upon it or the larger Christian-social purposes for which he had made the original admission.[43]

Now the English preachers were quite aware of what they were up against. They knew how some of their colleagues on the Continent had given way. If they had not heard more directly, it was impossible to miss the implications of such a plea as that which Philip Caesar addressed to those he styled "the governours of the Church" in Germany [44] against compromise and time-serving:

"But if suche be your wickednes, that for the favour and profite of greate men, you will, contrary to the manifest Scripture, contrarie to the judgement of all true preachers, and contrarie to your owne conscience, allowe, and by your auctoritie confirme this vice of Usurie, what worser men than you?" [45]

Still more impressive is the caution which Caesar's English translator, Rogers, in his adaptation of Hemingius commends to the preachers against usury. They should inveigh against all unlawful contracts, but

"they should with all diligence beware that rashly they do not reprove all contractes, which in their judgement doe seem unlawfull, allowed by the magistrate. . . . if they cannot reforme all abuses, which they shall finde in bargaines, let them take heede that they trouble not the Churche over muche, but commende the cause unto God, and beg of hym that he would set to his helping hand." [46]

Indeed, that sounds as if Hemingius had recognized the difficulty of eliminating usury from the life of the state, a conclusion that seems reasonable in the light of his answer to the objection already raised, that families and commonweals cannot be maintained without usury: "I graunt the same in this corruption of the worlde, where all manlines is excluded." [47] However, he adheres to his own conviction that both would be better served by free lending.[48]

But though the English translator of both Caesar and Hemingius, Rogers, is clearly aware of the ground already lost and of the dangers inherent in the whole situation, he is no less resolved to hold fast what he considers the sound Protestant line. This is clear from the plea which he prefixes to his translation of Caesar's arraignment of usurers already alluded to:

"Now that it maie bee knowen, that, as Philosophers through the force of reason; and the Prophetes, with other godlie men, through the Spirite of God, in all ages have condemned Usurie: So the Preachers in these daies can not, and good Protestantes will not allowe the same." [49]

In general, the English preachers answered his expectations. But there were doubtless many who took care to remember the advice which Rogers' Hemingius addressed to the proponents of the new order who should feel obliged to handle this by no means easy subject: "Yet are thei to use the wisedome of the spirit to their owne comfort, the profite of the Church, and the better advauncement of the glorie of God." [50] And if some of the preachers perhaps paid more attention to his warning than Hemingius intended, one can hardly be surprised in view of the intimate relations between the civil and the religious orders. For we must not forget that this was preëminently the age of patronage in the church as everywhere else. We have some very strong words on the subject from one of the sermons preached at Paul's Cross in the first quarter of the next century.[51] Interestingly enough in view of some of the things which the preacher, Charles Richardson, said in the course of the sermon, when he came to publish it, he dedicated it to Sir Julius Caesar, "Master of the Rolles, and one of his Majesties most Honourable Privie Counsell," acknowledging quite frankly that he owed to his patron's favor the main part of his support.[52] But he has, nevertheless, some very strong things to say in the course of his sermon of the kind of rich and prosperous churchgoer who has no intention of going to church to hear his own sins rebuked:

"So long as the *Minister* doth *daube with untempered morter,* so long as he will *heale their hurt with sweet words,* and stroke their head in their sinnes, so long as hee will not open his mouth against their sinnes, but rather will give them a *placarde* to continue in them; yea it may be, wil *runne with them to the same exercise of ryot:* hee is a Preacher for their tooth, then they love him and commend him: but if in conscience of his duety, hee will *rebuke them sharpely, and not suffer them to sinne,* then they cry out of him, as they did of the *Prophet Jeremy,* to be *a contentious man, and a man that striveth with the whole earth."* [53]

That is the sort of complaint which one usually hears from Puritan preachers, who were quite aware that they were judged by the more comfortable members of their flock to be unnecessarily austere, and who were, therefore, apt to put down any repugnance they encountered in any direction to such an unwillingness to meet their more strenuous demands. It would be rash to say that there were no English preachers who condoned usury in the sixteenth century. But, in general, the sixteenth-century English preachers seem to have maintained a firm line against it. It is significant that when laymen like Hales and Wilson came to discuss social matters, they defined the position of their clergymen as so firmly in opposition to usury. Certainly, the leaders among the preachers of the day did not hesitate to make clear where they stood. But they proceeded warily. For where even the most zealous acknowledged the magnitude and complexity of the problem, it is not surprising that the more cautious sometimes held back. Babington who was not a favorite preacher of Queen Elizabeth for nothing, we may be sure, has an amusing disclaimer on this theme:

"This matter of Usury is so largely handled by many, and so little regarded by moe, that I spare my labour in it. To allow all that some allow, or to condemne as much as some condemne, as yet I see no reason. Many are the cases, and intricate are the questions mooved and mentioned in this matter." [54]

Usually the preachers took pains to define what they meant by usury so that there might be no misunderstanding. "Usurie," said Philip Caesar through the mouth of Thomas Rogers, "is a gaine above the principall, exacted onely in consideration of the loane." [55]

Henry Smith is, characteristically, a little more explicit:

"Usurie is that gayne which is gotten by lending, for the use of the thing which a man lendeth, covenanting before with the borrower, to receive more then was borrowed." [56]

Jewel says the same thing a little more elaborately, although, perhaps, it should be pointed out that he includes in his definition the important acknowledgment that usury may be in kind as well as in money:

"Usury is a kind of lending of mony, or corne, or oile, or wine, or of any other thing, wherin, upon covenant and bargain, we receive againe the whole principall, which wee delivered, and somewhat more, for the use and occupying of the same. . . . It is filthy gaines, and a worke of darknesse. It is a monster in nature: the overthrow of mighty kingdoms, the destruction of flourishing States, the decay of wealthy Cities, the plagues of the world, and the miserie of the people." [57]

Again, this is quite traditional doctrine as may be seen if the Recusant Nicholas Sander's definition of usury is set beside the foregoing:

"Usurie is all maner of gaines, which is either bargained or hoped for by the force of the contract of geving to lone, whether monie be lent, or oile, corne, wine, or any like thing that is spent with the first natural and proper use thereof, for when the use of that thing which can be but once used of the borrower without the spending thereof and which by the very delivery to thend it may be used, is alienated from the lender, is payed for: that is real usurie, and when the lender hath a desire to be paid for the use of that thing, that is mental usurie." [58]

But, still more important, the basic notion of the nature of interest at the bottom of all these definitions is the same. It is the same conception which informed St. Thomas' famous answer to the question of the justice of taking usury for money lent:

"I answer that, To take usury for money lent is unjust in itself, because that is to sell what does not exist, and this evidently leads to inequality which is contrary to justice." [59]

And this old argument of St. Thomas turns up in a slightly different form, with even greater stress on the basic absurdity of interest, in Caesar's argument that to defend usury is to suppose that money of itself can produce any fruit:

"Now consider how greate is the blindenesse, or rather the madnesse of men in these dotyng daies of this worlde, that to a thyng frutlesse, barren, without seede, without life, will ascribe generation." [60]

That objection, of course, implies a very simple notion of the function of money.

Sander, who made a good deal of the unnaturalness of usury,[61] is strong on these objections that rest on the nature of things, claiming that since money is among the things spent in the first proper use of them,[62] the lordship of it for the time of the loan rests not in the lender but in the borrower; [63] so its ownership passes for the time being, and the owner can claim nothing for the time involved:

"But yf the monie would have lyen idely by you al that tyme (as commonly it should have done, because they are either riche, or shewthfull [sic], who geve to lone) then you do an injurie unto God, in selling the time whiche is none of yours." [64]

Some of the preachers were at pains, however, to meet the needs of the practical world of enterprise so far as they could without compromising their basic principles. A good example of this spirit of reasonable accommodation is to be seen in their handling of the problem of joint-stock companies. Mosse, for instance, in his very definition of usury provides for the exclusion of joint-stock companies from his condemnation:

"I doe thus define that Open, Outward, and Actuall usurie whereof I now intreate, and which I take to be forbidden by the worde of God. Usurie is a lending for gaine, by compact, not adventuring the principall. Or more plainly thus. Usurie is, when a man not adventuring the goodes which hee lendeth, covenanteth to receive againe more then he lendeth, even upon this consideration, because he lent them." [65]

This exclusion is the more important in that Mosse is quite explicit in his enumeration of the different ways in which men play the usurer in buying and selling.[66] He has clearly no intention of condoning the faults of trade just because they are so prevalent. Moreover, this exception of the joint-stock company is in itself thoroughly traditional. St. Thomas had made the same allowance, as may be seen in his answer to an objector of his time:

"On the other hand he that entrusts his money to a merchant or craftsman so as to form a kind of society, does not transfer the ownership of his money to them, for it remains his, so that at his risk the merchant speculates with it, or the craftsman uses it for his craft, and consequently he may lawfully demand as something belonging to him, part of the profits derived from his money." [67]

Much of the same character is the provision which Rogers' Caesar makes, this time on the authority of Melanchthon, for the taking of interest when it is a compensation for the damage suffered through the borrower's delay in repayment.[68] This, he explains, is a special exception to his condemnation of usury.

Another characteristic exception is that often made on behalf of charity. The field of benevolence has always had its special temptations for the pious, and the sixeenth-century preacher was no more immune to them than his medieval predecessor or his modern successor. Brinkelow in his famous scheme for the use of the goods of the bishops to the profit of the commonwealth had suggested something very much like what most of the preachers of the century were to condemn as usury, namely, that part of the temporalities of the bishops should be spent upon aiding the towns, "as part of it to be lent to poore occupiers" according to the number in each town. There should be no interest the first year, "but every yeare after, iii.pound of every hundreth pound, that the somme maye encrease and not decay." [69]

More common was the allowance made by Jewel when he declared that the putting out of the stock of an orphan or a helpless man was all right, and that in such a case the usury was allowed, for the whole transaction was a deed of charity.[70] Babington made the same allowance in the case of orphans and extended it to strangers and exiles for religion and other good reasons, with the justification that

"wee know the end of the Commaundement is love: so farre then, as borrowing and lending breaketh not that, but agreeth with it, moderate men doe what is fit for them, and no scope given to the condemned Usurer. To meete with one inconvenience, and to bring many others into the Common-wealth, was never wisedome." [71]

But Henry Smith who once said, "Sinne is never compleat untill it be excused," [72] would have none of it. Such allowances seemed to him of a piece with the customary excuses of the defenders of usury. He complained that just as some men distinguished different kinds of lying, so they distinguished different kinds of usury: "the Merchants usurie, and the Strangers usurie, and the Widowes usurie, and the Orphans usurie, and the poore mans usurie, and the byting usurie, and the charitable usurie and the necessarie usurie." [73]

Most of the preachers were not so uncompromising as Smith. Nevertheless, when they had made what seemed to them reasonable concessions, they held firm to their opposition to usury. Where their attacks are explicit, they show a surprising uniformity, and where they are implicit, they spring to a striking degree from the same basic conception of the matter as the systematic treatises. This becomes clear if we look at the ground-plans of the formal discourses on the subject that we have been studying. Thomas Rogers in his version of Philip Caesar gives us an extensive survey of the matter in the table of the principal chapters which he prefixes to that treatise:

"1. A Recityng of the causes, wherefore Usurie is founde faulte withall and condemned.
2. A methodicall declaration of Usurie.
3. Whether Usurie be lawfull.
4. Usurie what kinde of sinne.
5. A confirmation of the true opinion, that Usurie, as a deadly synne, is justly misliked and condemned.
6. The judgment of the Doctors of the pure Church in all ages concerning Usurie.
7. Of restitution.
8. Of Interest.
9. A refutation of certaine objections.
10. An exhortation to avoyde Usurie." [74]

That is the matter in extenso, as it were, with a certain amount of overlapping. One gets the matter more intensively in the announced plan of the seventh chapter of Hemingius, that on usury, again through the medium of Thomas Rogers:

"Firste wee will shewe that Usurie is forbidden, and wherefore.

"Then we will note the punishmentes of Usurers, that the remembraunce of them may somewhat asswage their greedines.

"Afterward we will shewe howe the dispensers of the misteries of God, that is, the preachers of the Gospell, should behave themselves in this matter of Usurie, that so they may neither be partakers of other mens offences, nor go about any thing that may turne to their owne destruction.

Last of all, wee will give certaine admonitions, the marking wherof in all bargaines, wilbe very profitable." [75]

Miles Mosse follows a similar plan with certain modulations in emphasis:

"In this treatise, are handled these foure principall poyntes.
1. Usurie *is described, what it is, and what are the kindes and branches thereof.*'
2. *It is proved to be manifestlie forbidden by the worde of God: and sundrie reasons are alledged, why it is justlie and worthily condemned.*
3. *The objections are answered, which are usuallie made out of the Scriptures, for the defense of some kinde of* usurie, *and towards some kinde of persons.*
4. *Diverse causes are shewed why* usurie *shoulde not bee practised of a christian (especiallie not of an English man) no not though it could be proved, that it is not simplie forbidden in the Scriptures.*" [76]

Though Jewel's order is different, with a resulting shift in emphasis, his scheme is basically much the same:

"I will shew you first, what Usury is: Then, whence it springeth, and what are the causes of Usurie: Thirdly, what commeth of it, what hurt it worketh to the Common wealth: and I will lay foorth such reasons, às may make any good man abhorre it: Then I will declare, what the Holy Fathers, and the Apostles, and Martyrs, and Christ, and God himselfe have thought and spoken of Usury." [77]

And so is that of Henry Smith:

"First I will define what Usurie is: Secondly, I will shew you what Usurie doth signifie: Thirdly, I will shew the unlawfulnesse of it: Fourthly, I will shew the kindnes of it: Fiftly, I will shewe the arguments which are alleadged for it: Sixtly, I will shew the punishment of it: Seventhly, I will shew you what opinion we should holde of them, which doo not lend upon Usurie, but borrow upon Usurie: Lastly, I will shew you what they should do which have got their riches by Usurie." [78]

Moreover, the brief catechetical or encyclopedic treatment of the subject follows in condensed form the same lines as the more extended development in the whole treatise.

Babington in spite of his disclaimer of any intention of going into the matter, gives a very good summary of the typical discussion in his development of the implications of the eighth commandment, using for his text Exodus 22.14:

> "*If a man* (saith the Lawe) *borrowe any thing of his neighbour, and it bee hurt, or else dye, the owner of it not beeing by, he shall surely make it good. If it bee an hyred thing he shall not make it good, for it came for his hyre.* In which Lawe if we well weigh it, we may first see, that if we have that thing which our neighbour would borrowe, and we able without our hurt well to spare it him, we are bound to do it, or else we sinne against this lawe of GOD, and we even steale from our brother, that which in right is his. . . . Secondly in this lawe as one very well hath noted, we may see a great light given to that hard controversie concerning usury of mony." [79]

Then upon the premise that money lent by the usurer is hired by the borrower, Babington proceeds to develop his second main point, that money does not die, and usually is not hurt in the process of loan. From that he goes on to his third point:

> "Thirdly, consider howe the Lawe will have an apparant hurt of the thing lent, or else it alloweth no recompence, but Usurers will have consideration for likely losse. For say they, if I had had my money, possibly I could have gained thus much with it: Yet are they not sure they could have done it, for God could have crossed their expectation, and being not sure that they could have gained, it is not apparant that they have beene hindred, but this Lawe of God provideth in equity onely for apparant harme, and therefore nothing for them. Fourthly, the equity of this law is onely this, that good will be no looser, and therefore provision is made for recompence, if the thing lent received hurt: but Usurers will have their good will as they call it, certaine and an excessive gainer. Fiftly, in this law of God the borrower is respected, that he should have helpe of his neighbour and not pay for it, unlesse he hurt the thing which he borrowed, but usury regardeth wholy the lender. Wherefore it seemeth that if this law of our God

had ever any equity, this usury of money had ever plaine injury, and that this kinde of lending is void of love, and therefore apparantly a breach of this Commaundement." [80]

That paragraph might be taken as a summary of all the treatises we have been looking at. It is not difficult to see in such a coincidence of pattern the fruit of a common tradition. Nor is the root of that tradition far to seek. For here, as usual, the preachers love to bring up their reënforcements. The subtitle which Thomas Rogers gave to Philip Caesar's treatise, *A General Discourse against the Damnable Sect of Usurers* [81] sums up their technique: "grounded uppon the worde of God, and confirmed by the auctoritie of Doctors both ancient, and newe." On his title-page Rogers put for texts Psalms 1.5 and Luke 6. And for human authority he ranged from Saint Jerome to Melanchthon.[82] In other words, the foundation of the theory is Scripture, but the development of it is the work of the scholastic doctors. This becomes clear if beside the outlines above are put the four "points of inquiry" which Thomas Aquinas put at the head of his discussion of the seventy-eighth question of the second part of the second part of *The Summa Theologica,* "Of the Sin of Usury":

" (1) Whether it is a sin to take money as a price for money lent, which is to receive usury? (2) Whether it is lawful to lend money for any other kind of consideration, by way of payment for the loan? (3) Whether a man is bound to restore just gains derived from money taken in usury? (4) Whether it is lawful to borrow money under a condition of usury?" [83]

And this conclusion as to the scholastic provenience of the case against usury is confirmed if we take a look at *A Briefe Treatise of Usurie* which Nicholas Sander published at Louvain in 1568.[84] The outline of that treatise as presented in the table of contents of the work might be taken as a summary of the outlines we have just been looking at:

1. "The occasion of this Treatise, and the argumentes which are commonly made for the defense of usury, and what is usurie."
2. "That usurie is forbidden by Gods lawe under the paine of everlasting damnation."

3. "Whence bargaines proceede, and why Almosdedes are so acceptable to God."
4. "Of geving to lone, or of lending, which are naturally free contractes."
5. "How much it importeth, that the boundes and limites of everie contract belonging to the law of nations, should be inviolably kept and maintayned."
6. "That the usurer in setting out his mony for gayne, doth, and can not but geve his monie to lone."
7. "How heynouse, and how much against the nature of geving to lone, and against the law of al Nations the vice of usurie is."
8. "That the Heathens condemned usurie."
9. "That the Civil lawe doth not acknowledge usurie to spring or arise of the nature of suche thinges as are geven to lone, but rather to be contrarie thereunto."
10. "Certaine examples of usurie, whereby yt may the better be knowen, what is usurie, and what is not: and of the restitution which the usurer is bound to make." [85]

This traditional character of the preaching against usury persisted through the sixteenth century and into the seventeenth. That is especially clear in a sermon which Charles Richardson, "Preacher at Saint Katherines neare the Tower of London" preached at Paul's Cross in December of 1614, and published in the following year under the classic title, *A Sermon against Oppression and Fraudulent Dealing*.[86] For the authority whom he invokes again and again is Thomas Aquinas. A particularly striking example is to be found in his vigorous arraignment of the oppression of the poor. He pronounces such oppression

"*theft,* and worse then *theft* as Thomas Aquinas doth well determine: *Oppression* and *theft* are both of them (saith he) to bee accounted sinnes, because they both spoyle a man of his goods against his will: yet so, as in *theft,* a man is wronged ignorantly, that hee knoweth not of it: but in *oppression,* he is wronged by violence; he knoweth it, and looketh on, and cannot tell how to helpe it. Now that is more directly against a mans will, that is done by violence, then that which is done ignorantly. And therefore, *oppression* is a more grievous sinne then *theft.* Againe (saith he) in oppression, beside the dammage done to the party, there is alwayes some indignity and reproch done to his person, which is farre worse then fraud or deceit, which is used in *theft.*" [87]

When the rope's-end disreputability of theft in this entire period is recalled, it is easy to recognize the note of contempt not so common among the arraignments of tyranny of the latter half of the century.

Richardson's is at once a reaction to and a fresh carrying forward of an older tradition. So through the baffling ebbs and flows of spiritual times and seasons the persistent struggle of the religious effort is renewed.

It is easy to smile today at the neighborhood view which the sixteenth-century English preachers took of the central issues of the rising capitalism that was so soon to overwhelm the feeble barriers they sought to erect in its path. But in fact they were dealing as always with the immediate world they knew day in and day out. In that world what impinged upon their immediate consciousness was not the large-scale operations of the Fugger's or the Pallavicino's, or even the financial operations of their own government. What they saw was the world of small-holders and independent craftsmen and petty tradesmen with their perennial need for capital to carry them till harvest, to buy raw materials, to furnish the beginnings of a shop.[88] And on the other hand, they saw the host of prosperous yeomen, innkeepers, tailors, drapers, grocers, mercers, and other substantial businessmen with a bit to spare, alert to any chance to pick up a little extra.[89] In such a world, still of the small neighborhood, they saw the more sharply the misery which hard-dealing on the lender's part might cause the unfortunate debtor, and they felt keenly the destruction of neighborhood peace and amity that might ensue.[90] So they clung the more tenaciously to their ideal of a Christian neighborliness of spirit that would prompt him who had a surplus to relieve the anxieties of his less fortunate neighbor without any thought of making his profit of the poor man's necessities.

In this they showed both striking agreement and striking faithfulness to tradition. Again, we find the clue in St. Thomas. For he had answered the objection that the injunction to lend is not an obligation but a counsel in the following terms:

"A man is not always bound to lend, and for this reason it is placed among the counsels. Yet it is a matter of precept not to seek profit by lending: although it may be called a matter of counsel in comparison with the maxims of the Pharisees, who deemed some kinds of usury to be lawful, just as love of one's enemies is a matter of counsel." [91]

So in an age when usury was widespread, and the temptation to make money in that way strong, the preachers insisted that those who had money should lend to those who had not as a form of alms; as Sandys put it in a sermon at York:

"Everie man is to his neighbour a debtor not onely of that which himselfe boroweth, but of whatsoever his neighbour needeth, a debtor not onely to pay that he oweth, but also to lende that he hath and may conveniently spare: to lend I say according to the rule of Christ, *Lend, looking for nothing thereby.*" [92]

This is the doctrine implicit in the advice which Greenham is said to have given to a usurer who seems for once to have been considering mending his way of life:

"A certaine man that was an Usurer, asking him how with a good conscience he might use his money. He sayd, occupie it in some trade of life, and when you can lend to the poore, doe it freely and willingly, and that you may henceforth labour aswell against covetousnes in occupying that trade, as before you desired to strive against usurie; especially use prayer, the word of God, and the companie and conference of his children: and whatseever [sic] you get by lawfull gaine, give evermore the tenth to the poore." [93]

And this obligation held even when there was fear that the money so lent might not be paid back, as Rogers "out of Hemingius" makes clear, prudently distinguishing two sorts of obligation to lending, the natural and the Christian:

"The naturall is whereby we are bounde by the lawe of nature to lende to sutche, as lacke our helpe. The Christian Obligation is whereby God doth binde hys to lende to the needie, that is, not onely to sutch as may doe the like at another tyme, but also to them whiche are unable to requite." [94]

Mosse, himself, after proving the taking of usury contrary to express scriptural injunction [95] went on to prove that the usurer breaks the law of charity, because he does not do as he would be done by.[96] For, obviously, anyone would prefer to have money lent to him free of charge for its use. Rogers' Hemingius drives that point home when in answer to the common defence of the usurers that they lend to men who are willing to pay their charges, he retorts that men borrow of necessity and not because they are willing, and that whatever good they gain from the usury could be better gained from lending.[97] Indeed, the very fact that usury does for profit what should be done for charity constitutes a serious injury to charity, as Caesar points out in his sixth objection to usury:

> "Because it quencheth charitie, whiche is the principall chaine of humaine societie: it taketh awaie the lawe of nature, from whence the positive lawes are taken, whiche also condemne usurie." [98]

But there was not only the taking of usury to be considered, but the giving of usury. St. Thomas, it will be remembered, had ruled that there was no sin in borrowing for usury from a professional usurer, provided it was for a good purpose.[99] Babington remembered "the words of *Jeremie,* who saith, *he hath neither given usury nor taken, and yet they hated him,*" [100] which he interpreted to mean that either would have been cause for self-blame and decided against it. Henry Smith was not so sure. Indeed, this is perhaps the only place where Henry Smith might be described as unduly prudent. He makes it quite clear that he would have preferred not to discuss the question for fear of misunderstanding.[101] For Smith was quite aware of the temptations of the needy here as elsewhere.[102] Like St. Thomas he recognized that it might be lawful to suffer injury where it would not be lawful to offer it.[103] So to the man who asks if he may borrow when in extreme need to save life or credit, always with the proviso that nobody will lend without usury, Smith answers:

> "I woulde answere him as the Prophet answered Naaman: neither doo, nor doo not, but *goe in peace.* I will not forbid thee, nor I will not condemne thee, but if thy conscience condemne thee not, I thinke thy sinne one of the least sinnes." [104]

But he is very anxious that this half-hearted allowance should not be taken advantage of:

"Some I know borrow for meere necessitie; if anie may be allowed, those are they: but there is a kinde of borrowers in this Cittie, which feede usurers as the bellowes kindle the fire, so they have no need to borrow but because they would be rich, and richer, and richest of all; therefore they will imploy all the money which they can borrow, thinking to get more by the use of it, then the usurie of it doth come to. This maketh them sell their wares so deare, because they must not onelie gaine the price, but the interest beside, and more then the interest too, or else they gaine nothing." [105]

Here, as always, Smith is quite aware of the shifts of poor rascals as well as of rich, and is equally uncompromising with both.

Indeed, it would be a grave mistake to conclude from the traditional character of the preaching against usury that the preachers of these sermons were unaware of the economic life of their time. Henry Smith, for instance, gives a very impressive survey of the commercial iniquities of his day in his list of the various kinds of usurers. The first group of all is made up of those who "will not take Usurie, but they will have the use of your pasture, or your land, or your orchard, or your teame," etc., and so make more money than they would otherwise. A second group will not take usury but will accept such commodities as plate or tapestry which lose more of their value in use than usury would amount to. A third group instead of usury will take a pawn worth more than the money lent, which will be forfeited if the money is not repaid by a certain day. A fourth group will not take usury but will buy something at a low price and then agree with the borrower that he shall buy it again at a certain day which the lender knows the borrower will not be able to meet. So for a small loan the lender receives a large return. Then there is the fifth group who likewise

"will not take Usurie, but they will lende out their money to occupiers, upon condition to be partakers in their gaines, but not in their losses: So one takes all the paines, and abideth all the venture, and the other that takes no paines, reapeth halfe the profit. This Usurie is forbidden in 2. Thess. chap.3.vers. 10 where it is said; *Hee which will not worke, let him not eate.*"

Smith's sixth bad example is the lender who will get a workman to work for him without pay for a certain period in return for a loan. One might be quite sure that the usurer loses nothing on this transaction either. The seventh class comprises those who

"if you have not present money to pay for their wares, they will set a high price of them, for the forbearing of the time, and so they doe not only sell their wares, but they sell time too: that is, they doe not onely sell their owne, but they sell Gods owne."

Next he lists the usurers who do not themselves lend but give their wives leave to do so. So he comes to his ninth and last group:

"But that I was informed of them since this Sermon was preached, I had left out our capitall usurers, which will not lend anie money, because they dare not require so much gaine as they would have; but if you would borrow an hundred pound, they wil give you wares worth threescore pound, and you shall answere them an hundred pounde for it." [106]

Similarly, Nicholas Sander shows that he is quite aware of the argument for investment when he explains the way in which a man with money to spare will argue to justify himself in using it to gain more than he could lawfully:

"I have (sayeth he) a poore stocke of money lawfully gotten, it lyeth by me idely, and it will quickly be spent, if it be not occupied. I was not brought up in the trade of merchandise, I have wife and children, who are like to begge, unlesse I provide some perpetuall reliefe for them. In this case what shal I do with my money but imploye it so, that it might not be lost, and yet might bring me some yearely profite?

"Agayne, I lend it to such a merchant whom I knowe to take commoditie and no hurt therby: why then may I not take profite of mine owne money together with him? or why should he enrich him selfe with my money, and not be bounde to geve me some part of his gaine?" [107]

But though Sander thus shows himself to be quite aware of the case for investment, he will none of it but reiterates flatly his thesis that "usurie is utterly against God and Nature, even as mankilling is." [108] Then he proceeds to take up point by point the usual claims of the investor. Not only does the man who gives usury suffer, but the whole commonwealth suffers. For the merchant who borrows is constrained to sell all his wares at a higher price to cover the cost of the usury. So everyone who buys the wares suffers.[109] Again, it often happens that the merchant is not able to raise the money to pay the yearly sum due the usurer. Then the merchant loses his credit until finally he becomes bankrupt. The result is general disaster, for

"he not only leeseth his principal who looketh for gayne: but also manie other men, who made lawful bargaines with the sayd merchant, are defrauded of their right and thereby made unable to keepe towche with others, whereupon ariseth from man to man, an infinite confusion and losse both of credit and of goodes." [110]

Then he rounds on the gentleman with an argument too often reserved for those in humbler positions in society: "Furthermore, how manie idle men doth usurie cause to be in a realme?" and suggests that if it had not been for the hope of usury, they would have found some other way of making their living to their own honor and the profit of the commonwealth.[111] The preachers in England would in general have found little good to say of Nicholas Sander, but on this rebuttal of the case for investment they would have agreed with him. Especially would they have sympathized with Sander's appeal to social utility. For though the English preachers grounded their thought on Scripture as on a rock and then reënforced it with the authority of Church Fathers and Reformers, they were quite aware of the secular character of the spirit with which they were contending, and tried to cope with it on the basis of the law of nature and secular experience. So Bishop Jewel, when he had brought up both Scripture and Church Fathers to his support, concludes with the universal statement of his proposition that "there was never any religion, nor sect, nor state, nor degree, nor profession of men, but they have disliked it." [112] And Mosse when he has lined up the schoolmen behind his position turns even more emphatically to the teachers of the secular order:

"And therefore, wee finde that the great common wealth men of all ages, though they knewe, and sawe evidently, how without diverse kindes of bargaining and contracting, societie among men could not possibly be maintained: yet they have alwaies prohibited, and condemned usurie, as a thing carrying with it so great inequallitie, that it, and the publique good, could not well stand together." [113]

But Mosse and Sander alike must have realized the odds against which they were preaching. It is this consciousness of preaching to stone walls that accounts for a note of social iconoclasm that every so often creeps into the usury sermons. It is to be heard in Smith's *The Sinners Confession.* After reminding his auditors that the Law of God in the Old Testament required that the man who stole a sheep should restore four for one, and Roman Law that usurers should forfeit four times what they took for usury, Smith comes to the present:

"If the same law were now to use agaynst our theevish Usurers, as it was sometime among them, wee should not have such complaining of the poore both in prisons and streetes. But if these great theeves (I meane our biting Usurers) that rob and spoyle without ceasing when they have no neede, might finde no more favour, than those pettie theeves which rob and steale sometime, when they are driven thereto by extreame necessitie, then surely the Common-wealth would soone be disburdened of that pestilent brood of Caterpillers wherewith it is pestered." [114]

This is searching enough, but there is something even sharper in the question with which Thomas Rogers in the dedicatory address to Sir Christopher Hatton of his translation of Philip Caesar's *A General Discourse against the Damnable Sect of Usurers* concludes a swift survey of the harm done by that class:

"And when I consider these thinges, I marvell with my selfe why suche enquirie is made for vagabondes, and none at all for these men, why poore wretches are straightlie examined how they do live; and these fellowes come not into question. . . . For if simple theeves, whiche robbe most commonly for neede, against their wils, in feare, in out places, secretlie, straungers, deserve suche a death, how should they be handled, whiche have no neede, and yet will steale, and that impudently without blushing, in famous places, openly, and from their freindes?" [115]

And yet probably the majority of the preacher's auditors would have agreed with them. The best-known layman's treatise on the subject sums up their preaching with an optimism about its potential effectiveness that most of them would hardly have hoped for. It is Dr. Thomas Wilson's *A Discourse upon Usury* which he completed in 1569 and published in 1572.[116] Wilson had had an extensive and varied experience of the world, as student, traveler, humanist, civilian, member of Parliament, and diplomat, and he had had abundant opportunity to observe the impact of the new commercial point of view at home and abroad. All of these varied elements enter into the form of his discourse, a dialogue in the best humanist tradition between the rich, worldly merchant, the godly and zealous preacher, and the temporal and civil lawyers. The preacher and the doctor of the civil law do square off for long and set orations, with an appropriately shorter effort by the less speculative merchant, but there is, especially at the beginning, the atmosphere of the give and take of life that is the great charm of the humanist dialogue. It is in that tradition that the setting is given, and in that atmosphere that the dialogue opens. The merchant has heard the sermon against usury in his parish church and has asked the preacher home to dinner. From the terms of the invitation one gathers that the merchant has been listening to the preacher and perhaps thinking over what he has said, but there is no sign that he is in any way abashed by what he has heard.[117] And the brief account of the dinner with its cheerful boasting of "the good order of the Cytie" bears out that impression.[118]

In such a comfortable atmosphere the preacher's opening assertion that the world is nearing its end naturally falls very heavily.[119] One can easily understand the merchant's rejoinder: "Tush, what amounteth your care for the worlde? You have discharged your duetye: let the worlde care for it selfe, and let every one aunswer for his owne doinges. Lorde god, what should you be so muche greved inwardlye?" [120] It is the voice of the new individualism challenging the old view of social responsibility.

It is more than that. It is the voice, too, of a new compartmentalism in human relations. The lawyer backs up the merchant by pointing out that those who live in the world must do as the world does.[121] And when the preacher tries to take the ground from under worldliness by pointing out that "a verye litle thyng satisfieth nature," the merchant rounds on him stoutly by saying that while that is very well for him whose profession it is, to despise the world, "Plenty belongeth to us, that are worldlings." [122] But the lawyer goes further, pointing out that the preacher embarrasses men with preaching against usury, and yet he does not know what usury is.[123]

So the stage for the argument is set, and the merchant settles down to listen to it, protecting himself, however, by warning the disputants that he will listen to them as they argue it out, but when it is over, however it goes, he will do what he thinks fitting, a candid repudiation of theory thoroughly in keeping with the highly pragmatic habits of mind of his class.[124] The argument that follows proceeds, so far as the preacher is concerned, along the lines with which we are already familiar. The preacher opens by setting up his social ideal. All Christians should live together as brethren, helping each other according to their need.[125] The man who lends for gain not only breaks that amity but actually steals his neighbor's goods.[126] The preacher marshals the Scriptures and the Church Fathers to support this indictment.[127] Then he appeals to more immediately practical considerations, pointing out that covetousness ruins the commonweal, for the usurer does nothing yet gains all.[128] He goes into the stock objections to the selling of time, and he expatiates on the liberality of lending freely.[129] There is nothing milk and water about the preacher. He would have "some penall lawe of death made against the usurer." [130]

The merchant is impressed,[131] but the lawyer clings to the fact that all commonweals in the world are actually governed otherwise. He thinks the preacher must be misinterpreting Scripture, and he still insists that it is not in the power of preachers to judge precisely what usury is.[132] He attempts in his oration further to disqualify the preacher by pointing out that since the profession of the preacher is divinity, his whole sermon "soundeth of God" and asks what man cannot perform.[133] Then he plunges into the establishment of his own thesis that usury is wrong only when "it byteth." [134] He admits readily that a man should give some of his surplus to the relief of the poor, but he insists that he should then use the rest for his own advancement.[135] In his turn he cites the Roman law and the common law and even Scripture for the allowance of gain.[136] And he rounds out his case with the conclusion that where charity is kept, there is no usury.[137]

The merchant is much briefer, but unmistakable. He begins his oration by the characteristic observation that to say and to do are two very different things.[138] And he defends his order on the ground that he and his fellows lend not for usury but for interest and exchange, and that to the benefit of the higher classes and of the state.[139]

The preacher holds fast to his position—anybody who takes a penny of gain is a usurer.[140] One admission he does make, and that is that the lender should have recompence for delay in paying.[141] But he will have none of the rest of the merchant's arguments. When the preacher concludes his "Replicacion," the civilian takes a hand with an informed discrimination between what is usury and what is not.[142] He invokes the schoolmen with their stress on intent or purpose.[143] And then he proceeds to sum up the case against usurers, especially those who practice dry exchange,[144] drawing upon canon law [145] and the pagan law writers [146] for the condemnation of these offenders with a vigor that gives much pleasure to the preacher.[147]

It has been a long oration, this of the civilian, and we need hardly be told that the merchant has often nodded during it; indeed, he acknowledges the fact with gratitude to the speaker because he has given him a good chance to digest his dinner.[148] The lawyer, as one would expect, prefers Justinian to the canon law, because Justinian favored provision for a moderate return of interest.[149] The civilian thereupon cites the reformers who were not against moderate usury,[150] but the preacher sticks to Scripture,[151] and he refutes the argument from Calvin and Bucer by saying that they enlarged the law to help religious fugitives.[152] He still insists that to give alms and to lend freely are the ways in which a Christian should use his surplus,[153] and he pointedly reminds the merchant that he is but the steward of his riches.[154] At last the preacher makes an end with an appeal to a consideration which seems always to have been especially moving to the imagination of the sixteenth-century man, whatever his place in society, the uncertainty of life—the rich die as soon as the poor.[155] Perhaps that oldest of all the arguments in the preacher's arsenal proved the most effective. But whatever it is, the resistance he has hitherto encountered crumbles. The civilian admits that he wishes he had put more time into the study of Scripture.[156] The lawyer confesses the error of his belief that it was better to suffer rather a mischief than an inconvenience seeing how loath men are to lend for nothing.[157] The merchant admits the world is a very tempting thing and that merchants put most of their thought on getting rich. He repents and promises to mend his ways.[158] So the dialogue ends with the preacher very properly rejoicing.[159]

Well might John, Bishop of Salisbury, on the twentieth of August, 1569, express his approval of the work.[160] But in its context of the preaching against usury, the distinction of the work lies not so much in its presentation of the potency of the preacher's case as in the full and vivid presentation of what the preacher was up against. As the merchant had very wisely observed, to say and to do are two very different things. Many a merchant must have been impressed by the Sunday sermon, but whether that impression would survive the plunge into the world of Monday morning was another matter.

For a dichotomy of which Calvin most certainly never dreamed had come into the thinking of even the church-going merchant. It is admirably illustrated by the story which George Phillips tells of the poor city man who got rich and sent his son to the university and then with great pride and no disturbance of conscience received the news that his son had preached against usury at Paul's Cross, saying:

"I cannot justly blame my Sonne for that he hath done, for it is as well his profession, to speake against usury, as it is my occupation to follow it, otherwise hee might want matter to speake on, and both my selfe and my Son might lacke money to live on: proceed therefore my Sonne, quoth this goldfinder, and see you spare not to invent damning arguments against such as live by loane, and I hope that in time this wil become my trade alone." [161]

This story certainly has a distinctive flavor of the triumphant middle class, very different from what one would find in a medieval exemplum.

CHAPTER VII

CONTENTATION

BUT impressive as is this sustained attack of the sixteenth-century English preachers upon usury, even more impressive is their arraignment of the spirit that underlies and prompts the varying manifestations of that ancient sin. Perhaps the most complete indictment of that spirit is to be found in a single tense and packed sentence of Jewel:

"As the Sea is never filled with water, though all the streames of the world run into it: so the greedinesse of an Usurer is never satisfied, though he gaine never so unreasonably." [1]

That is the really important issue in this campaign of the sixteenth-century preachers against usury. For the attack on usury, not only the deliberate and extensive attack like that just studied in the tracts and sermons on the subject, but the implicit and incidental condemnation and arraignment are really part of something larger and more basic to the whole orientation of the preachers. And that is their attack on the spirit behind the alarming growth of usury, the absorption of the time in the acquisition of wealth.

Interestingly enough, the Puritan preachers, Greenham and Chaderton and Perkins, have rather less to say about usury itself than some of their more traditionally minded contemporaries. That is not because they are indifferent to the subject. Rather, it is that they are more interested in the analysis of the state of mind behind the phenomena described by the old term, and they are more interested in the dynamics of that psychology than in its classification. It is clear that they have before their eyes as they preach, the aggressive, self-confident, expansive middle class and that even as they throw the full force of their moral conviction and the very considerable resources of their eloquence across its path, they have caught the dynamic of that social thrust that was to carry the world they knew into a very different order of life.

The character of the spirit which informed that remarkable advancement of the middle classes is a subject that has much engaged the attention of modern economic historians. One of the most interesting efforts to define it is that of the Italian author, Amintore Fanfani:

"Modern man, who is capitalistic, regards wealth as the best means for an ever more complete satisfaction of every conceivable need; he also regards it as the best means for improving his own position. He considers goods as instruments to be used *ad libitum* by their possessor. He does not recognize any claim on them on the part of third parties not their possessors, still less does he think it unlawful for their possessor to use them so as to obtain an unlimited increase or their reproduction at ever diminishing cost." [2]

The result of the operation of this spirit is described even more succinctly by Max Weber: "Man is dominated by the making of money, by acquisition as the ultimate purpose of his life." [3]

As Signor Fanfani very wisely reminds us, the distinctive spirit of modern capitalism is not an invention of the sixteenth century. Examples of individuals possessed of such a spirit are to be found long before our period. The important contribution of the sixteenth century to the history of this aspect of capitalism is the increase in the number of individuals possessed steadily and with confidence of this spirit and the increase in their social influence and, eventually, power.[4]

It is very doubtful if most of the sixteenth-century preachers knew much about economics, and still less probable that they suspected any basic change in the foundations of social life to which they were accustomed, but they were familiar with the passions of the human spirit, and by precept and experience they knew a good deal about the passion of greed. And there can be no doubt that they saw very clearly that they were face to face with a tremendous manifestation of it. They set themselves to do battle with it, not just as it threatened their own interests, though as we shall see, they were involved, but as it threatened all of the values of the society of their day.

Moreover, it was not the issue of social justice which primarily engaged the attention of the preachers of this period even in their arraignment of usury. It was the spiritual state of the usurer, for here as always, the greatest concern of the preacher was for the condition of the soul of the man to whom he was preaching. His first business was not to save society but to save the souls of those in his charge.

The question, then, for the preacher was, what is wrong with the soul of the usurer? Of the answer the preacher had no doubt. It is to be found in one word, "covetousness." There is nothing new about that word any more than there is about the thing which it describes. The psychological and moral reality back of it is probably as old as man, and undoubtedly preachers have been hammering at the theme ever since man began to be preached at. The preachers of the sixteenth century, of course, knew quite well that the love of gain was one of the standing temptations of humanity. For instance, Henry Smith says of David's effort to win his fellow-men to the ways of virtue: "To make us love godlines, he calleth it by the name of that we love most; that is, *Gaine.*" [5] For this spirit many of the preachers used the word "covetousness" itself as preachers had done for generations. It was, for example, the first of the long list of strikingly unsavory ingredients which Jewel identified in the composition of usury:

"Covetousnesse, desire of mony, unsatiable greedinesse, deceitfulnesse, unmercifulnesse, injury, oppression, extortion, contempt of God, hatred to the brethren, and hatred of all men, are the nurses and breeders of usury." [6]

Henry Smith found in covetousness the root of usury when he complained that "covetousness makes an usurer and extorner [sic] and deceiver." [7] Turnbull went even further when in one of his sermons to the parishioners of "S. Mari-Colechurch in Chepeside" he charged them to avoid covetousness "as the roote and mother of all wickednesse." [8] Smith would certainly have thought Turnbull was making the right remark in the right place, for he himself located it in the social scene with precision when he called it "the Londoners sinne." [9]

That is what one might call the classic, traditional approach to the matter, and doubtless in most of the sermons of the day there was very little that was any fresher, any less conventional. But in the greater preachers of the time like Jewel and Smith and others whom we shall come to presently one finds a profounder awareness of the distinctive spirit of the age. For to their firm grasp on their common ethical tradition, they add a sense of the dynamic of an active life and a very detailed and penetrating preoccupation with the psychological processes of its leaders. The combination is illustrated admirably in Greenham's appeal to the devoted money-maker who does not like to plead guilty to the charge of covetousness:

"In heaping up thy riches, thou saist thou art not covetous, because thou givest to every one his owne, and takest nothing but that the law will give thee. But all this thou maist do, and yet be covetous. If then thou wouldest know thy heart, thou maist hereby trie it: If thou bee ever musing how thou maist get thy goods: if it cheere up thy heart when thou doest encrease them, then thou art covetous though thou see it not, thy mind is on thy money, though thou perceive it not." [10]

That combination of the classical and the contemporaneous permeates their entire analysis of the spiritual disaster of usury. They begin as usual with the scriptural injunction. For instance, in *The Whole Treatise of the Cases of Conscience,* Perkins invokes the seventeenth chapter of Deuteronomy with its command to the king "that he *should not multiply his horses, or his silver or his golde.*" [11]

But the preachers were not content for all their stress on Scripture and scriptural authority to let the matter rest simply on the unlawfulness of covetousness. Rather they set about trying to convince the covetous man of the futility and the folly of his ways. Perkins himself had followed up the scriptural injunction with the warning that the "seeking of abundance is a hazard to

the salvation of the soule by reason of mans corruption." [12]
Rogers' Hemingius said the same thing but went into more
detail in his final charge to preachers:

> "Last of all, let them with diligence admonishe the ritch men, that
> they suffer not themselves to be entangled with the showe of ritches,
> and that they take heede, lest beyng seduced by the subtile arguments
> of the seducing flesh, they loose their faithe, and fall into the snares
> of Sathan." [13]

But Babington went even further. What concerned him was the
spiritual blindness of the covetous. Calvin had long ago recognized
this basic sickness of the worldling when he told those of the
new faith who had been unable to withstand persecution:

> "The care of this present worlde carrieth thee away: and that is
> bicause thou hast no taste of the worlde to come. Covetousnesse
> burneth thee: verely bicause thou knowest not yet, which are the
> true riches." [14]

Babington clearly agreed with this diagnosis of Calvin's but
with a difference in emphasis. For what most impressed him was
that the attachment to gain is not only the fruit of blindness
but that in itself it is the effectual cause of spiritual blindness,
in itself darkening the whole soul; as he put it in his notes on the
tenth chapter of the book of Exodus:

> "Even so over hote desires of gaine hurteth the inward light, as we
> know, both by that which hath beene said touching the world, and
> by that which Saint *Paule* saith . . . And then, the inward eye being
> out, nothing but darknesse is there, and so a falling into all dangerous
> Courses that may leade to destruction and perdition. Then *Usury* is no
> sinne; no, not usury upon usury; oppression and deceit be no sinnes,
> stealth and robbery, (if it may be any way coloured) is wisedome, and
> well; yea, murther and blood bite not." [15]

Greenham says the same thing in more psychological terms with
an emphasis on insight and its effect on the will that is characteristic of him.

> "It is harder to beleeve in the abundance of worldly meanes, then
> it is in the want of them: for they as it were, are vailes set betwixt God
> and us, they stay our sight in them that it cannot pearce to God." [16]

But perhaps the most interesting account of the harm which the preoccupation with riches does to the covetous is to be found in the third count of Perkins' arraignment of covetousness. It is put with great succinctness in the exposition to which we have already had occasion to refer. It is that the "seeking of abundance, is a fruit of diffidence in the providence of God." [17] That is of a piece with Caesar's objection to usury on the ground that the usurer comes to trust not God but himself and puts his own wisdom in the place of the divine wisdom:

"Now they, whiche put no affiance in the giver and bestower of every good thyng, but by their owne forecaste and wisedome, yea by unlawfull trades, neglectyng the meanes whiche bee ordained of God, provide for themselves, attribute that glorie whiche is due unto God, unto themselves, and their usurie." [18]

That is very close to that "security," that overweening confidence in oneself that so troubled the preachers when they came to consider the eleemosynary habits of the age. But in this field it was not so much the destructive quality of that spirit as its futility that called forth their reprobation. Here again the Puritan preachers may be said to take the lead in that they are at once more direct and practical in their appeal and more searching in their psychology. An excellent example of the practical attack is to be seen in what Henry Smith has to say to the covetous. The basic premise of his argument was revealed when in his sermon on contentation he pointed out that "the covetous man makes a foole of himselfe, He coveteth to covet." [19] But in the first of his two sermons on usury he brings the futility of the matter home in terms of the gossip of the city about them:

"A Usurer dooth receive two incomes, one of the borrower, and another of the revenger: of the borrower he lookes for gaine, but of the revenger he lookes for punishment. Therfore all the Scripture prophecieth evill unto him, as Michaiah did to Achab. Salomon saith: *He which encreaseth his riches by Usurie, gathereth for them which will be mercifull to the poore.* . . . Now marke whether this prophesie of Salomon be true, I know not how many in this Cittie doe encrease by Usurie, but this prophesie seemeth to be verified of many: for it is noted, that the riches and lands of Aldermen and Merchants, and other in London, do not last so long, nor indure so well, as the riches and lands of other in the countrie, and that their children doe not proove so well as others, nor come to that place in the Common weele, which for their wealth their parents looked that they should come to. . . . All riches are uncertaine, but the riches which are evill gotten, are most uncertaine." [20]

And the end of all the usurer's scheming is futility itself:

"This is the end of the Usurer and his money, if they stay together till death, yet at last there shalbe a division. The divell shall take his soule; the earth shall take his bodie, the strangers shal take his goods, and the mourners shall rejoyce under their blacks, and say, Wickednesse is come to the grave." [21]

Perkins takes much the same line on the futility of the ways of the covetous, but his emphasis is more penetrating in his analysis of human feeling and human motive. The covetous are fools because they overburden themselves unnecessarily and to no purpose. It is in the prefatory address to his discourse on *How to Live, and That Well,* that Perkins most effectively appeals to the stirring and driving merchant of his day:

"It is the common fashion of men, to multiplie their cares out of measure, and thereby to make their lives most miserable. For first of all, beside necessarie labours, they take upon them many needlesse and superfluous businesses. Secondly, their manner is, to care not only for the labours to be done but also for the event and successe of their labours, that they may alwaies prosper, and never bee crossed: but this care belongs to God alone. Thirdly, they content not themselves with their lot and condition, but seeke by all meanes to increase their estate, and to make themselves rich. Lastly, they exercise themselves not only in disposing of things present, but they fore-cast many matters in their heads, and plot the successe of things to come." [22]

This is strikingly reminiscent of St. Thomas' answer to the question "Whether we should be solicitous about the future?" There is a proper time to be solicitous about anything, answered the thirteenth-century thinker with characteristic moderation, but to worry ahead of time, say about the vintage in summer instead of autumn "would be needlessly forestalling the solicitude belonging to a future time. Hence Our Lord forbids suchlike excessive solicitude." [23] So the thirteenth-century and the sixteenth-century preachers agree on the folly of the common spirit of men, loading themselves with many cares.

But covetousness was not the only menace to contentation in that age of widening opportunity for some of the most energetic classes of society. Ambition was quite as potent, and that Perkins attacks no less severely in the same treatise on vocations to which we have had occasion to refer before:

"Ambition is a vice, whereby any man thinking better of himselfe, then there is cause hee should, becomes malecontent with his particular calling, and seekes for himselfe an higher place, and a better estate." [24]

Now there was nothing new in this attempt of Perkins' to stem the ambition of the time. As far back as 1549 Latimer and Crowley had been trying to do the same thing, albeit with landlords rather than merchants:

"If the Revenues and yerely Rentes of thy patrymony and landes, be not inough, nor sufficient for thi fyndyng, and wyl not suffice thy charges, then moderate thyne expences, borrow of thy two next neighbours, that is to say, of thy backe and thi belly. Learne to eat with in thy teather. Pul down thy sayle." [25]

In the same spirit Crowley adjures those landholders who had oppressed their tenants to improve their position or their heir's:

"Wishe that you had contented your selves with that state wherin your fathers left you, and strive not to set your children above the same, lest god take vengaunce on you boeth sodenly, when ye be most hastie to clime." [26]

And like Crowley, Latimer is hard even on the most pathetic and the most heroic of the forms of self-aggrandizement, the desire of parents to see their sons better off than themselves. Crowley had jingled especially against the prosperous merchant's desire to match his daughter above his station in life:

"Let it suffice the to mary
Thy daughter to one of thy trade:
Why shouldest thou make hir a lady,
Or bye for her a noble warde?" [27]

But Crowley had thought it a pity when the economic stresses
of an oppressed agricultural life had made it impossible for the
boy of good aptitude for liberal studies to go to the university
and prepare himself for learning and the church,[28] and Latimer
had, as we have seen, recalled with pride how his father's thrifty
handling of his modest estate had made it possible for him to set
his promising son to learning.[29] That example the preachers could
hardly fail to approve. But the desire of the ambitious parents
of the time to see their sons better placed than themselves, better
endowed with worldly wealth, was from their point of view one
of the mainsprings of the greed of the time, and both condemned
it heartily. Most men in his day, complained Latimer, did not
use their goods as God intended:

"They wil not loke on the poore, they muste helpe their children,
and purchase them more land then ever their grandfather had before
them." [30]

Crowley and Latimer were mainly concerned over the harm
which ambition led to, the oppression of the poor by the already
prosperous in too much of a hurry to better their estate. But in the
disorders of the middle of the century the effects of ambition
among the poor, naturally, came to seem even more threatening to
the stability of society. Indeed, when the author of *An Homelie
against Disobedience and Wylfull Rebellion* of about 1571 tries
to analyze the causes of rebellion, he finds ambition one of the
two main ones, the other being ignorance. He then proceeds to
define ambition in terms very much like Perkins': "By ambition,
I meane the unlawful and restles desire in men to be of higher
estate then God hath geven or appoynted unto them." [31] The
fact that shortly after, he qualified this indictment of ambition
to admit by implication that men may climb by lawful and peaceable means suggests that what is distressing him is not so much
the economic or spiritual hazards of ambition as the danger to

the peaceful maintenance of the established order. That this aspect of the matter was present in Perkins' mind, too, is shown in the second of the lessons which he draws in one of his sermons from the history of Korah, Dathan, and Abiram, it will be remembered, one of the favorite exempla of the preachers of submission. The first lesson is the traditional one, the warning of the punishment to rebels. Then he goes on to draw his second, that "hence we are taught to beware of ambition." [32]

The issue of social order, is, then, in Perkins' mind; but in general that is not the aspect of the matter that preoccupies his thoughts. There was very little danger of rebellion among the prosperous merchants and tradesmen to whom he usually preached. Much more was it the temptation of money-making. And to that, next to the appetite for power the most insatiable and inexhaustible of the appetites, he preached contentment. Perkins was quite as aware as the dramatists and the satirists of the ensuing years that the middle classes had cast their eyes upward. When, therefore, he attacked the problem of limitation upon the spirit of acquisition, he very adroitly refrained from going straight to the middle classes, anxious to ape the gentry, but turned rather to a sweeping survey of the whole social scene from this point of view. He began at the top of the social scale with the ambition of princes and kings, and showed how even they were restrained by the principle of contentment with what God gave, and then went down the scale to the citizens who were going to read what one of their favorite preachers had to say on the theme of the vocations:

"If God send aboundance of things more then necessarie to Princes, they may receive them at the hand of God, and they are to be thankfull therefore: but kings themselves may not seeke for more, then which is sufficient for their estates.

"Now if this be the dutie of the Prince, then much more is it the dutie of the people: and subjects in kingdomes should content themselves, if they have as much as will provide them foode, and rayment, and thus much lawfully may they seeke for. As for example, a master of a family, may with good conscience seeke for that measure of wealth, as shall in Christian wisdome be thought meete to maintaine him and his family with convenient food and raiment: having obtained thus much, a pawse must be made, and he may not proceed further, to inlarge his estate, by seeking for that aboundance that may well serve his own house, and a second, or many families more . . . we must estimate sufficiencie, not by the affection of covetous men, for then nothing shall ever be sufficient . . . for a sufficiencie in things of this life, our rule must be the common judgement and practise of the most godly, frugall, and wise men with whome we live: and that which they in good conscience judge sufficient and necessarie for every man, according to his place and calling, that is to be esteemed sufficient." [33]

Even to those ingenious citizens who pleaded, doubtless with a reminder of some of Perkins' own preachments on the subject of charity, that they wished to increase their incomes to play the role of benefactors to church and state, Perkins was adamant in his insistence upon staying within one's calling:

"I answer, we must doe good indeed, but yet within the compasse of our estates and callings, and according to our abilitie." [34]

But the motive of bettering one's estate in order to do greater good to the commonwealth and the church was, as Perkins well knew, not the usual mainspring of middle-class ambition. A far more common incentive was that of which in discussing the liberty of lawful use of things indifferent, in *A Discourse of Conscience*, to which we have so often had occasion to refer, Perkins had complained:

"And it is a common abuse of this libertie in our daies, that the meane man will be in meate, drinke, apparell, building as the gentle-man; the gentleman as the Knight; the knight as the Lord or Earle." [35]

For covetousness and ambition are not the only foes to contenta-tion. Quite as important is the passion for luxury. Indeed, in some ways it is even more widespread in its operations, for it involves not only those who are on the make but those who are already in possession of wealth and position. The cry against luxury is as we have seen from *Piers the Plowman* an old one, with its classic lines of indictment and remedy long drawn up. But the attack on it in the preachers of the later sixteenth century is no traditional formality but a very lively onslaught upon what is obviously regarded as an actual and immediate and widespread threat to Christian life.

And it is to be found in the sermons and writings of preachers of very different outlook, speaking to very different audiences. Henry Smith strikes one note when, comparing the manner of living of the England of his day with the manner of living of biblical times, he notes the advance of luxury, illustrating it especially in the matter of food, with the complaint that the taste of his day demanded that food be prepared for the eye as well as the stomach.[56] Archbishop Sandys is obviously thinking of a very different level of society when in discussing in a sermon at Paul's Cross the grand enemies of hospitality, covetousness and profuseness, he complains that some of the rich are eaten up with the three H's: "Horses, Haukes, and Harlots," while others spend their substance on vain apparel, building and banqueting.[37]

Perkins obviously has the levels of city society in mind when he charges that the rich spend on sports or gaming what they should give to the church, while those of lower position spend the gifts they owe on fine apparel and "good cheare." [38] Henry Arthington implied much the same criticism when he put "All excessive proude persons in apparell" first in his list of "the poore makers." [39] For Churchyard's famous complaint of the love of the time for fine feathers is appropriate to the middle-class man as well as to the courtier of whom he first wrote in the second stanza of a ballad which was licensed for printing in 1565–66:

> "The Byrde can spare no plumes
> That fethers gaye wolde have
> The Courttyer all consumes
> Who makes hymeselfe so brave." [40]

Closely allied to this love of fine clothes is the passion of the landlord class for luxurious building, that most princely of temptations. As Warren put it in a jingle of the first decade of the seventeenth century:

"It's sumptuous lodge, rich vesture, daintie fare,
  That robbe the purse, and make Revenewes bare.
Double and Treble Chimneis mounting faire,
Observe the single Hospitality,
All spent to build, and buildings to repayre,
Which should support oppressed misery,
    Great halls, large tables, gold, plate, little meate,
    Feed but the eye, while mouth hath nought to eate." [41]

That is, again, a classic complaint that is going to go on with undiminished vigor and, we may be sure, undiminished occasion into the next century. Charles Richardson, "Preacher at Saint Katherines neare the Tower of London" will in a sermon published in 1615 still be making the same old complaint when in trying to find the causes of the landlords' oppression of their tenants, he discovers one in the desire of the ambitious gentlemen of the time to cut a figure in brave apparel. Indignation at this vanity inspires one of his most vivid and most metaphysical passages, "And when by these meanes they have emptyed their cofers, they must coyne new money on their poore tenants skinnes," [42] a combination of the homely wrath of Latimer and the ingenuity of Donne that does credit to Richardson's age. And though Richardson is less picturesque in his statement, he is no less indignant in his arraignment of "sumptuous building":

"It is one of the vanities of this age, that every man, of any degree, must build like Princes. . . . And then not onely their owne *Tenants,* but all the Country about them shall bee tyred out with carriages. Poore men are glad to toyle themselves and their cattell, sometimes in the deepe of winter, yea sometimes in the midst of harvest, to bring timber or stones, or other provision, and all for feare of a further displeasure: for if any man refuse to come at their call, they will bee sure to sit on his skirts, and to pay him home, eyther by raysing him in the *Subsidy,* or by doubling his charge for the warres, or any way or other." [43]

This insistence that the luxury and the pride of the rich are at the expense of the poor is, of course, in the best medieval tradition.
  But it is the general position as well of the sixteenth-century

preacher. Henry Smith, who seems to have been especially troubled by the luxury in food of his time, accuses the rich worldling who sits down to a meal of ten or twenty dishes of meat when half of that might relieve the poor, of having no conscience.[44] Of course, he is not unaware that there are other forms of luxury, for he pays his respects to that luxury in dress that was the theme of every satirist of the time in drama and sermon alike:

"If the proud would leave their superfluitie in apparell, their excesse in imbrodery, their vanitie in cuttes, gardes, and pownces, their excesse in spangling their fantasticall feathers and needlesse braverie, the greater part would suffice towardes the reliefe of the poore, and yet have sufficient to suffise nature." [45]

But he soon returns to the subject of food:

"Let the glutton seeke onely to suffice nature and leave his dayly surfetting in belly cheere, then might the poore be fed with that which he oftentimes either lothsomely vomites forth, or worketh as an instrument to shorten his owne life." [46]

Doubtless this was to bring the relation between luxury and want closer home to the sober middle-class Londoner than all the animadversions on the courtier's splendor.

In all this, it will be noticed that it is not the seeking of riches but the spirit in which they are sought that is condemned. By and large the preachers of the second half of the sixteenth century did not hold with the blanket criticism of wealth that has so often played a part in Christian radicalism. For Christianity has never been able quite to forget that Christ himself once at least made a very discouraging prognostication as to the chances of the rich man's entering heaven.[47]

Very few of the English preachers are as pessimistic as the *Booke of Christian Exercise* on the camel and needle's eye text:

"The reason of which saieng (and many mo) standeth in this, that a rich man or worldling attending to heape riches can not attend to doe that which he came for into this world, and consequently never attaine heaven, except God work a miracle, and so cause him to contemn his riches, and to use them only to the service of God." [48]

Rather, this is one of the points on which the English preachers most strikingly made an effort to meet the circumstances of their day in what seemed to them a reasonable spirit. Henry Smith, for instance, glosses the famous text thus: "This hee saith not, because no rich man shal be preserved, but because the mercilesse riche man shall be damned," [49] and he turns the text to the support of his plea for greater charity on the part of those who are equipped with the necessary means. Turnbull goes to even greater pains, elaborating especially the opportunities of the rich man to put his wealth to good use:

"Wherefore as when Christ had tolde his disciples that it was easier for a Camell to passe through the eye of a needle, then for a riche man to enter into the kingdome of heaven; he expoundeth his meaning: for he meaneth not of all rich men in generall, but of such as trusted in their riches: which he plainely protesteth to his disciples: who tooke an occasion thereby to doubte of the salvation of many: even so when the Apostle threateneth riche men, whose utter destruction and calami- tie he denounceth, he ought not to be understood of all rich men with- out exception: for there be many rich, who use their riches to Gods glorie, and the comfort of their poor brethren: who are to be exempted from this commination of the Apostle." [50]

It would be easy to see in such passages a convenient rationaliza- tion of the preachers' familiar anxiety for the provision of the necessary resources for their work of teaching and preaching and for the increase of the provisions for charity in which they were so deeply interested. But to conclude so would be to overlook what seems to be their prevailing conviction about the nature of riches.

In general the preachers made no effort to condemn wealth in itself as evil. Rather it was something indifferent, which a Christian might use without scruple if he used it in the proper manner. Rogers' Hemingius, as usual, employed rather abstract and formal terms: "For welthy men have instrumentes both to vertue and wickednes, according to their disposition." [51] And Greenham expressed the same idea, but more personally, more in terms of attitude and feeling:

"The love of the creatures hindereth us in good things, but the use of them furthereth us therein. Gods children look to the spiritual use of those things, which the worldlings use carnally." [52]

In other words, it was not the riches but the way in which they were handled that was the most important thing. Here, it is probable that William Perkins of all the English preachers did the most careful job of thinking through the problem and formulating the necessary discriminations. And significantly he did this in *A Discourse of Conscience*,[53] his great effort to translate the basic Christian principles of conduct as he saw them into terms of day-to-day action, in order to meet the challenges of ordinary life lived in the actual world of his day. He began with the reasonable recognition of a realm of things indifferent which Christians might use without scruple if they used them in the proper way. And in his definition of the proper way he recognized what we should call today two levels of use, the natural and the spiritual.

The first he defined with more liberality than the Puritans are always given credit for: "The natural use, is either to releeve our necessities, or for honest delight." [54] The second was more complicated, and for that Perkins drew up four rules or principles:

"The first, that all things must be done to Gods glorie, I. Cor. 10.31. *Whether ye eate or drinke, or whatsoever ye do, do al to the glory of God.* And that this may bee performed, things indifferent must bee used as signes and tables, in which we may shew forth the graces and vertues that God hath wrought in the heart. . . . The second, Wee must suffer our selves lawfully to be limited and restrained in the overmuch or over common use of things indifferent. . . . Now the restrainers of our use, are two; the first is the law of charitie. For as charitie gives place to pietie; so Christian libertie in the use of outward things, gives place to charitie. And the law of charitie is, that we should not use things indifferent to the hurt or offence of our brother. I. Cor. 8.13. . . . The second restrainer, is the wholsom lawes of men, whether Civill or Ecclesiasticall. For howsoever things indifferent, after the law is once made of them, remaine still indifferent in themselves: yet obedience to the law is necessarie, and that for conscience sake. Act. 15.28.

"The third, We must use things indifferent so far forth as they shall further us in godlines. . . .

"The fourth. Things indifferent must be used within compasse of our callings, that is, according to our ability, degree, state, and condition of life." [55]

In other words, Perkins recognized two things which modern students have marked as characteristic of the capitalist spirit, its tendency to operate without regard to context in an autonomous realm of its own, and its disposition to push beyond any restraint on its expansive energy.[56] And in his effort to check its depredations, he sought to impose two restraints, the restraint of larger moral and spiritual context to which constant reference must be maintained, and the restraint of limitation. The spirit of wealth-making must not be suffered to operate without regard to any end but itself, and there must be observed certain limits beyond which it shall not go.

So essential are these principles to Perkins' teaching that he returns to them again in his *The Whole Treatise of the Cases of Conscience,* there to discuss them at considerable length and in detail. It is in the fourth chapter of the third book "Of Questions concerning Temperance," that he asks the key question: *"How farre a man may, with good conscience proceed in the desiring and seeking of Riches?"* [57] He answers as one would expect, only in so far as they are necessary to the realization of the purpose of a godly life.[58] He then proceeds to define the term "necessary" with the same moderation, suggested above, and with the same respect for the distinctions of a hierarchical society that we have already seen is in general characteristic of these men:

"Goods and riches are two waies necessarie; necessarie to nature, or necessarie to the person of a man. Goods necessarie to nature, are those, without which nature and life cannot bee well preserved; and these are most needfull. Necessarie in respect of a mans person, are those goods, without which a mans state, condition, and dignitie wherein hee is, cannot be preserved." [59]

He is, of course, aware that he has introduced a dangerously relative criterion. He therefore resorts to a social standard when he says that the question of what is necessary to a man's state in life is to be settled "not by the affection of the covetous man which is unsatiable, but by two other things; the judgment of wise and godly men, and the example of sober and frugall persons." [60]

In other words, one cannot make one rule for all classes of men, but one can set up a sliding scale, as it were, of reasonable and sober standards.

On the basis of such premises, then, he is ready to answer the question which he took up at the beginning of this discussion, and that he does categorically as follows:

"Man may with good conscience, desire and seeke for goods necessarie, whether for nature, or for his person, according to the former rules: but he may not desire and seeke for goods more than necessary, for if he doth, he sinneth." [61]

In other words, Perkins has tried to put a brake on the spirit of acquisition, by invoking two principles, the principle of limitation and the principle of reference to a larger context. Indeed, the principle of limitation invoked is that of reference to a larger context. It is, therefore, necessary to understand that context if we are to do justice to Perkins' intention.

Perkins invoked that larger context when he began his discussion of the Christian use of goods in a *Discourse of Conscience* with the basic principle "that all things must be done to Gods glorie." [62] That is the ultimate purpose of all Christian activity. But in the Calvinist view of things with its tendency to exclude rigorously all incidental implications and modulations and involvements, that purpose is on the whole more a factor of limitation than of expansion, of exclusiveness than inclusiveness. As such it dominates and informs immediately all the Calvinist's thinking about his daily life.

Indeed, it is the ultimate, continuous preoccupation of Calvinist thought about this life. It finds its immediate daily implementation in a doctrine which played a very large part in the preaching of Perkins as in the preaching of all the Puritans of the sixteenth century, as it was also to play a major part in the preaching of their successors in the seventeenth century. And that was the doctrine of the calling, the belief that every man has been appointed by God to a certain work in the world, and that his doing that work in the spirit God intended is his way of doing his part to insure that the will of God shall be fulfilled in him. That doctrine has been in general credited with no small amount of the responsibility for that devotion to business and that self-confidence in pushing on one's business that is so conspicuous a feature of the middle-class spirit of the time and as much as anything else, it is generally held, responsible for the tremendous advance of the middle class at this time. Indeed, Max Weber goes so far as to conclude from his very profound and sustained study of the history of the Calvinist doctrine of the calling that "the religious valuation of restless, continuous, systematic work in a worldly calling, as the highest means to asceticism, and at the same time the surest and most evident proof of rebirth and genuine faith, must have been the most powerful conceivable lever for the expansion of that attitude toward life which we have here called the spirit of capitalism." [63]

There is no doubt, I think, that the preaching of the doctrine of the vocation did have this effect. And yet there is no doubt either that a good deal if not most of the preaching of Perkins on this subject had a very different end in view. The very terms in which he defines the doctrine of the calling in *A Treatise of the Vocations* suggest a spirit very different from that of the rising middle class:

"A vocation or calling, is a certaine kinde of life, ordained and imposed on man by God, for the common good. First of all I say, it is a certaine condition or kinde of life: that is, a certaine manner of leading our lives in this world. . . . In a word, that particular and honest manner of conversation, whereunto every man is called and set apart, that is (I say) his calling. . . . God is the Generall, appointing to every man his particular calling, and as it were his standing: and in that calling he assignes unto him his particular office; in performance whereof he is to live and die. And as in a campe, no souldier can depart his standing, without the leave of the Generall; no more may any man leave his calling, except he receive liberty from God. Againe, in a clocke, made by the arte and handy-worke of man, there be many wheeles, and every one hath his severall motion, some turne this way, some that way, some goe softly, some apace: and they are all ordered by the motion of the watch. Beholde here a notable resemblance of

Gods speciall providence over mankinde, which is the watch of the great world, allotting to every man his motion and calling: and in that calling, his particular office and function. Therefore it is true that I say, that God himselfe is the author and beginning of callings." [64]

In itself such a passage is striking enough in its implications, but it becomes more so when it is set in its proper context, the whole social view of the time. The character of this, as we have already seen in the chapter on "Submission" was in its essence, hierarchi- cal.[65] Pricke in the catechetical dialogue to which we have already had occasion to refer,[66] expressly points out that the theory of submission to the power of the king involves not only the king but the magistrate and the superior and, in the case of servants, the master. Pricke insists that the servant should obey the master, even when he is a cruel master, for "albeit the Maister doeth abuse his place and estate: yet it is the Lords, and from the Lord: and therefore in yeelding service to an evill and cruell Maister, he doeth it to the Lord, who will shewe himselfe good and gratious unto him." [67] This doctrine of superiority and subjection is the rationale of a whole plan of social organization, viewed as ap- pointed by divine authority, yet not so much prescriptive as organic. The figure of the body is a favorite one used to describe the basic plan, but the preachers in their use of this figure put no less stress upon the distinction of the component members than upon their cooperation. This view of society was taken for granted by Perkins and most of the Puritan preachers of his day as a matter of course, quite as completely as by men like Sandys or Babington or Jewell. Perkins himself expressly defended the recognized distinctions of society on the familiar ground that al- though love binds society together, God himself has appointed that

"there should stil remaine a distinction betweene man and man. . . . Now looke as the inward gifts of men are severed, so are the persons distinguished in their societies accordingly. Secondly, persons are dis- tinguished by order, whereby God hath appointed, that in every societie one person should be above or under another; not making all equall, as though the bodie should be all head and nothing else. . . . And by reason of this distinction of men, partly in respect of gifts, partly, in respect of order, come personall callings." [68]

Most of his colleagues would have quite agreed with Perkins.

This respect for the hierarchical character of society is not something to which the preachers pay conventional lip service. It is rather something constantly in their thoughts no matter what the topic they are discussing. Perkins, for instance, in all his discussions of greed or luxury takes care in his discrimination between what is necessary and superfluous to specify that due regard shall be had to the demands of a man's "place and calling." [69] Again Richard Turnbull in his lectures or sermons on "The Canonicall Epistle of Saint James" protests very strongly the way in which the world is governed by "respect of persons," treating the rich with reverence and the poor with contempt,[70] but he immediately takes pains to avert any suspicion of leveling views by explaining that the apostle is not to be understood as wishing to take away the respect which is due to men of "honour or worshippe." [71] Then, as if this were a matter on which a prudent man would not take any risks of being misconstrued (he has dedicated his treatise to the Archbishop of Canterbury),[72] he underscores his caution by going on to point out that

"neither preacheth the apostle disordered confusion, as the Libertines and Anabaptists in former times have, and now Phantastical and unbrideled spirites doe: who would remove degrees of honour and calling, not onely out of the Church, but I feare out of the common wealth also." [73]

In other words, even though in the year 1591 the leveling menace could be viewed by a London preacher as a thing of the past, still he was clearly unwilling to seem to give any countenance to such views.

Perkins to whom the challenge of the Anabaptists was apparently much more of a living issue was even more explicit, for in answering those who contended that the believer should not be subject to any ruler but God and Christ he drew a very sharp distinction between the two orders of the church and the world:

"There be two kinds of governments upon earth: one spirituall and inward, this is the kingdome of heaven and of Christ within man, standing in peace of conscience, and joy in the holy Ghost: in regard of which regiment of Christ, there is no distinction of persons, no difference of bond or free, Master, servant, father, sonne; but all are one in Christ. The other is a civill regiment, wherin orders and distinctions of men must be maintained; as some must be Princes, some subjects, some fathers, some children, some masters, some servants." [74]

This is typical. There is no suggestion in all this literature that the kind of society to be desired is one in which everybody is equal. Rather it is the kind of society epitomized by Perkins' master, Greenham, when in one of his *Grave Counsels* he summed up the whole complicated business of government in a single pithy sentence: "Care in superiours, and feare in inferiours, cause a godly government." [75] When the doctrine of the calling is set in the context of such a view of society, it is very clear that it was viewed by the preachers at least as something very different from an instrument of individual advancement. Though it is recognized that the worker will through the fruit of his labor secure the necessities of his life, Perkins is insistent that the final end or cause of even the humblest calling is *"the common good:* that is for the benefite and good estate of mankinde." [76] It is not for the aggrandizement of the individual, as Perkins makes very clear:

"Here then we must in generall know, that he abuseth his calling, whosoever he be that against the end thereof, imployes it for himselfe, seeking wholly his owne, and not the common good. And that common saying, *Every man for himselfe, and God for us all,* is wicked." [77]

Since therefore a man's calling is assigned to him, and since upon his fulfilling of its duties and obligations depends the fulfillment of God's purpose in him, and the maintenance of the welfare of society, it is important that he should be faithful to it, not neglecting it or forsaking it. Constancy in one's calling is one of the prime requisites of the Christian life. A man may, therefore, change his calling only for very weighty reasons, either of private necessity or of common good.[78] Mere hopes of personal advantage cannot in any sense be accepted as adequate excuse. So viewed in the light of the hierarchical, organic conception of society which all these men accepted for the secular world, the doctrine of the calling is seen as an instrument of social stabilization of great potential importance.

It was a heroic remedy for that time, the restlessness of which was proverbial. Perkins would not have agreed with Carpenter as to the satisfactoriness of the present state of the Church of England, but he would certainly have agreed with him when in *A Preparative to Contentation* he lamented the restlessness of the age in which he found himself:

"Alas, why is it then, that now men waxe wearie of prayer? wearie of Gods service? wearie of the word of God? wearie of true obedience? wearie of peace and quietnesse? wearie of goodnesse? wearie of God? and how commeth it to passe, that English men in lieu of forraine pleasures, doo disdaine their home commodities? How is it, that so many of them have such unquiet consciences, such strange conceits, and are never contented with whatsoever good thing the Lord God in his mercie enricheth them?" [79]

Carpenter knows, as he has implied in part of the full title of his work that there are "Discontentations which are incident to everie particular vocation and condition of men in this life," [80] but though he is willing to offer that consideration as an argument to patience, he is clearly not satisfied with it as an explanation of the present situation.

The personal remedies which Carpenter offers for the restlessness of the time are characteristic. He summed them up in a brief statement at the top of one of his chapters: "Everie man is to take the benefite of time: to keepe within the bounds of his vocation, and to depend on the divine providence." [81] The stress put upon this injunction to keep to the vocation is, of course, due to two very important features of the time. The first is the tendency in some of the more radical of the Puritan groups for lay people to take a very important part in the religious agitation to which men of Carpenter's general position so very vigorously objected. But still more it is due to what is a very important feature of the social life of the time, the probable increase in the number of and the certain increase in the attention paid to those who had risen in the world economically and socially, often at the expense of their previous calling and social position.

Now the preachers were quite aware that to ask some men to be content with the position in which they found themselves was asking a good deal. Indeed, it is on this theme of the unequal rewards of the vocations that Henry Smith penned what is perhaps after Crowley's the most brilliant expression of social indignation to be found in this literature. It is on the ancient theme of those agricultural wrongs which so exercised Crowley, but Smith's account of the injustice suffered by the poor farmer is set forth, significantly enough, more in terms of the exploitation of the middleman than the tyranny of the landlord. Yet whatever the changes in circumstances, the farmer's lot is still as in Crowley's day a hard one, and the preacher's compassion is no less lively because he expects him to bear it with patience:

"The time was when Adam digged and delved, when David kept sheepe, and all the house of Jacob were called men occupied about cattell: but as they for this were abhominable to the Egyptians (as Moses saith in the same verse) so they which doe like them, are abhorred of their brethren: and they which live by them, scorne them for their worke, which would be chastened themselves, because they worke not: There was no Arte nor Science, which was so much set by in former times, and is now profitable to the common-wealth, bringing lesse profit unto it self, that may so justly complaine of her fall without cause, and her despight from them which live by her, as this painfull Science of husbandrie: that it is marveil that any man will take paine for the rest, to be contemned for his labour, and be a scorne for the rest, which might hunger and starve, if he did not labour for them more then they do themselves. No marvel then though many in the poore countries, murmure and complaine that other cannot live by them, and they cannot live themselves: but it marvell if their complaint doe not growe in time of rebellion, and pull other as lowe as themselves: for why should the greatest payne yeeld the least profit? yet this is their ease, [sic] for if you marke, you shal see that the husbandman doth bate the price of his fruits so soon as the dearth is past, though he rayseth it a little, while the dearth lasteth; but they which raise the price of their wares with him, seldome fall againe, but make men pay as deere when the dearth is past, as if it were a dearth stil. Thus a plentiful yeere doth damage him, and a hard yeere dooth vantage them. So this painefull man, is faine to live poorely, fare meanely, goe barely, house homely, rise early, labour dayly, sell cheape and buy deere, that I may truely say, that no man deserveth his living better, no man fulfilleth the law nearer: that is, thou shalt gette thy living in the sweate of thy browes; then this poore sonne of Adam, which pickes his crums out of the earth: therfore he should not be mocked for his labor, which hath vexation enough, though all men spake well of him, and in my opinion, if any deserve to be loved for his innocencie, or for his trueth, or his paine, or the good which he brings to the common wealth: this Realme is not so much beholding to any sorte of men (but those that feede the soule) as those which feede the body, that is, those that labour the earth: yet you see how they live like drudges, as though they were your servants to provide foode for you, and after to bring it to your doores: as the beasts serve them, so they serve you; as though you were another kinde of men. I cannot thinke upon their miserie, but my thought tels me, that it is a great part of our unthankfulnesse, that we never consider what an easie life and living God hath given unto us in respect of them." [82]

Quite clearly Henry Smith saw that to ask the poor farmer to be patient when those who were more fortunate than he were so obviously not content was to ask much of human nature. And it was still harder when those in more fortunate positions in life were, as so often happened, obviously much less deserving than the poor. We may be sure that idealists like these preachers had often enough found life fall short of expectation in this respect to command their sympathy for all the undeserved privations of the godly poor.

The brutal argument that riches being the gift of God must argue the love of God for the happy possessor was not unknown in the sixteenth century, for Greenham explicitly denies it, and also the converse, that the want of riches indicates the displeasure of God with the poor. [83] And most of the preachers of the time would have agreed with him. For they were too much accustomed to think in terms of the war between the world and the spirit to be at all surprised to hear that the godly were having a difficult time while the ungodly were thriving. Indeed, they would have agreed as a matter of course with Carpenter as to the special need of the godly for patience in this ungodly world:

"But the godly and best disposed persons, in whatsoever time, place, or calling they live, are constrained with *Simon* of *Cirene* to beare the

Crosse after their Maister Christ. For why, there be not only ministred unto them many mightie causes of *Discontentation,* through those greevous oppressions urged on them by the ungodly . . . but also the holie spirit in them is moved, through the horrible sinnes and greevous offences of the ingratefull against God, to drive the mestive mill of lamentation, with flouds of weeping teares." [84]

But even Carpenter was not without some comfort for fallen human nature, for he held before the eyes of those who had been so disturbed at the contemplation of the prosperity of the wicked beside the poverty of the good the prospect of the time when the wicked would at last know the judgment of God. [85] Similar comfort was offered by Turnbull when he cited the example of the apostle Saint James, who after listing the wrongs which the poor suffer,

"comforteth them, exhorting them patiently to beare the crosse imposed, and to suffer with quietnes, the manifolde troubles of this life: earnestly expecting in their mindes the comming of the Lord Jesus Christ, who shall plentifully avenge their injuries upon the heads of their oppressors." [86]

But however comforting to the unregenerate such promise of vengeance might be, the preachers of the second half of the sixteenth century were like their predecessors too much concerned about the patience part of the Apostle's argument to spend much time on anything so inflammatory as thoughts of vengeance. Rather, they put their stress on what might be called a more positive form of comfort in the suggestion of God's remembrance of the suffering of the poor in the compensations of the future. Such was the implication of Babington's assurance that "the Lord of Heaven" is "most careful of their good, who heere in this life have had least, and are indeed yet unprovided for." [87]

Indeed, Babington is sure that the very greatness of their misery may be taken as a pledge of their future victory:

"Consider now with your selfe and forget it never, how able the Lord is to turne the wrongs of his children to their good, and their disgraces to their greater honor. . . . Surely the causelesse wrongs of men, truly fearing God, are many, and even by such done many times as of all other should not: but God is the same still, as loving and mercifull, as mightie and powerfull to right you as ever. Looke unto him, and relie upon him in patience, you shall see his pleasure in good time." [88]

This emphasis on the more positive side of the action of Providence was not entirely a matter of prudence. For the preachers were concerned with more than social stability in their preaching of patience. Even more important to them was the spiritual side of the doctrine. For the preachers of the sixteenth century had not by any means lost the medieval disposition to treat the poor as independent sinners to be held to account as firmly as anybody else. Indeed, the poor like every other class have their characteristic and particular sins. Henry Arthington summed them up with traditional and immediate vigor:

"The proceeding sinnes from the poore themselves, whereby they provoke the Lord to pinch them, are these six especially:
1. First, their misspending of former times in idlenesse, when they might have wrought.
2. Secondly, their wilful wasting of their goods when they had them, in bibbing and belly-cheare.
3. Thirdly, their impacient bearing of their present want, complaining often without cause.
4. Fourthly, their dayly repining at others prosperitie, to have so much, and they so little.
5. Fiftly, their banning and cursing, when they are not served as themselves desire.
6. Sixtly, their seldome repairing to their parish Churches, to heare and learne their duties better." [89]

That indictment of the tendencies of the sinful poor does not differ so much from that of Langland with regard to wastefulness and idleness,[90] but there is in 1597 more stress on the failure to come to church and be preached to than in the fourteenth-century arraignment.

But the most striking and the most distinctive element in Arthington's list of the shortcomings of the poor is the stress put upon lack of patience. Fully half of the six counts are devoted to some aspect of this fault. That is typical of the time, as may be seen in a treatise of Gervase Babington's which was clearly intended to give comfort to the poor, *A Conference betwixt Mans Frailtie and Faith.* In this dialogue, Faith, recalling Christ's comfort, *"Blessed are the poore, for theirs is the kingdome of God,"* defines Christ's poor as

"the poore in spirit. That is, such as using godly meanes, yet are of purpose by their God kept under, and being under, doe not swell with pride, arrogancie, and conceite, but even as the begger knowing his want, and no way having of his owne to trust to, confesseth others mens helpe needfull for him, humbleth himselfe before them, beggeth their aide, and giveth them (as instruments) the praise of his living; so they humbled, tamed, schooled and reformed by their want towards all men, carry a lowly heart, and onely at the Lords hands looke for both comfort in this world, and salvation in the world to come." [91]

But the preachers were not unaware of the fact that the argument enjoining patience upon the poor might be abused. George Phillips turns roundly on those rich men who complacently expect patience from the poor without looking to their own part: "How then would you have them content that possesse nothing, seeing your selves live mal content, which enjoy al things?" [92] But from the preachers' theory of the matter there was not much that the poor could do but be patient. For the redress of the wrongs from which they suffered, the preachers turned to those who could do something about it, the prosperous and the powerful, whose insatiate greed had caused so much of the misery of the poor. To them they preached contentation, as Perkins with a terseness worthy of Latimer phrased it, "to be contented with that condition of life wherein God hath placed us, not seeking things beyond our estate." [93] Long ago Latimer had counselled the economic fathers and grandfathers of the audience of Perkins and Smith and Jewell that they should be satisfied with an economic mediocrity, commending it to them as the surest guarantee of a quiet life, a noble but hardly a congenial ideal for one of the most aggressive ages of English history. [94]

On the whole, Perkins is very sound but a little austere on the subject of contentation. There is, to borrow one of those prophylactic figures so dear to the heart of the time, a good deal more of the poultice than of the salve in his treatment of this vexing subject. Henry Smith, whose famous *Three Sermons* on the theme of contentation first appeared in 1599,[95] is more on the positive side. He is no less severe with the covetous than Perkins, but he tries harder to persuade his hearers of the advantages of contentment, for instance, pointing out that "no man hath enough, but he which is contented." [96] Indeed, a lyric note not common in Smith comes into his commendation of this virtue:

"Such a commaunder is contentation, that where-soever she setteth foote, an hundred blessings waite upon her; in every disease she is a Phisition, in every strife she is a Lawyer, in every doubt she is a Preacher, in every griefe she is a comforter: like a sweet perfume which taketh away the evill sent, and leaveth a pleasant sent for it." [97]

If one did not know the spirit of the audience with whom these men were pleading, one might wonder if sometimes they did not come perilously close to quietism. There is a passage in one of Perkins' sermons that is even stronger in its promise of surcease of care:

"Now faith, when we have done the workes of our callings, according to the prescript of the word of God, faith (I say) maketh us commend to God the blessing, successe, and event thereof by prayer and affiance in his promises, not doubting but he will give us all things necessarie. And if we want the blessing and successe we looke for, yet faith makes us to renounce our owne desires and in silence to quiet our hearts in the good pleasure of God. And thus many worldly cares are cut off." [98]

But such a passage as this must be read not only in the light of the audience to which these men spoke but, as we have had occasion to observe before, in the context of their preaching as a whole. In that there was certainly no encouragement to idleness. The belief in the duty of all men to labor for their sustenance and for the maintenance of society was too deeply engrained in their thinking for that.[99] Babington spoke for all when he said of idleness: "All countries and all people . . . that have lived under any good government, have abhorred it." [100] Perkins, so firm in his denunciation of the oppressions of the rich, so quick in his perception of the injustices which the poor had to suffer, was yet most emphatic on the foul disorder that would result if beggars and rogues and vagabonds were tolerated in the commonwealth. That is why he so wholeheartedly commended that famous statute of the thirty-ninth year of Elizabeth which has so often excited the compassion of the modern humanitarian:

"And therefore the Statute made the last Parliament for the restraining of beggars and rogues, is an excellent Statute, and beeing in substance the very law of God, is never to be repealed." [101]

There was no question that everybody, except perhaps the idle poor, would agree with this stress on the necessity of labor for the poor. But the preachers, especially the Puritan preachers, were not content to leave things there. Henry Smith in particular emphasized the inequity of the usual stress on the idleness of the poor without regard to that of the rich:

"If the Apostles rule were kept, they which doe not worke should not eate: but now they which do not work eate most: and the husbandmen which worke eate not; but are like Bees, which prepare foode for other and pyne themselves. Let us consider this, for they had not one lawe and wee another, but the same curse which was denounced upon Adam, was denounced upon all his children, that every man should get his living in the sweat of his browes. Although I knowe there bee divers workes, and divers gifts, and divers callings to worke in; yet alwayes provided, they which doe not worke should not eat, for in the sweat of thy browes, that is, in labor and travel, thou king, and thou Judge, and thou Prelate, and thou Land-Lord, and thou Gentleman, shalt gette thy living as Adam thy Father did: or else thou doest avoyde the curse, and a greater curse shall follow; that is, they which will not sweat in earth, shall sweate in hell." [102]

And when Perkins summed up the positive obligations of the doctrine of the calling, he made no exceptions to his universal rule:

"And the ende of a mans calling, is not to gather riches for himselfe, for his family, for the poore; but to serve God in serving of man, and in seeking the good of all men; and to this ende men must apply their lives and labours." [103]

In other words, Perkins is trying to substitute for the expansive, striving, self-assertive spirit of his day one of quiet labor within the limits of one's appointed place in the world, leaving the outcome in the hands of the Lord, who gives and withholds the gifts of this world. In so doing he was, of course, throwing himself across the main line of advance of his day, especially among just those classes of the community to which he looked for the most sympathetic support of his general religious position. And this is all the more striking because Perkins was in general so timely in his appeal, so sure and even shrewd in his assessment of the interests and motives of his age, so practical in his grasp of the moral and psychological problems of his time. It cannot have been through inadvertence or through unawareness. Moreover, we have no reason to believe that his doing so lost him any very widespread support among his hearers, and we have no reason to believe that his preaching in this area was of more than very limited effectiveness.

CHAPTER VIII

ALMS

THE relief of the poor was one of the main themes of the social discussion of the sixteenth century, both lay and clerical. The shortcomings of the old religious order in this area had been, as we have seen, one of the favorite themes of reformers of all stripes of opinion at the opening of the century. And the tremendous increase in begging and vagrancy attendant upon the dislocations of the years that followed constituted one of the social problems that most engaged the thoughts of men of every party.[1] Such was the urgency of the problem that for once speculation had to issue in practical action.

This took two forms, measures for the repression of vagrancy and begging, that the numbers to be relieved by charity might be reduced as much as possible, and measures for increasing the admittedly insufficient provisions for relief. There can be little doubt that both problems were aggravated by the spoliation of the monasteries, but they were in no sense created by them, as may be seen from the experience of countries in which the old religious order was still relatively undisturbed.[2]

Of these two developments, only the second, the increasing of the means of charity concerns us here. That took two directions in the period we are studying. The first was the widening of the basis of eleemosynary effort by the recognition of community responsibility; the second was the systematic organization of relief on a considered plan.[3] Mr. F. R. Salter has shown that this was a European development, of which the English manifestation is to be seen in the growth of poor law legislation from 1495 to 1601, from the clear recognition of the distinction between the able-bodied and the impotent poor to the enactment of a compulsory poor rate.[4] The increasing secularization and the systematization of relief alike were a general European development.[5]

Probably the most widely celebrated Continental example of the development is the famous relief scheme set in operation in the Flemish city of Ypres in 1525. The main principles of that organization are to be found in a treatise of the Spanish humanist, Juan Luis Vives, *De Subventione Pauperum*. Although this work was not published until 1526, it is, of course, quite possible that the proponents of this plan had been able to consult him in person. Though Vives had begun this treatise during his residence in England, it is not known to have been translated into English during our period.[6] But an official description of the Ypres scheme, *Forma Subventionis Pauperum quae apud Hyperas Flandorum Urbem Viget*, was published at Antwerp in 1531,[7] and this was translated into English by William Marshall and published in 1535.[8]

It is significant of the spirit of the time that Marshall invokes both the "comen comoditie and profyte" of the realm and Christian charity to commend the example of Ypres to the Queen (Anne Boleyn), to whom the book is dedicated.[9] The propriety of these terms of commendation becomes apparent when one turns to the text of *The Forme and Maner of Subvention or Helping for Pore People*, itself. For almost at the beginning of the treatise, two premises of the plan are clearly laid down, the first the obligation of both the ecclesiastical and the political or civil rulers to provide for the poor, and the second, the general social obligation, set forth in the terms with which we are already familiar:

"For lyke as by the reson that the partes of mans body are naturally knytte and joyned togyther eche to other therfore if one of theym be greved the other also feleth grefe: even so we that are membres of Chrystes mistycall body joyned by faythe and charyte ought wyllyngly and mercyfully to offre helpe to such as have nede." [10]

But however lofty the basic social notions of the Ypres apologist, there is no question of the realism of his approach to the problem. He is quite aware of the strains human nature itself puts on the idealism of the average man. There is, for instance, the widespread fear that liberality to the poor may be wasted because of the unworthiness of the recipients.[11] So like all writers of the time, this one is anxious to cut down on begging, but he is not ready to forbid all begging, because he is afraid of suffering in those cases in which no other provision may be open to dire need.[12] At the same time he is quite aware that it is rash to trust to begging in these days "whan cristen charite is so colde and holynes and devotyon so sore decayed." [13]

On the other hand, he is not blind to the shortcomings of the poor. There are those who could well work who prefer the easier way of begging, and leave employers short of necessary labor.[14] And there are even more who have very little capacity for managing their own affairs prudently or effectively,[15] and these need the help of other men if they are to escape suffering.[16] So provision is made for prefects to keep an eye on the reckless and the idle,[17] to provide for the education of the young either in schools or at crafts, according to their gifts,[18] and to compel the strong beggars to useful labor.[19] These provisions, quite typical of the time, are tempered by the injunction that the public officials shall give courteous hearing to the complaints of the poor,[20] with the doubtless much-needed reminder: "Poore men no doubte are membres of the cyte as wel as ryche." [21]

So much for the giving of alms. As for the raising of the necessary funds for the supplying of these alms, regular provision for the collection of alms is made, and the curates and preachers are asked to urge their parishioners to respond generously to these collections, but the contribution is still apparently quite voluntary.[22] Such is the basic scheme. There are other features, of course, of a good deal of interest. There is a sympathetic provision for the seeking out of the proud poor with respect for their feelings.[23] There is the less encouraging reminder: "A poore man shulde after his degre (which is small and lytell) be contented with lytell," [24] probably compounded of a recognition of the limitation on means and of the point of view of the average citizen who contributed to the funds.

There is no question that the latter is in the forefront of the writer's mind when he comes to enumerate the "commodyties that the Cytyzens fele by the meanes of this polycy," ranging from the swelling of the labor supply to the removal of the ugly sights and smells that used to be encountered at the porches of churches.[25] But at the end the author returns to his initial premises when he cites as the final benefit the improved condition of the poor man, "for all men busely labour to helpe him as one that is sente of god upon whom every man maye fynde mater and occasion to practise vertue." [26] This last note in particular is typical of the transitional position of the translator's period, for it is, as we shall see presently, a distinctively Catholic attitude toward the business of alms-giving, that is here commended in a work presented by a man thoroughly committed to the reform.

But the main ideas with regard to community responsibility and the rationalization of the provision for and administration of relief represented by the Ypres scheme continued to exert an influence upon the thought of sixteenth-century England. A thoroughly Protestant and at the same time still more secularized version of the Ypres scheme is to be seen in a work by another man associated with that city, Andreas Gerardus, the Protestant reformer, who is known to history by the name which he took from his birthplace, Hyperius. An English minister, Henry Tripp, translated Hyperius' book into English and published it under the title, *The Regiment of the Povertie* in 1572.[27]

The breadth of view with which a man in Tripp's position might approach this problem is to be seen in the dedicatory epistle which he addressed to the Bishop of Rochester as a preface to his translation. This statement is especially interesting from our point of view because even in the following condensed form it gathers up several strands of the preaching tradition which we have been studying, with a side glance at the Utopian tradition as well:

"If the . . . unsatiable desyre or appetite of our own privat commoditie wer once rooted out of mens mindes, and the contrary persuasion settled, to wit, that it is as unlauful to live as to our selves, not profiting our brethren, as it is to seeke our commoditie by an other mans hinderance. . . . Sure I am, that neither *Plato, Aristotle,* etc. nor any other that have travailed most to bring the politique government to perfection, were ever able to describe or paint out such a live-like patterne of a common wealth as this one errour once reformed, wold restore unto us." [28]

This is one of the classic views of the world, but there is a converse to it, not nearly so widespread, namely, that the welfare of the individual is indispensable to the welfare of the whole. This Henry Tripp gives with no less vigor and completeness:

"But I would to God we did so consider and vew our own bodies, that we might lern ther by, and the better conceive what belongeth to the common wealth or the churche of God: wherof the one by the Philosophers: the other by the Apostle is compared to a bodie, wherein (as in eache of our bodies) *symetria et sympathia, id est,* due proportion and right placing of eche member, in respect of the whole bodie, and a mutual passion or sense of feeling, diffused thorow every part, must be preserved. For whether soever of these two shall happen to be empaired or disturbed, forthwith there foloweth eyther griefe, or a deformitie, or utter confusion to the whole bodie."

And this principle is ratified by a whole battery of authorities, including Paul, Plato, and the Stoics. [29]

But he knew well that this was Utopia of which he was talking, and so, we may be sure, did the Bishop of Rochester. His answer to the practical and immediate problem, therefore, is to be found in the treatise which he translated and presented to the bishop and the public with the foregoing address. This work is highly traditional, as we shall see, in many of its principles and its recommendations, but it is nonetheless fresh and practical in its approach to an enduring problem. To begin with, the author professes two motives to his study, his devotion to the glory of God in the churches and to the help of the poor. [30] He insists strongly throughout his book on the obligation of the church to the poor. Much of its treasure was collected to the end that it might be able to fulfil that obligation, [31] and the principle that a fourth of all church goods should go to the relief of the poor was early established by ancient canons. [32] But Hyperius saw clearly that the poor "are alway the greater part in any societie." [33] So it is not surprising that he insisted that the church cannot without help take care of the task of relief, much less the ministers alone. For the obligation extends to everybody that calls himself Christian. Therefore the elders of the church and the magistrates should get together and see what they can do to solve the problem.[34]

It is clear that the cooperation of both authorities would be needed for the realization of his suggestions for the raising of money for relief. The increase in "earnest pennies" in bargaining, in buying and selling, and in the making of marriages is one method. Another is a voluntary contribution from all public officers and functionaries upon their assumption of office, another the increasing of fines by a contribution to the poor box. More money still may be raised by the abolishing or curtailing of plays and games, banquets, feasts of brotherhoods and colleges, etc.[35] But this seems to him the least of his concerns.

Much more urgent is the problem of administration. And here the author displays a certain realism that is at once strongly reminiscent of the realism of the medieval writers and thoroughly characteristic of the sixteenth century. Not all the poor are worthy by any means in the eyes of this theorist of poor relief any more than they were in the eyes of Langland. Henry Smith, faced with this problem in the excuses of those who hesitated to relieve a beggar because they did not know whether he was what would be today called a deserving case, advised them, if they did not know that the beggar was bad to take a chance on relieving him, and if he were undeserving of the aid he received, let his sins fall on his own head.[36] But Hyperius is not so easily content. Indeed, the first thing needed, he thinks, in any effective scheme of poor relief is some sort of sorting-out. The valiant beggar that haunted the rehabilitation schemes of Piers Plowman still plagues the sixteenth-century social reformer, and Hyperius has some good stories to tell of the enterprises of these perennial rascals.[37] But clearly he does not think that the rogues count for much beside the victims of genuine poverty.[38] Nevertheless, careful investigation is necessary to give men what will really help them, careful investigation both of their needs and their resources. Especially is this necessary when it comes to providing them with the indispensable work which Hyperius, in common with the earlier students of the subject, believes all men who are able-bodied need.

Indeed, one of the most interesting passages in the book concerns the provision of work for the handicapped. Here the author cites at length the activities of a college for the blind at Bruges,[39] where the pupils were taught to play on organs and musical instruments, to make brooms and baskets, and to work in wine presses and operate hand mills.[40]

Quite as interesting are the provisions for the teaching of promising children in good literature, especially Scripture, but something of the timidity of the time with regard to numbers is reflected in the author's reassurances as to the number of likely candidates being small in any one place.[41] Probably the explanation of this caution is very simple, awareness of the limited resources to be counted on. For the same regard to the limitations of resources is apparent in the provision for illness and other special needs so far as the treasury will permit.[42]

But this regard for the limitations of resources is to a certain extent counterbalanced by the insistence of Hyperius on a careful attention on the part of the overseers of the poor to their complaints as well as their needs. Hyperius took grumbling for granted, admitting that, "to say the truth, all povertie (almost) are naturally wrangling, grudging and disdainful." [43] So he bids the overseers do all they can to forestall complaints, especially by being as equitable as they can in the distribution of alms.[44] Moreover, the overseers are to meet once a week for the purpose, among others, of hearing the complaints of the poor.[45] And any demands which they shall make are to be heard courteously and met so far as possible.[46] Especially are the overseers to exercise constant patience in seeking out the proud poor who will be ashamed to make their wants known.[47]

This humanity of Hyperius is one of his outstanding traits. But he is no less aware of the psychology of those who afford the means of support for the poor. He cautions the overseers that they should watch the morals of their clients, especially of young widows, so that the prosperous of the community will not complain that their wealth is being spent on harlots.[48] Those who enjoy the provisions for relief that he has described should be content with the state to which God has called them.[49] That is a return which one would expect the psychology of the time to exact. But here again Hyperius shows more respect for the moral independence and freedom of the poor than do some of his contemporaries, for he appeals to the poor to help support their own morale: "Moreover, lette them comforte one another, and encourage one another to modestye, sobrietye, and taciturnitie." [50]

On the other hand, Hyperius has his arguments to convince substantial citizens of the advantages to all citizens of adequate poor relief. They are freed of clamor, of fear of outrages, of the sight of ugly bodies, of exposure to contagion, and they are assured of a much greater readiness to work on the part of those whose troubles have been relieved.[51] The result is a greater sense of security in all classes [52] and better relations between them—"the riche man without offence or disdayne wil salute the poore man: and agayne the poore neighbour will not be ashamed to resalute the riche, and to wishe him well." [53] This is a very different spirit from that of *An Act for the Punishment of Vacabundes, and for the Releefe of the Poore and Impotent* of the fourteenth year of Elizabeth, an act of which Henry Tripp in his dedicatory epistle expresses his entire approval.[54] That was, however, an advance over that of the first act of Elizabeth, and Tripp may very well have looked forward to an advance still further in the direction of Hyperius.

But whatever the hopes of the preachers for the improvement of the public handling of the problem of the relief of the poor, their first and characteristic concern was with the obligation of the individual Christian to do his duty in this as in every other realm. Nowhere is their preoccupation with what today would be called "personal morality" more clearly demonstrated than in their general concentration on the problem of private and individual alms-giving in their approach to this problem.

For alms-giving was not just a matter of provision of resources for the relief of suffering. Rather what they had to say on the duty of alms-giving was the final expression of their theory of wealth.

As we have already seen, they did not condemn wealth but pronounced it neutral, something which man could use or abuse.[55] The proper use of riches becomes therefore a concern of the deepest moment to the godly Christian, if he is to fulfil his duty and make sure of his own spiritual safety. Here the preachers stand ready to help him. The Hemingius of Rogers is succinct and objective. The problem of the disposition of resources is clearly what absorbs his attention:

"The firste and principall use of ritches, should bee to maintaine religion, and to set forth̬e the glorie of God. . . .

"The seconde use of ritches ought to bee, to adorne the Commonweales wherein wee are, accordyng to our habilitie. . . .

"The thirde good and lawfull use of ritches is, that everie man do keepe hymselfe accordyng to his power honestly, and maintaine his houshold.

"The fourth and the last use of ritches good and commendable, is to releive the poore." [56]

On the other hand, Perkins is, as usual, concerned with the spiritual state of the steward, with his attitude toward his charge; especially is he anxious to ensure that that attitude will meet the requirements of his position in the total scheme of God's purpose. It is in *The Whole Treatise of the Cases of Conscience* in answer to the question *"How a man may with good conscience, possess and use Riches?"* that he lays down his four rules for the proper use of riches:

"I. Rule. They which have riches are to consider, that God is not onely *the soveraigne Lord,* but the *Lord of their riches,* and that they themselves are but *the stewards of God,* to imploy and dispense them, according to his will. Yea further, that they are to give an account unto him, both for the having and using of those riches, which they have and use. . . .

"II. Rule. We must use specially moderation of minde, in the possessing and using of riches, and be content with our estate, so as we set not the affection of our heart upon our riches, Psal. 62.10.

"III. Rule. We must, upon the calling of God, forsake our riches, and al that we have in this world, not onely in disposition of minde, but in deed. . . .

"IV. Rule. We must so use and possesse the goods we have, that the use and possession of them, may tend to Gods glorie, and the salvation of our soules." [57]

As for the more particular directions for the proper apportionment of riches, Perkins substantially agrees with Hemingius: "Our riches must be imploied to necessarie uses." These Perkins proceeds to define as, first, "the maintenance of our owne good estate and condition," second, the good of others, especially our family or kindred, third, "the reliefe of the poore, according to the state and condition of every man," fourth, "the maintenance of the Church of God, and true religion," and fifth and last, "the maintenance of the commonwealth." [58]

It is because of this stewardship theory of riches that the preachers arraign so severely the greedy and the ambitious and the luxurious who use their riches to their own comfort and pleasure and do not share them with the poor. These men have mistaken the purpose of their possessions. They are not theirs to do with as they please. They are the gift of God. They are given by God that they may be used for the good of all, especially of those to whom they have not been given, for in the words of Sandys:

"To serve in justice is the duetie of everie man: The riche man is a servaunt to the poore to releeve and comfort him as he is able. For that is right and to that end God hath made him rich, that he as a faithful steward might bestowe those riche blessings upon the familie and houshold of God." [59]

The covetous man and the luxurious man who use their riches to their own comfort and pleasure are, therefore, guilty of a basic injustice to those with whom they refuse to share what God has given them. That is the heart of George Phillips' arraignment of the oppressive rich of his day:

"All men doe know that there is enough delivered out to the great Stewardes, to suffice the whole housholde: but they have made that which they have received, riches of iniquity; whilst by iniquity they witholde that from their brethren, which was delivered for their brethren, themselves being but Stewardes of it, at the most." [60]

Indeed, Turnbull on the authority of Saint Chrysostom does not hesitate to go so far as to declare that:

"In as much therfore as the rich are not lords of their riches, but the stewards of God, to imploy them to the glory and pleasure of their master: and the overplus of their riches none of theirs, but the poores, whom they slay and murther, asmuch as in them lieth, when they detaine it: therefore, when they suffer the poore to perish; the naked to sterve; the needie to die for want of necessary succour: when in the meane time, their garmentes are moth eaten, and their gold and silver cankered, the consumption, canker, and corruption of these things shall stande up in judgement against them." [61]

And with less splendor but more hard-headed realism Henry Arthington reminds the prosperous among his auditors that "God might have made our estate like unto the poore: that his more bountifull dealing with us, should open our hearts to be so much the more beneficiall to them, or else wee shew our selves unworthy of his blessings, and deserve in justice to be deprived of them." [62]

Alms, then, are a basic obligation of the man of any means, and the execution of that obligation one of the basic concerns of the preachers, just as important in their eyes and just as imposing in the total effect of their preaching as the attack on covetousness. It is one of the topics which they most often treat formally, one of the themes of the Christian life to which they most commonly return explicitly and by implication. It is one of the topics treated in the second tome of the homilies of 1563, in *An Homely of Almes Dedes, and Mercyfulnesse towarde the Poore and Nedye.*[63]

The formal approach of this homily is worth noting because it is so typical of the contemporary approach to the problem. The author at the very beginning explains just what he is going to do:

"Fyrste, I wyll shewe howe earnestlye almyghty God in his holye woorde, doth exacte the doinge of almes dedes of us, and howe acceptable they be unto him.

"Secondly, howe profitable it is for us to use them, and what commoditie, and fruite they wyll brynge unto us.

"Thirdlye and last, I wil shewe out of Gods worde, that who so is liberall to the poore, and relieveth them plenteously, shal notwyth-standyng: have sufficient for hym selfe, and evermore be wythout daunger of penurye, and scarsitie." [64]

That this is again what might be termed a classic approach becomes apparent when we find that a very similar plan was fol-lowed in the treatises and sermons of other writers of the period. It is laid out quite explicitly by Rogers' Hemingius in the intro-duction to his discussion of the theme of alms:

"Wherefore I will firste of all shewe how we should begin to deale our almes, and what are the kindes thereof. Afterwarde I will recite the causes, whiche may provoke the godlie to bestowe their Almes. Then I will signifie with what mind one should deale his almes, and withall I will prescribe a manner of giving almes. Last of all, I will shew what are the endes of true Almes, and the commoditie redound-ing to the mercifull." [65]

Much the same approach is implicit in Henry Smith's definition of alms:

"Almes is a charitable reliefe given by the godlie to the sick, to the lame, the blinde, the impotent, the needy the hungrie and poorest persons: even such as ar daily vexed with continuall want: to whome even of duty, and not of compulsion, we ought to impart: some part of that which God hath mercifullie bestowed uppon us." [66]

The explanation of this identity is to be found in the fact that here as in their preaching on usury, for all their differences of approach and of emphasis, the preachers still in the main adhere to tradition. If one turns to Thomas Aquinas' discussion of "Almsdeeds," one will find that their groundplan has been drawn out of the characteristically more extended analysis of the scholas-tics:

"We must now consider almsdeeds, under which head there are ten points of inquiry: (1) Whether almsgiving is an act of charity? (2) Of the different kinds of alms. (3) Which alms are of greater account, spiritual or corporal? (4) Whether corporal alms have a spiritual effect? (5) Whether the giving of alms is a matter of precept? (6)

Whether corporal alms should be given out of the things we need? (7) Whether corporal alms should be given out of ill-gotten goods? (8) Who can give alms? (9) To whom should we give alms? (10) How should alms be given?" [67]

And this indebtedness becomes still more apparent, if we take up the specific answers which the medieval author returns to these questions. For example, to the question "Whether Almsgiving is an Act of Charity?" [68] he replies: "External acts belong to that virtue which regards the motive for doing those acts. Now the motive for giving alms is to relieve one who is in need," and he concludes that it is to be regarded as an act of mercy. [69] But this conclusion raises another question: "Whether Almsgiving is a Matter of Precept?" That Thomas answers in the affirmative too: "As love of our neighbour is a matter of precept, whatever is a necessary condition to the love of our neighbour is a matter of precept also." [70] Indeed, many of the reasonable limitations and qualifications which we shall presently find the sixteenth-century preachers conceding are anticipated by the thirteenth-century writer. For instance, when he says that we should give of our surplus to those in need, this obligation is limited to those alone who could not be succoured if we did not give. [71]

In the same spirit he answers the question: "Whether one ought to give alms out of what one needs?" by defining what things are necessary in such terms as to go beyond what is needed for the bare maintenance of life: "Secondly, a thing is said to be necessary, if a man cannot without it live in keeping with his social station, as regards either himself or those of whom he has charge." [72] This spirit of moderation extends to the recipients of relief as well. Although St. Thomas grants that alms should be given to the needy not that he may live an easy life but that his necessities may be relieved, yet he reminds the too-often exacting giver of alms: "Nevertheless we must bring discretion to bear on the matter, on account of the various conditions of men, some of whom are more daintily nurtured, and need finer food and clothing." [73]

But whatever the support of authority at their back, the preachers of the sixteenth century had their work cut out for them when they undertook to persuade men who had so many good uses for their money as the newly prosperous classes of the sixteenth century to part with it to others. Indeed, one of the things that most worried the preachers was the lack of charity of the time, as evinced both in inadequate support of the church and inadequate relief of the poor. The disappointment of the disestablishment was now a good ways back and might be assumed to have been assimilated in that general acceptance of loss and gain which men instinctively make in periods of social transition. The repudiation of the monastic ideal was quite complete, and the soundness of the strategy of the destruction of that stronghold of the old order generally accepted among the supporters of the new. But the charity associated with the old order, so bitterly attacked by the early reformers for its inadequacy, too late recognized for at least more than the inheritors of their property were likely to provide after the disestablishment, seems with the passing of time to have gained rather than lost appreciation in the public memory. The lament for times past, is of course, the proper field of the ballad, but there is something more than that in a ballad probably to be assigned to the beginning of the next century yet in its spirit typical of this period:

> "I read in ancient times of yore,
>   That men of worthy calling
> Built almes houses and spittles store,
>   Which are now all down falling;
> And few men seek them to repair,
>   Nor none is there among twenty
> That for good deeds will take any care." [74]

So too, the tradition of the old hospitality, arraigned as it was in its day for waste and encouragement to certain social disorders, lingers on in a glow of wistful remembrance investing the old secular society of the countryside as well as the monastic. An example is to be found in another ballad, probably of the second half of the sixteenth century, printed by John Payne Collier, without name of author or date of publication in the same collection:

"Christmas beefe and bread is turn'd into stones,
Into stones, into stones, into stones,
                    and silken rags;
And Ladie Money sleepes and makes moanes,
And makes moanes, and makes moanes, and makes moanes,
                    in misers' bags:
Houses where pleasures once did abound,
Nought but a dogge and a shepheard is found,
                    Welladay!
Places where Christmas revells did keepe
Are now become habitations for sheepe.
          Welladay! Welladay! Welladay!
                    where should I stay?" [75]

That is, of course, the helpless complaint of the romantic spirit in which nostalgia has taken the place of indignation. But there seems to have been a widespread feeling from the middle of the sixteenth century on, that men were not so forward with works of charity as they used to be, that the present was not so well provided with institutions and habits of charity as the past. Sandys in a sermon which he preached at Paul's Cross when he first came to be Bishop of London in 1570, complained: "In former times here hath beene provision for the poore, and some as yet remaineth: but it is for the most part much abused." [76] It was, however, more than the loss of the provision that had existed, which had so much troubled the earlier preachers, as we have seen, that now troubled their predecessors. It was that the springs of charity seemed to have dried up.

Henry Smith is certainly not to be suspected of either a romantic or a religious tenderness for the old order, but he asks:

"Where is the large liberallity become, that in time past was rooted in our forefathers, they were content to be liberal, though they applied it to evill purposes, the successours of those which in time past gave liberallie to maintain Abots, Friers, Monks, Nunnes, Masses, Durges, Trentals, and all idolatrie: seeing the abuses thereof, may now bestow it to a better use: namely to foster and feed the pore members of Christ." [77]

Here Smith is bringing up again the old hope of the first reformers that the resources which had been misapplied to the support of the old regime might be converted to the promotion of the new.

But it did not prove so easy to affect that transfer. In spite of the complaints of suffering in the mid-century tracts, there seems to have been a feeling of prevailing prosperity in the later decades. At least the preachers seem to have felt that, possibly because so many of these sermons that deal with social problems are the work of London preachers in touch with the prosperous merchant classes of the capital. Smith certainly did, as he says in his answer to his own question above:

"The worlde is as great as it hath beene, the people now are more rich then they have beene and more covetous then they have beene: yea, they have more knowledge then ever they hadde: yet want the desire they have had to become liberall and seeme therein most wilfull ignorant." [78]

And Smith's complaint is supported by that of other preachers.[79]

This was in itself bad enough and would have grieved the preachers in any case. But they were quite aware of the fact that those whose attachment to the ancient order was more than a matter of sentiment would be at no loss for an explanation of the change. Parsons, for instance, in his attack on Foxe in *The Third Part of a Treatise Intituled of Three Conversions of England* in 1603 charges that the old tradition of alms-giving and such good works as the building of schools and bridges has been given up by the new saints. They will not be bothered with them; nor do they think them any way to Paradise, for they count on faith alone to bring them there.[80]

Parsons' adversaries were sensitive to such taunts, as may be seen from Henry Arthington's rebuttal of the general charge:

"Neither let the Papists untruly reproach us, that we deny good workes, or deedes of charitie, for (as they may perceive by that which hath bin said) we urge them to all Christians, upon paine of damnation to those that refuse them, because they can not without them approve themselves to be true beleevers, and with out faith no man can please God, yet we do not put them in Christs place, as the cause or matter of our salvation, but as effects only proceeding from faith, whereby we make it manifest, that we do belong unto his redemption, because we desire in all things to please him." [81]

There is no need of asking here whether Arthington described correctly the theory of works which he repudiated. The important thing for our purposes is what he has to say of his own theory. There is no question that the discriminations he makes in the passage above are real discriminations, but they were in practice not easy to teach. In many ways they were not so easy to teach as the ideas that had prompted the munificence of the old regime. For the men who had given to the foundation of the ancient charities had believed that in so giving they were doing something to the honor and glory of God and, subject to certain conditions of repentance for their sins and resolution to amendment of life, something that would promote the salvation of their souls. Sinners had welcomed the opportunity to make some degree of amends for their misdeeds, and even the best of men, viewing their faulty performance in the light of their professions, had been glad to make an offering to heaven in petition for grace to persevere. These were quite simple ideas, running certain risks of misunderstanding and abuse and corruption, it is quite true, but also fairly comprehensible to the average man and obviously very potent in their appeal to frail and aspiring humanity. Nicholas Sander could and did in *A Briefe Treatise of Usurie,* published at Louvain in 1568, not only urge upon the Catholic possessioners the consideration that his demand that they give only what was "superfluous and more than is needful" was very moderate compared with the ideal of perfection of giving away all they had and following Christ, but he could also cite the eleventh chapter of Luke and other places in Scripture to show "that even our dayly sinnes and inward uncleannesse, are made cleane by Almosdedes." [82] That argument the Protestant preachers had thrown away in scorn.

And they had done so on two grounds. The first was, as Arthington made clear above, that any suggestion that what a man did helped to procure his salvation diminished the just honor due to Christ as the Saviour and Redeemer of mankind. The second is admirably summed up in a sentence of the sermon which

Sandys preached at his first coming to York in 1576: "Therefore daungerous and desperate is that doctrine of the Papists which doth teache us ever to be doubtfull and in suspence of our salvation." [83] Rather the Protestant ideal was Babington's: "Stand wee therefore in the truth of God with assured comfort of our happy end, when once we finde we are truely come to Jesus Christ by the Fathers giving." [84]

Now that security was a tremendously impressive moral phenomenon, and the source, obviously of much strength. But it did raise its problems. Though the preachers made great efforts to enforce upon their congregations the necessity of constant moral endeavor, they seem always to have been uncertain of their success. Chaderton, one of the greatest of what might be called the pre-Puritan leaders, complained that

"the most parte of Protestantes are altogether secure, and carelesse, touching the obedience of faith, rather presuming in the pryde of their hearts of the mercies of God for their salvation, then by humble and trembling heartes to worke, ratifie, and confirme unto their owne consciences the certaintie of their election." [85]

And Perkins, the greatest of the Puritan divines of the sixteenth century, in *A Salve for a Sicke Man* declared that he was shocked at the way in which men waited until they came to die before thinking of salvation, a complaint by no means unknown among the defenders of works, and he drew the following conclusion: "This one sinne argues the great security of this age, and the great contempt of God and his word." [86]

But there was another explanation of the security of the day, less theological but perhaps even more human. Greenham in commenting on the Jews who looked back wistfully to the flesh-pots of Egypt in his sermon, *Of Murmuring*, makes an observation in spirit not unlike Perkins' complaint of the dilatory pentitent:

"Many are like minded to these people now adaies: for we see divers upon their death-beds very senseles and secure, who can be contented with open mouth to record the goodnesse of GOD towards them in things concerning this present life: but in the meane time, being without hope, sense or feeling of the sweet joyes to come, do die thus by their flesh-pots." [87]

One who paid more attention to the role of the imagination in human action than did the sixteenth-century preachers might have interpreted this state of mind as lack of imagination. But Greenham found a direr explanation of what was to him no mere psychological curiosity. It seemed to him that such men must be, whatever their profession, practical atheists. Like Chaderton Greenham was deeply concerned about this basic faithlessness of his time.

"He feared," said his sixteenth-century editor, "rather Atheisme than Papisme in the Realme: for many having escaped out of the gulfe of superstition, are now too farre plunged and swallowed up of prophanenes, thinking either that there is no God, or else that he is not so fearefull and mercifull, as his threatnings and promises commend him to be." [88]

That this experience of the English Calvinists was not unique is to be seen in what Calvin has to say on the same topic when in the words of the 1561 English version of *The Institution of Christian Religion* he admits that

"those who complain of the moral danger in the doctrine of predestination are not altogether wrong, for there be many swine, whiche with filthy blasphemies defile the doctrine of predestination, and by this pretense also do mocke out all admonishmentes and rebukynges, sayeng, God knoweth what he hath ones determined to do with us. But Paul telleth that we be to this ende, that we should leade a holy and faultlesse life. If the marke of that election is directed unto be holinesse of life, it ought more to awake and sturre us up cherefully to practise that holinesse, than to serve for a clokyng of slouthfulnesse." [89]

In other words, here, as so often in the religious field, the reformer found it easier to drive men from one extreme to another than to achieve what he considered the mean of his aim.

This is especially understandable in the case of the doctrine of predestination, because in the beginning it had seemed so important to the reformers to destroy what they considered the trust in works of the old order. Their ideal is clearly stated in that brief sentence in which William Tracie in his testament summed up the testimony of both Tyndall and Fryth on this point, to the effect that "a good worke maketh not a good man but a good man maketh a good worke." [90] Such men as these thought of the good work as the natural flower of the faith of the good man. But when it came time to write *An Homely of Almes Dedes* for the second tome of the homilies of 1563 even convinced Calvinists knew that for the generality of men the problem was not so simple. For this work begins with a vigorous commendation of alms, citing the twelfth chapter of Luke, and the fourth chapter of the Book of Tobit, and the ninth [seventh?] of Ecclesiasticus as support for the view of alms as medicine for the safety of the soul.[91] But the ever-present fear of misunderstanding on the score of "works" presently checks this enthusiasm with the caution that those places of Scripture that extol the profit of almsdeeds are not to be taken to mean that giving alms washes away sin.[92] Rather

"the good deedes of manne, are not the cause that maketh man good, but he is first made good by the spirit and grace of God that effectually worketh in him, and afterwarde he bringeth foorth good fruites. And than as the good fruite doth argue the goodnes of the tree: so doth the good and merciful dede of the man, argue and certainly prove the goodnesse of him that doth it." [93]

Now the notion that good works are proof of the state of a man is unmistakably implied in that last sentence. It is much more explicitly stated in a textbook of the time which sets forth the position of the Continental Calvinists on such matters, as understood and defined by some of the students of Beza and Faius. An English translation of this work under the title, *Propositions and Principles of Divinitie,* was published in 1591. The first of the "Principles Concerning good Workes" are there set forth as follows:

"1. Good workes are as necessary for the sound and the undoubted discerning of true sanctification in a regenerate man, (whereof we have spoken) as are good fruits in a tree that beareth, to shew that it hath bin rightlie graffed.

2. We call good works, the effects of those actions onelie, which in the regenerat by the working of the Spirite of God through faith, are squared according unto the prescript rule of Gods law, that in them God might be glorified, and our neighbours helped." [94]

Now all this was no mere dispute over fine points of theory. For men who believed that the conviction within that one was of the elect was necessary for a saving faith, the possibility of such a conviction was a matter of the deepest and profoundest urgency, all the more so because some of the most sensitive and thoughtful spirits of the time were not always sure that they had that firm faith and inner certainty that they were of the Elect. It is the awareness of this fact that makes Turnbull go a step further in his sermons to his parishioners in Cheapside, published in 1591. For he suggests that the doing of good works is a testimony that we are of the elect.

"And for asmuch as it is not onely a matter of most great account in all times, to have this godly care of bringing forth fruites of true sanctification unto Gods glorie: but is also the most lively testimonie of our election, who are therefore called of God, that we might be irreprehensible through love: and the sure signe of our regeneration and new birth, whose chiefe end is to walke in good workes, which God hath prepared for us." [95]

But Laurence Chaderton who was frankly worried that the "Papistes" might triumph over good Protestants in the matter of works [96] had long before this gone much further. For in a sermon of 1578 he had not hesitated to draw the obvious conclusions, and in the teeth of the prevailing Protestant suspicion of "works" he had stressed their necessity,[97] when he explained that good works were required not only for the doing of the Father's will

"but also for the declaration of our faith, for the confirmation of our hope, for the separating of us from all infidels and hypocrites, for the example of those which are without, and within the Church, for the relieving and succouring of all, especially of those which are of the houshoulde of fayth, for to justifie our religion to be pure and undefiled before God the Father, for to testifie our obedience and thankefulnesse to God the author thereof, finally to prayse and magnifie the great power, Justice, and mercie of God the Father, his Sonne, and the holie Ghost, one God, and three persons in the whole and perfect worke of our redemption." [98]

He even went so far as to bring up the indispensable scriptural examples to enforce his principles, Abraham sacrificing Isaac, and Rahab the Harlot sending the messengers another way, both of these protagonists presented as justified through works: "Knowe therefore for a certeintie, all you that professe the feare of God, that fayth professed without woorkes is dead." [99]

But Chaderton goes farther in the direction of an emphasis on works than most of his contemporaries in the Protestant field would go at that time. Most of them kept closer to their own territory and tried within the framework of their own commitments to justification by faith to establish alms-giving as a part of the Christian life. Their first and most basic argument, of course, is that God commands it. That is why Sandys in a sermon delivered at Paul's Cross when he first came to be Bishop of London in 1570 could say:

"I shall therefore exhorte you the citizens of London, and in Christ Jesus require it at your handes that such order may be taken that the poore may bee provided for and not suffred to crie in your streetes." [100]

Moreover, God demands alms-giving not alone of the rich, but as Perkins in *The Whole Treatise of the Cases of Conscience* insists, of the poor as well. But since he knows that this obligation is not so generally acknowledged as the obligation of the rich to give alms, he appeals to Scripture. The oblations demanded for the maintenance of the altar in the Old Testament were expensive, and they were demanded of the poor as well as the rich. But now the material altar has been taken away, and "yet," he goes on to point out, "we have something in the roome therof, namely, those that are poore and destitute, which all men are bound, in conscience to releeve and maintaine, as once they were to maintaine the Altar." [101] This is a favorite doctrine of Perkins', on which he insists again by implication in *A Warning against the Idolatrie of the Last Times:*

"And they which are of any ability at all be it never so smal, should give something, be it never so little, in regard that reliefe is the honouring and worshipping of God." [102]

And it is a doctrine which Sandys likewise assumes when in *A Sermon made at the Spittle in London*, he holds up the example of Cornelius the Captain in the tenth chapter of Acts:

"He gave much almes to the people. This is that sacrifice which God doth require chiefly of a christian." [103]

But all the preachers seem instinctively to feel that this is not enough. Rogers out of Hemingius assembles a half dozen causes "moving to mercifulnes." The first is our Christian profession: "For this doth require that wee excell in all good woorkes, and that we make of, and cherish one another as the members of one bodie whose head is Christe." [104] The second is God's command to help the poor. The third is the example set by Christ and his members, the fourth the "dignitie and account whiche God maketh of our almes devoutly conferred." The fifth is "our neighbour hymselfe," and the sixth, "the sondrie punishementes for suche as bee harde harted." [105]

Perkins himself offers a not dissimilar series of "inducements," beginning with the commandment of God. Then he points out that spending on relief is the best kind of thrift, for it is a giving and lending to the Lord, a point which he reiterates in his third inducement when he styles relief the best exchange, for it changes earthly treasure into heavenly. The fourth recapitulates the argument already discussed, that

"releefe is a signe of Gods mercie to us-ward. Salomon saith; *By mercie and truth, sins are forgiven,* that is, within our consciences we know them to be forgiven. . . . The mercie and bowels of compassion, that is in us, is as it were a print and stampe of the mercie of God set in our heartes: and therefore by the little sparke of mercie in us, we know the fulnesse of his mercie." [106]

And the series ends with the argument that by relief comes the right use of goods. All this, he concludes, adds up to the excellency of works.[107]

But although all these arguments may be found again and again in the sermons and tracts of the times, the one which is most common is the one that might be counted on to appeal most to the sound investment instincts of the merchant of the time, and that is the idea that he who gives to the poor lends to the Lord, for as George Phillips put it, "Our Saviour accompteth that done to himselfe, which is done to poore Christians." [108]

The author of the homily on alms apparently had run into the argument that the giving of alms might impoverish the generous often enough to take time to reassure such timorous souls that God had promised that those who give to the poor will never want.[109] And he backed up his persuasion by the classic scriptural example of the poor widow who helped Elias.[110] And then he swung the argument back to the spiritual level with a paraphrase of a sentence of Saint Cyprian: "Whilest we are carefull for dymynishyng of our stocke, we are altogether carelesse to diminishe our selves." [111]

This is the classic outline of the argument as presented over and over again by the preachers of the time. Henry Smith follows the plan of the homily with unusual fidelity and, for him, unoriginality.[112] Sandys sums up the whole argument in a single terse sentence: "He that giveth to the poore lendeth to the Lorde, a sure discharger of his debts to the uttermost." [113] But it remains for Perkins to reduce the whole argument to pounds and shillings practicality:

"A man upon good security lends to another an 100. pounds hoping for the principall with the increase at the yeares end: yet dare not he skarse deliver an 100. pence to the poore members of Christ, upon the promise and bond of God himself, who saith, *Prov.* 19.17. *He that gives to the poore, lends to the Lord,* and he will returne the said gifts with a blessing." [114]

But it was enough that the Christian whether moved by scriptural example or hope of heavenly usury should give alms to the poor. It was essential that he should do so in the right spirit. Rogers' Hemingius was content to remind the alms-giver that he should avoid hypocrisy and vainglory.[115] It was not like Perkins to let the matter pass so casually, nor did he. In *The Whole Treatise of the Cases of Conscience* he drew up six requirements for the giving of alms in order that they may be good works, pleasing unto God:

"First, a man must consecrate himselfe, and all the gifts that he hath and enjoyes, to God and his honour. . . . Secondly, we must give almes *in faith* . . . first, we must be perswaded, that we are reconciled to

God in Christ, and stand in his favour: and then our almes shall be accepted. . . . Thirdly, we must give *in simplicitie* . . . that is, of meere pitie and compassion, . . . Fourthly, we must give in love. . . . Fiftly, *in justice.* For we must not give other mens goods, but our owne truely gotten. . . . Sixtly, with a bountiful and *chearefull mind.*" [116]

Here, of course, Perkins has in mind something of which the preachers of the time have a good deal to say, and that is the contempt of the rich for the poor. John Stockewood, in recommending to the clergy that they show toward their parishioners a "loving affeccion" feels obliged to add that that means not only toward the "riche and mighty," but also toward "the poore and simple people, and so much the rather towardes them, as their necessitie is the greater, and the number the fewer that in their calamities are willing too doe them good." [117] It is in the light of such contempt that Henry Smith asks the more fortunate not to despise the poor or call them names like "base rogues." [118]

Bishop Babington is even more positive in his injunctions to magistrates and rulers, judges and governors, in one of his sermons at Paul's Cross:

"O cast them not away as neare as you can, without your comfort. Their spirits are troubled, their injuries be great, their skill but small to move your affections by any orderly tale." [119]

In such a passage Babington shows a real capacity for putting himself into the place of a man in a situation very different from his own. There is no more sympathy, but there is even greater delicacy of imagination in the reminder of a sentence in Smith's *The Poor Mans Teares:* "And let us be mindfull that povertie and want compelleth many an honest person to take in hand the performance of much vilde and slavish businesse." [120]

One could hardly expect the preachers to develop the resentment of the poor against this contempt when, as we shall see in a moment, they were as concerned about promoting the proper spirit in the poor as the rich. But Arthur Warren, whose jingles often give a more popular expression of the preachers' social charges and complaints, does not feel any such inhibitions but puts into the mouth of the poor a very lively protest.

> "Poorelings but Caterpillers they account,
> Their proffits destinated to devoure,
> That Seas of sorrowes shall our Soules surmount,
> While Pride gainst Poore doth flouds of malice poure,
> Adjudging us but Burthens of the Earth,
> And Canker-wormes increasing Countries dearth." [121]

And it is typical of Warren that he does not hesitate to call the attention of the rich to the absurdity of this attitude on very secular but no less fundamental grounds, namely that the poor are really the support of the rich:

> "Diggers, and Dikers, Drudges, Carters, Swaines;
> Sheepheards, and Cowards, friend thee at thy neede,
> The poorest persons worke thy richest gaines,
> Thy Dropsie with Commodities to feede,
>   Coblers, and Curriers, Tinkers, Tanners all
>   Support thy state, else would thy fortresse fall." [122]

In general the approach of the preachers to this problem of making the rich respect the poor is, as one would expect, on more conventionally religious grounds. The basic plan is to be seen in *An Homely of Almes Dedes* in the homilies of 1563, where the homilist reminds the hesitating alms-giver that Christ himself in his life in this world was poor and needy, and that he promised to send the poor to us to supply his absence as an object of the charity all good Christians would want to have shown him. And he proceeds to develop this theme on the classic lines that the poor are dear to Christ, and in helping them we please him.[123] These points are made over and over again by the preachers on the theme of alms-giving. Turnbull gives a slightly prudential turn to the argument, when he reminds the despisers of the poor, men, as he had already pointed out, only too prone to pay homage to power and possession,[124] that "God hath chosen the poore to be heires of his kingdom." [125] But perhaps even more effective from the prudential point of view are the comminatory reminders to the proud. Jewel puts his warning in more general terms, as one would expect, in his command that "no man oppresse or defraude his brother in any matter, for the lord is an avenger of all such things." [126]

And yet for all their promises and all their threats, the preachers knew perfectly well that in commending alms-giving as in condemning usury, they were rowing against the current of their day. In a world in which the various provinces of man's activity were more and more establishing their autonomy, and the secular activities of everyday life, especially, were making good their independence of the old religious contexts, they held up the ideal of a unified plan of life to realize the plan of God, a plan to which every activity must be subservient. On the fiercely expanding energies of a very considerable class of men who were just coming to feel the pride of their strength they tried to impose a brake of social and religious limitations. To an age, of which large sections were already glimpsing the prospects of a comfort and even a splendor and a luxury which they had never known before, they held up the spiritual ideal of a very different sort of riches.

How far did they succeed and how far did they fail? That is a very difficult question to answer with any hope of precision or completeness. Certainly, in the specific field of usury they failed, as the successful expansion of the new age of industry and commerce bears witness. As regards the spirit of covetousness, that is a still more difficult question to answer, for too many imponderables are involved. That more people · devoted themselves to making money and devoted more of themselves to it would, I think, be conceded by most students of the sixteenth century. How far the preachers succeeded in mitigating that spirit is a question impossible to answer.

On alms it is easier to return a definite answer. Whatever of real purpose to effect a more equitable distribution of the world's wealth had been in the minds of the earlier preachers on behalf of the poor had certainly been pretty much attenuated in the minds of their successors. They clearly had no hope of any immediate change in the world's picture on that score. But they had hopes of moving some of the new rich to sharing their surplus with the needy, and they strove manfully for the realization of those hopes. Here it is clear that they enjoyed some real measure of success. One striking example may prove illuminating, especially since one of the preachers thought enough of it to call the attention of the public to it in a pamphlet. Most of the time, in the nature of things, preachers have to spend their eloquence talking to their failures and about their failures. It is pleasant therefore to find an Elizabethan preacher talking about what may fairly be called one of his successes, indeed, a prize exhibit. For that is what Abraham Fleming is doing in *A Memoriall of the Famous Monuments and Charitable Almesdeedes of the Right Worshipfull Maister William Lambe, Esquire*, published in 1580.[127] William Lambe, Citizen of London, had been a gentleman of the chapel in the reign of Henry and a member of the company of cloth-workers. He must have been a very rich man, to judge from the roster of his beneficences, but he was one of that saving remnant of rich men who use their wealth for the benefit of the needy.[128] He was a very religious man, given to meditation on pious literature [129] and zealous in attending sermons:

"For he hath bene seene and marked at Powles crosse, to have continued from eight of the clocke, untill eleven, attentively listening to the Preachers voice, and to have endured the ende, being weake and aged, when others both strong and lustie went away." [130]

But he was also a very practical person, possessed of considerable initiative and even originality. He certainly performed what might be called the classic works of mercy, as Fleming summed up his good deeds toward the end of his little book:

"some in relieving desolate widowes, some in succouring fatherlesse children, some in comforting impotent people, some in providing for poore prisoners, some in supporting decaied occupiers, some in amending honest maides marriages, some in susteining his housholde serv-- ants." [131]

But he went beyond these to meet, also, the special industrial needs of his day. For having seen during the course of his lifetime "the decay of sundrie trades," [132] he gave what were for those days very considerable sums of money, three hundred pounds in all, Fleming tells us, to three groups of poor clothiers, in Suffolk, at Bridgenorth in Shropshire, and at Ludlow, "for their supportation and maintenance at their worke and occupation." [133] This was a very practical form of relief. But his most famous good work was the building at his own cost without any aid from anybody else the Conduit in Holborn, a work completed in 1577.[134]

This was not, however, the limit of his beneficent public-spiritedness, as Fleming went on to point out:

"And yet further note the wisedome and providence of this Gentleman, who considering that the right use of a good thing might cut off many occasions of unthriftines and idlenesse, and knowing that we are placed in this worlde to followe the vocation whereunto wee are called: besides that, seeing the hardnes of this age wherein we live, that many would worke if they had means, many neglect and care not for worke though they have meanes, some would willingly withstand povertie if they might; some had rather begge and doe worsse than give themselves to labour, hath beene thus beneficiall to poore women that are glad to take paine, as to bestow upon them a hundred and twentie pales, wherwith to carrie and serve water: an honest shift of living, though somewhat toilsome." [135]

These works primarily concerned the body. Master William Lambe was not content to let his service to his fellow-Londoners stop there:

"For he was not onely carefull that it should goe well with the bodie, but also mindfull of the safetie of the soule. Which to be true, I fetch my confirmation from his own person, whose daily custome it was to meditate upon a Praier booke, called The Conduit of Comfort, published under his name: that with the water thereof his soule, as with the other his bodie, might be refreshed. The benefite of which booke, being bought for a litle monie, he was willing should be generall, even as the Conduit which he founded not severall but common." [136]

No wonder Fleming, himself a writer of devotional books as well as sermons, regarded Lambe with such admiration: "And thus you see what monuments this Gentleman hath left behinde him, to

beare witnesse to the worlde of the fruitfulness of his faith." [137]
No wonder, either, that he took such pains to make sure that so
sound an example of what a rich man might be was not lost.

For he wrote not only this very serious and formal treatise of
memorial, but he composed, also, "An Epitaph, or Funerall Inscription, upon the Godlie Life and Death of the Right Worshipfull Maister William Lambe Esquire" which he published in
broadside form, probably about the same time.[138] It is William
Lambe "Founder of the new Conduit in Holborne," whom he
commends to the broadside-reading public as "Rich in his life,
poore at his death, a steward of the Lordes." This effort is in
verse, rhyming fourteeners of the general literary level of the
verses in his *Diamond of Devotion.*[139] About half of the poem is
devoted to the elaboration of the theme suggested in the first
half of the first line: "All Flesh is grasse." The remainder is devoted to the praise of Mr. Lambe. Something of its literary quality
may be gauged by the following expression of the regret of the
poor for the dead philanthropist:

"Now such as had his wooll to weare, lament of him the lacke,
  His flesh did fill their bellies full, his fleese kept warme their backe,"

and by the close with its modest expression of confidence in Mr.
Lambe's present status, and its prayer that his good example may
be followed:

"His soule in Abrahams bosome restes, in quietnesse I trust:
 ⎧A place allotted unto Lambs, there to possesse in peace,
 ⎨Such blessings as this Lambe enjoyes, whose like the Lord increase,
 ⎩For Jesus sake the spotlesse Lambe. And here my penne shall cease."

But whatever the precise degree of credit to be given to either
the beneficent cloth-worker or his clerical panegyrist, Mr. Lambe
was, fortunately, not unique. There is another broadside of the
time which commemorates the charity and practical benefactions
of "Master Robert Rogers, Marchant Adventurer and Leatherseller of London, deceased, who declared the fruites of his faith,
by his most christian and charitable workes" and who died in
1601.[140] The broadside poet emphasizes especially his careful

stewardship of his wealth and his bestowal of it for the relief of his fellows.

There is certainly no need of multiplying examples of the public spirit of the newly risen middle classes. The history of the various forms of benevolence and charity of the time abounds in such cases, especially toward the end of the century. This increase of middle-class benevolence clearly helped to repair some of the ravages of the destruction of the monuments and endowments of the old philanthropy, and it achieved new splendors of its own. For this the preachers may clearly, I think, be given a fair, if not the major, share of credit. But it can hardly be said that this was any innovation in the life of England. Rather it was the carrying forward of an ancient tradition into new conditions and circumstances.

NOTES

CHAPTER I

THE PIERS PLOWMAN TRADITION

1. See, for instance, M. Beer, *Social Struggles in the Middle Ages*, trans. H. J. Stenning (London, 1924), chap. ii.
2. G. R. Owst, *Literature and Pulpit in Medieval England* (Cambridge, 1933).
3. William Langland, *The Vision of William concerning Piers the Plowman*, ed. W. W. Skeat (Oxford, 1886) pass. vii, 11. 104–5. Unless otherwise specified, all references are to the B text.
4. *Ibid.*, pass. iii, 11. 121–68.
5. *Ibid.*, pass. xvi, 1. 27.
6. *Ibid.*, pass. xv, 11. 304–7.
7. *Ibid.*, pass. xi, 11. 274–76.
8. *Ibid.*, pass. iv, 11. 108–14 (C text).
9. *Ibid.*, pass. v, 11. 209–18.
10. *Ibid.*, iii, 1. 78.
11. *Ibid.*, pass. ix, 11. 98–106.
12. *Ibid.*, pass. vi, 11. 25–29.
13. *Ibid.*, pass. xix, 11. 432–36.
14. *Ibid.*, pass. i, 1. 202.
15. *Ibid.*, pass. ix, 11. 199–200.
16. *Ibid.*, pass. xvii, 11. 244–70.
17. *Ibid.*, pass. i, 11. 186–87.
18. *Ibid.*, pass. xvii, 11. 344–48.
19. *Ibid.*, pass. vii, 11. 68–72.
20. *Ibid.*, pass. vi, 11. 70–77.
21. *Ibid.*, pass. xiv, 11. 271–72.
22. *Ibid.*, pass. x, 11. 69–70.
23. *Ibid.*, pass. xiv, 11. 164–65.
24. *Ibid.*, pass. xiii, 11. 437–52.
25. *Ibid.*, pass. vi, 11. 47–49.
26. *Ibid.*, pass. x, 11. 332–37.
27. *Ibid.*, pass. xiv, 11. 279–319.
28. *Ibid.*, pass. xiv, 11. 104–110.
29. *Ibid.*, pass. xvii, 1. 21 (C text).
30. *Ibid.*, pass. x, 11. 458–59.
31. *Ibid.*, pass. x, 11. 456–57.
32. *Ibid.*, pass. xv, 11. 192–94.
33. *Ibid.*, pass. xv, 1. 206.
34. *Ibid.*, pass. x, 11. 112–113 (A text).
35. *Ibid.*, pass. xiv, 1. 99 (C text).
36. *Ibid.*, pass. xiv, 11. 259–60.

37. *Ibid.*, pass. xi, 11. 52–54.
38. *Ibid.*, pass. xv, 11. 223–26.
39. *Ibid.*, pass. xx, 11. 376–77.
40. *Ibid.*, pass. xviii, 11. 233–38 (C text).
41. *Ibid.*, pass. x, 11. 13–21 (C text).
42. *Ibid.*, pass. x, 11. 89–90 (A text).
43. *Ibid.*, pass. viii, 11. 305–6 (C text).
44. *Ibid.*, pass. xix, 11. 242–43.
45. *Ibid.*, pass. x, 11. 300–1.
46. *Ibid.*, pass. vi, 11. 9–19.
47. *Ibid.*, pass. vi, 11. 185–89 (C text).
48. *Ibid.*, pass. xx, 1. 274.
49. *Ibid.*, pass. xiii, 11. 12–13.
50. Owst, *op. cit.*, pp. 548–49.
51. See Herbert B. Workman, *John Wyclif: a Study of the English Medieval Church* (Oxford, 1926), Vol. II, Book III, chaps. iv. and viii.
52. John Wyclif, *Epistolae Dominicales*, XXVIII, in *Select English Works*, ed. Thomas Arnold (Oxford, 1871), II, 303.
53. Wyclif, *Sermons on the Gospels for Sundays and Festivals*, LXXXVI, in *Select English Works*, I, 299.
54. *Ibid.*, CXIII, p. 380.
55. Wyclif, *De Blasphemia, contra Fratres*, Pars III, in *Select English Works*, III, 420–22.
56. Wyclif, *Vae Octuplex*, in *Select English Works*, II, 379–85, editor's marginal summaries.
57. Wyclif, *Vae Octuplex*, p. 386.
58. *Ibid.*, p. 387.
59. *Ibid.*, p. 388.
60. Wyclif, from *De Papa*, cap. x, in *Select English Writings*, ed. Herbert E. Winn (Oxford, 1929), p. 83.
61. Wyclif, *Sermons on the Gospels for Sundays and Festivals*, LXIV, p. 199.
62. Wyclif, *De Apostasia Cleri*, cap. ii, in *Select English Works*, III, 433.
63. *Ibid.*, cap. iv, p. 438.
64. Wyclif, [*Church Temporalities*], cap. ii, in *Select English Works*, III, 215–16.
65. Wyclif, from *De Officio Pastorali*, cap. ix, in *Select English Writings*, pp. 84–85.
66. Wyclif, from *The Grete Sentence of Curs Expouned*, in *Select English Writings*, pp. 34–35.
67. Wyclif, *Sermons on the Gospels for Sundays and Festivals*, L, p. 147.
68. Wyclif, from *De Officio Pastorali*, cap. ix, in *Select English Writings*, p. 84.
69. Wyclif, *The Church and Her Members*, cap. ix, in *Select English Writings*, p. 133.
70. Wyclif, from *De Officio Pastorali*, caps. vi and vii, p. 81.
71. Wyclif, *Sermons on the Gospels for Sundays and Festivals*, CXV, p. 386.
72. Wyclif, *Epistolae Dominicales*, L, p. 364.
73. See Wyclif, *Sermons on the Gospels for Sundays and Festivals*, LXVI, p. 209, and LXXXV, pp. 291–92.
74. See Workman, *John Wyclif*, II, 94.
75. Wyclif, *Sermons on the Gospels for Sundays and Festivals*, XXIII, p. 58 and LXV, pp. 202–3
76. *Ibid.*, LXIV, pp. 200–1.
77. *Ibid.*, LXXXV, p. 292.
78. Wyclif, *Of Mynystris in the Chirche*, in *Select English Works*, II, 414.
79. Wyclif, *Sermons on the Gospels for Sundays and Festivals*. LXIII, p. 176.

80. *Ibid.,* LXIV, p. 200 and LXXXIII, p. 282.
81. Wyclif, *The Church and her Members,* cap. ix, p. 133.
82. Wyclif, *Sermons on the Gospels for Sundays and Festivals,* XLII, p. 119.
83. Wyclif, [*Church Temporalities*], cap. ii, p. 215.
84. Wyclif, *De Blasphemia, contra Fratres,* Pars II, p. 416.
85. Wyclif, *Epistolae Dominicales,* XV, p. 269.
86. Wyclif, *Church Temporalities,* cap. iii, pp. 216–17.
87. Wyclif, from *A Petition to the King and Parliament,* in *Select English Writings,* p. 65.
88. Wyclif, *Epistolae Dominicales,* XXV, p. 296.
89. Wyclif, *Church Temporalities,* cap. i, p. 214.
90. Wyclif, *Sermons on the Gospels for Sundays and Festivals,* LXXIX, p. 265.
91. Wyclif, [*Church Temporalities*], cap. i, pp. 213–14.
92. Wyclif, *Sermons on the Gospels for Sundays and Festivals,* LXVII, p. 212.
93. *Ibid.*
94. Wyclif, *Epistolae Dominicales,* XLV, p. 353.
95. Wyclif, *Sermons on the Gospels for Sundays and Festivals,* X, p. 26.
96. Wyclif, *Sermons on the Ferial Gospels and Sunday Epistles,* CCXXVIII, in *Select English Works,* II, 200–1.
97. Wyclif, from *Of Servants and Lords,* in *Select English Writings,* p. 101.
98. Wyclif, from *Five Questions on Love,* in *Select English Writings,* p. 111.
99. Wyclif, [*On the Seven Deadly Sins*], cap. xx, in *Select English Works,* III, 147.
100. Wyclif, from *Of Servants and Lords,* p. 100.
101. Wyclif, *Epistolae Dominicales,* XXV, p. 296.
102. Wyclif, from *Of Servants and Lords,* p. 104.
103. Wyclif, *Sermons on the Ferial Gospels and Sunday Epistles,* CCXII, p. 180.
104. Wyclif, *Epistolae Dominicales,* VIII, p. 245.
105. Wyclif, from *Of Servants and Lords,* p. 103.
106. *Ibid.*
107. Wyclif, from *The Grete Sentence of Curs Expouned,* p. 104.
108. Wyclif, *Epistolae Dominicales,* IV, p. 233.
109. Wyclif, *Sermons on the Ferial Gospels,* CXL, p. 28.
110. Wyclif, *Sermons on the Gospels for Sundays and Festivals,* LXXXI, p. 272.
111. *Ibid.,* CXIV, p. 384.
112. *Ibid.,* CXVII, p. 392.
113. See Workman, *John Wyclif,* II, 8 ff.
114. Wyclif, *Sermons on the Gospels for Sundays and Festivals,* LXXV, p. 245.
115. *Ibid.,* VIII, p. 21
116. *Ibid.*
117. Wyclif, *Sermons on the Ferial Gospels,* CCII, p. 164.
118. Wyclif, *Sermons on the Gospels for Sundays and Festivals,* XIV, p. 35.
119. Wyclif, from *Of Confession,* in *Select English Writings,* p. 94.
120. For Wyclif's realism see Workman, *John Wyclif,* Vol. I, Book I, chap. iv, "Wyclif's Place among the Schoolmen."
121. Wyclif, *De Blasphemia, contra Fratres,* Pars III, p. 427.
122. [*Wyclif's Confessio*], in *Select English Writings,* p. 87.
123. Workman, *John Wyclif,* II, 118.
124. Wyclif, *De Blasphemia, contra Fratres,* Pars I, p. 407.
125. Wyclif, from *The Church and her Members,* cap. vi, p. 129.
126. Wyclif, *Epistolae Dominicales,* LV, p. 376.
127. Wyclif, *Sermons on the Gospels for Sundays and Festivals,* VI, p. 15, and XL, p. 111.
128. *Ibid.,* XXXII, p. 85.

129. Wyclif, *Epistolae Dominicales*, II, p. 227, XLVII, p. 358.
130. *Ibid.*, XXXII, p. 318.
131. Wyclif, *De Blasphemia, contra Fratres*, Pars II, p. 418.
132. Wyclif, from *A Petition to the King and Parliament*, p. 64.
133. Wyclif, *Epistolae Dominicales*, LV, p. 376.
134. *Ibid.*, XIX, p. 279.
135. Wyclif, *Of Mynystris in the Chirche*, p. 420.
136. Wyclif, *Sermons on the Gospels for Sundays and Festivals*, LXVI, p. 209.
137. *Ibid.*
138. Wyclif, *Epistolae Dominicales*, XXVII, p. 300.
139. Wyclif, *Sermons on the Gospels for Sundays and Festivals*, LXIX, pp. 220–22.
140. Wyclif, *Epistolae Dominicales*, LIII, p. 371.
141. *Ibid.*, p. 370.
142. Wyclif, *De Apostasia Cleri*, cap. ii, p. 434.
143. Wyclif, *Of Mynystris in the Chirche*, p. 421.
144. Wyclif, *Sermons on the Ferial Gospels*, CXLIX, p. 50, and *Sermons on the Gospels for Sundays and Festivals*, LVIII, p. 176.
145. Wyclif, *Sermons on the Gospels for Sundays and Festivals*, LXI, p. 186.
146. Wyclif, [*On the Seven Deadly Sins*,] cap. xviii, p. 143.
147. Wyclif, from *Of Feigned Contemplative Life*, in *Select English Writings*, pp. 92–93.
148. *Ibid.*, p. 90.
149. *Ibid.*
150. Wyclif, *Epistolae Dominicales*, VI, p. 240.
151. *Ibid.*, XLIII, p. 347.
152. Wyclif, *Sermons on the Gospels for Sundays and Festivals*, LXXIV, p. 241.
153. Wyclif, *Of Mynystris in the Chirche*, p. 394.
154. *Ibid.*, p. 395.
155. Wyclif, from *The Church and her Members*, cap. iii, p. 124.
156. Wyclif, *Sermons on the Gospels for Sundays and Festivals*, LXI, p. 189.
157. Wyclif, from *The Church and her Members*, cap. x, p. 135.
158. Wyclif, *Sermons on the Gospels for Sundays and Festivals*, VIII, p. 19.
159. *Ibid.*, XLV, p. 128.
160. Wyclif, *Epistolae Dominicales*, XXVI, p. 297.
161. Wyclif, *Sermons on the Gospels for Sundays and Festivals*, XLI, pp. 113–14.
162. Wyclif, from *De Papa*, cap. x, p. 83.
163. Workman, *John Wyclif*, I, 7, 12.
164. Roberte Langelande, *The Vision of Pierce Plowman* (London: Roberte Crowley, 1550).
165. *Ibid.*, sig. *2.
166. Roberte Langelande, *The Vision of Pierce Plowman*, "nowe the seconde time imprinted," (London: Roberte Crowley, 1550), sigs. *3–¢4.
167. *Ibid.*, sig. *3.
168. *Ibid.*, sig. D4.
169. *Ibid.*, sig. K3.
170. *Ibid.*, sig. Ff3.
171. *The Praier and Complaynte of the Ploweman unto Christe* (n.p. 1531 [Antwerp: M. Lempereur, 1531?]).
172. *Ibid.*, sig. E5v.
173. *Pierce the Ploughmans Crede* (London: Reynold Wolfe, 1553).
174. *The Praier and Complaynte of the Ploweman unto Christe*, sig. B7v.
175. *Ibid.*, sig. F2.
176. *Ibid.*, sigs. E6v–E7v.

177. *Pyers Plowmans Exhortation, unto the Lordes, Knightes and Burgoysses of the Parlyamenthouse* (London: Anthony Scoloker [1550]).
178. *Ibid.*, sigs. A1v–A2.
179. *Ibid.*, sig. A4.
180. *Ibid.*, sigs. A5–A5v.
181. *Ibid.*, sig. A2v.
182. [Francis, Thynne], *Newes from the North* (London: John Allde, 1579).
183. *Ibid.*, sig. B3.
184. *Ibid.*
185. *Ibid.*, sig. B4.
186. *Ibid.*, sig. C3v.
187. *Ibid.*, sig., K1v.
188. *I Playne Piers* [N. Hyll? 1550?].
189. *Ibid.*, sigs. A7v–A8.
190. Percy Simpson, *Proof-reading in the Sixteenth, Seventeenth, and Eighteenth Centuries* (London, 1935), p. 69.
191. *A Godly Dyalogue and Dysputacyon betwene Pyers Plowman, and a Popysh Preest concernyng the Supper of the Lorde* (n.p. [, 1530?]).
192. *Ibid.*, sig. A3.
193. *Ibid.*
194. *Ibid.*, sig. A7.
195. *Ibid.*, sig. A8.
196. *The Praier and Complaynte of the Ploweman unto Christe*, sigs. B7v and F2.
197. *Ibid.*, sigs. F4–F4v.
198. *I Playne Piers*, sigs. E3v–E4.
199. *The Praier and Complaynte of the Ploweman unto Christe*, sig. C5.
200. *A Godly Dyalogue and Dysputacyon betwene Pyers Plowman, and a Popysh Preest*, sigs. A3v–A7v.
201. *The Praier and Complaynte of the Ploweman unto Christe*, sigs. B3–B4.
202. *Ibid.*, sigs. A1v–A2v.
203. Francis Thynne, *The Debate betweene Pride and Lowliness* (London: John Charlwood for Rafe Newberry [, 1570]).
204. *Ibid.*, sig. A5.
205. *Ibid.*, sig. E3.
206. Geffray Chaucer, *The Plowmans Tale* (London: Wyllyam Hyll [, 1545?]).
207. Geffrey Chaucer, *The Plough-mans Tale* (London: G. E. for Samuell Macham and Mathew Cooke, 1606)—Huntington Library Photostat 232493 of Bodleian Library copy, Malone, 315.
208. Geoffrey Chaucer, *Jack Up Lande* (London: for John Gough [,ca. 1540?]).
209. *Ibid.*, sig. A1v.
210. *Ibid.*, sigs. A5v–A6.
211. *Ibid.*, sigs. A6v–A7.
212. *Ibid.*, sigs. B4v–B5.
213. *Ibid.*, sig. B2v.
214. *Ibid.*, sig. B5.
215. *Ibid.*, sig. B8v.
216. Chaucer, *The Plowmans Tale*, sig. D1.
217. See above, pp. 6 and 10–11.
218. Chaucer, *The Plowmans Tale*, sig. A2v.
219. *Ibid.*, sig. A3.
220. *Ibid.*, sig. A3.
221. *Ibid.*, sig. A3v.
222. See above, p. 27.

223. Chaucer, *The Plowmans Tale,* sig. C8v.
224. *Ibid.*
225. *Ibid.,* sig. D4v.
226. *Ibid.,* sig. B2v.
227. *Ibid.,* sig. D3v.
228. *Ibid.,* sig. B8.
229. *Ibid.,* sig. B8v.
230. *Ibid.,* sigs. B6–B6v.
231. Chaucer, *The Plough-mans Tale* (1606).
232. *Pyers Plowmans Exhortation unto the Lordes, Knightes and Burgoysses of the Parlyamenthouse,* sigs. A4–A4v.
233. *Ibid.,* sig. A2.

Chapter II

The Utopia and Commonwealth Tradition

1. R. W. Chambers, *Thomas More* (London, 1938), pp. 125–31.
2. Sir Thomas More, *A Fruteful and Pleasaunt Worke of the Beste State of a Publyque Weale, and of the New Yle called Utopia,* trans. Raphe Robynson (London: Abraham Vele, 1551), sig. B3.
3. *Ibid.,* sig. B2v.
4. *Ibid.,* sig. B8v.
5. *Ibid.*
6. *Ibid.,* sigs. E4v–E5.
7. For instance, *ibid.,* sig. Gl.
8. *Ibid.,* sig. C3v.
9. *Ibid.*
10. *Ibid.,* sig. C4v.
11. *Ibid.*
12. *Ibid.,* sigs. C6v–C7.
13. *Ibid.,* sigs. C7v–C8.
14. William Langland, *The Vision of William concerning ···ers the Plowman,* ed. W. W. Skeat (Oxford, 1886), pass. xx, 1. 274.
15. More, *op. ci·.,* sigs. E4v–E5.
16. *Ibid.,* sig. I2v.
17. *Ibid.,* sig. M5.
18. *Ibid.,* sig. H8.
19. *Ibid.,* sigs. F5–F5v
20. *Ibid.,* sigs. E2v–E3.
21. *Ibid.,* sigs. O7–O7v.
22. *Ibid.,* sig. B8v.
23. *Ibid.,* sig. F3.
24. *Ibid.,* sigs. G7–G7v.
25. *Ibid.,* sig. F3.
26. *Ibid.,* sigs. G7–G7v.
27. *Ibid.,* sigs. H6v–H7.
28. *Ibid.,* sig. Il.
29. *Ibid.,* sigs. G3v–G4.
30. *Ibid.,* sigs. L2v–L3.

31. *Ibid.* sig. H4v.
32. *Ibid.*, sig. I2v.
33. M. Beer, *Social Struggles in the Middle Ages* (London, 1924), pp. 13, 29 ff.
34. More, *op. cit.*, sigs. G1–G1v.
35. *Ibid.*, sig. R7.
36. *Ibid.*, sigs. G1v–G2.
37. *Ibid.*, sigs. R7v–R8v.
38. *Ibid.*, sig. S1.
39. *Ibid.*
40. *Ibid.*
41. See above, pp. 10–11.
42. More, *op. cit.*, sig. I1v.
43. *Ibid.*, sigs. I1–I1v.
44. *Ibid.*, sig. G2v.
45. *Ibid.*, sig. G3 ff.
46. *Ibid.*, sig. S3v.
47. *Ibid.*, sig. Q2.
48. *Ibid.*, sigs. S3v–S4.
49. *Ibid.*, sig. O2.
50. *Ibid.*, sigs. Q1–Q1v.
51. *Ibid.*, sig. L5.
52. *Ibid.*, L5v.
53. *Ibid.*, sig. Q4.
54. *Ibid.*
55. Chambers, *op. cit.*, pp. 134–46.
56. More, *op. cit.*, sig. Q7.
57. *Ibid.*, sig. Q7v.
58. *Ibid.*, sig. R1.
59. *Ibid.*, sig. R1v.
60. *Ibid.*, sig. R1.
61. *Ibid.*, sig. Q3.
62. *Ibid.*, sigs. Q3–Q3v.
63. *Ibid.*, sig. Q4.
64. *Ibid.*, sigs. Q4v–Q5.
65. See above, p. 11.
66. Langland, *op. cit.*, pass. xii, 1. 275 ff.
67. More, *op. cit.*, sig. I5.
68. Raphe Robynson, Dedicatory Address to More, *op. cit.*, sig. +4.
69. *Ibid.*, sig. +5v.
70. *Ibid.*, sig. +2.
71. *Ibid.*, sig. +3v.
72. More, *op. cit.*, sig. Q4v.
73. *The Prayse and Commendacion of Suche as Sought Comen Welthes: and to the Contrary, the Ende and Discommendacion of Such as Sought Private Welthes* (London: Anthony Scoloker [, 1548?]), sig. A7v.
74. *Ibid.*, sig. A2.
75. *Ibid.*, sig. A2v.
76. *Ibid.*, sig. A3v.
77. *Ibid.*, sigs. A4–A4v.
78. *Ibid.*, sigs. A4v–A5.
79. *Ibid.*, sig. A5v.
80. *Ibid.*, sigs. A7–A7v.
81. *Ibid.*, sig. A7v.

82. *Ibid.*, sig. A8.
83. *Ibid.*, sigs. A8–B2.
84. *Ibid.*, sig. B2.
85. *Ibid.*, sigs. B2–B4.
86. Thomas Starkey, *A Dialogue between Cardinal Pole and Thomas Lupset, Lecturer in Rhetoric at Oxford* in *England in the Reign of King Henry the Eighth*, Part II, ed. J. M. Cowper, E.E.T.S. (London, 1878).
87. *Thomas Starkey's Life and Letters* in *England in the Reign of King Henry the Eighth*, Part I, ed. J. M. Cowper, E.E.T.S. (London, 1878), p. x ff.
88. *Ibid.*, p. vii.
89. Starkey, *Dialogue*, p. 6.
90. *Ibid.*, p. 196.
91. *Ibid.*, p. 197.
92. *Ibid.*, p. 26.
93. *Ibid.*, p. 163.
94. See, for instance, *ibid.*, pp. 96–100.
95. *Ibid.*, p. 60.
96. *Ibid.*, p. 35.
97. *Ibid.*, p. 77.
98. *Ibid.*, p. 156.
99. *Ibid.*, p. 200.
100. *Ibid.*, pp. 72–73.
101. *Ibid.*, pp. 76–77.
102. *Ibid.*, pp. 86–87.
103. *Ibid.*, p. 77.
104. *Ibid.*, p. 97.
105. *Ibid.*, p. 42.
106. *Ibid.*, p. 119.
107. *Ibid.*, p. 19.
108. *Ibid.*, p. 56.
109. *Ibid.*, p. 33.
110. *Ibid.*, p. 180.
111. *Ibid.*, p. 167.
112. Saint Thomas Aquinas, *The "Summa Theologica,"* trans. Fathers of the English Dominican Province, Part II (Second Part), Second Number, X (London, 1918), Q. 42. Art. 2, 518.
113. Starkey, *Dialogue*, p. 163.
114. *Ibid.*, p. 107.
115. *Ibid.*, pp. 107–8.
116. *Ibid.*, p. 163.
117. *Ibid.*, pp. 181–82.
118. W[illiam] S[tafford], *A Compendious or Briefe Examination of Certayne Ordinary Complaints, of Divers of Our Country Men in These Our Dayes* (London: Thomas Marshe, 1581).
119. [John Hales], *A Discourse of the Common Weal of this Realm of England*, ed. Elizabeth Lamond (Cambridge, 1929), p. 107.
120. *Ibid.*, p. 150, editor's note.
121. *Ibid.*, pp. xxii–xxiii.
122. *Ibid.*, pp. 10–12.
123. *Ibid.*, p. 10.
124. *Ibid.*, pp. lvi–lvii.
125. *Ibid.*, p. 21.
126. *Ibid.*

127. See Beer, *op. cit.*, pp. 107, 178–79.
128. Hales, *A Discourse of the Common Weal of this Realm of England*, p. 21.
129. *Ibid.*, pp. 131–32.
130. *Ibid.*, pp. 132–33.
131. *Ibid.*, p. 49.
132. *Ibid.*, p. 50.
133. *Ibid.*, p. 51.
134. *Ibid.*, p. 52.
135. *Ibid.*, p. 57.
136. *Ibid.*, p. 115.
137. *Ibid.*, p. 49.
138. *Ibid.*, pp. 138–39.
139. *Ibid.*, p. 31.
140. *Ibid.*, p. 29.
141. *Ibid.*, p. 132.
142. For instance, *ibid.*, pp. 63, 107.
143. Stafford, *A Compendious or Briefe Examination of Certayne Ordinary Complaints:* see above, ftn. 118.
144. *Ibid.*, sig. **2.
145. *Ibid.*, sigs. **2–**2v.
146. Hales, *A Discourse of the Common Weal of this Realm of England*, p. xxxiii and Stafford, *A Compendious Examination of Certayne Ordinary Complaints*, sig. C3v ff.
147. *Politique Discourses, treating of the Differences and Inequalities of Vocations, as well Publique, as Private*, trans. Aegremont Ratcliffe (London: for Edward Aggas, 1578).
148. *Ibid.*, sig. A3v.
149. *Ibid.*, sig. I3v.
150. *Ibid.*, sigs. A2–A2v.
151. *Ibid.*, sigs. V4v–X1.
152. Thomas Floyd, *The Picture of a Perfit Common Wealth* (London: Simon Stafford, 1600).
153. *Ibid.*, sig., A1.
154. *Ibid.*, sigs. B9v–B10.
155. *Ibid.*, sigs. B12v–C1.
156. *Ibid.*, sigs. O9–O10.
157. Gerrard de Malynes, *A Treatise of the Canker of Englands Common Wealth* (London: Richard Field for William Johnes, 1601), sig. A2.
158. Gerrard de Malynes, *Saint George for England, Allegorically Described* (London: Richard Field for William Tymme, 1601), sig. A2.
159. *Ibid.*, sigs. A6–A6v.
160. Malynes, *A Treatise*, sigs. B1–B1v.
161. *Ibid.*, sigs. G7–G7v.
162. *Ibid.*, sig. I6v.

CHAPTER III

The Reformers and the Wealth of the Church

1. [Henry Parker], *Dives and Pauper* (London: Richarde Pynson, 1493), sig. e8v.
2. *Ibid.*, sig. iia.

3. *Ibid.*

4. *Ibid.,* iiav.

5. *Ibid.,* sigs. A5v–A6.

6. *Ibid.,* sig. B3.

7. *Ibid.,* sig. B2v.

8. *Ibid.,* sig. m6v.

9. *Ibid.*

10. See above, pp. 26–27.

11. Parker, *op. cit.,* sig. m6v.

12. *Ibid.,* H2.

13. *Ibid.,* sig. H1.

14. *Ibid.,* sig. o1v.

15. *Ibid.,* sig. n4.

16. *Ibid.,* sig. H1.

17. *Ibid.,* sig. H1v.

18. *Ibid.,* sig. f5v.

19. *Ibid.,* sig. f6.

20. *Ibid.*

21. *Ibid.,* sig. f6v.

22. *Ibid.,* sigs. I5–I5v.

23. *Dictionary of National Biography* (London, 1895), XLIII, 237.

24. Symon Fyshe, *The Supplication of Beggers* (n.p., 1524).

25. R. W. Chambers, *Thomas More* (London, 1938), pp. 254–55, 258–62.

26. John Foxe, *Actes and Monuments of These Latter and Perilous Dayes, touching Matters of the Church* (London: John Day, 1563), sig. Ss3v.

27. *Ibid.,* sig. Ss1ff.

28. Fyshe, *op. cit.,* sig. c8.

29. *Ibid.,* sigs. d8–d8v.

30. Hugh Latimer, *The Fyrste Sermon . . . whiche he preached before the Kynges Majest. wythin his Graces Palayce at Westmynster* (March 8, 1549) (London: Jhon Daye and William Seres [1549]), sig. C2v.

31. William Langland, *The Vision of William concerning Piers the Plowman,* ed. W. W. Skeat (Oxford, 1886), pass. x, 11. 300–1.

32. See above, p. 10.

33. John Wycliff, *Sermons on the Gospels for Sundays and Festivals,* CXVII in *Select English Works,* ed. Thomas Arnold (Oxford, 1871), I, 392.

34. Foxe, *op. cit.,* sig. PPPp3v.

35. Chambers, *op. cit.,* pp. 259–62.

36. Henry Brinkelow, *The Complaint of Roderyck Mors, sometime a Gray Fryre, unto the Parlament House of Ingland* (Geneve: Myghell Boys [London: A. Scoloker and W. Seres, 1548?]), sig. C3.

37. *Ibid.*

38. *Thomas Starkey's Life and Letters* in *England in the Reign of King Henry the Eighth,* Part I, ed. J. M. Cowper, E.E.T.S. (London, 1878), pp. xlviii–lxiii.

39. *Ibid.,* p. liv.

40. *Ibid.*

41. *Ibid.,* p. lviii.

42. *Ibid.*

43. Thomas Lever, *A Fruitfull Sermon made in Poules Churche at London in the Shroudes, the Seconde Daye of Februari* (London: Jhon Daie and Wylliam Seres, 1550), sig. B7v. See also *A Godlie Treatice concerning the Lawful Use of Ritches* which Thomas Rogers took "in effecte" out of Nicolas Hemingius' *Commentaries* and published in 1578 (London: for Andrew Maunsel), sig. Q3, where the same point of view is presented.

44. Henry Gee, *The Elizabethan Prayer-Book and Ornaments* (London, 1902), p. 23.
45. *Ibid.*, p. 207.
46. *Ibid.*, p. 208.
47. [Robert Crowley], *An Informacion and Peticion agaynst the Oppressours of the Pore Commons of this Realme* ([London: J. Day, 1548]), sig. A2.
48. Thomas Lever, *A Sermon preached at Pauls Crosse, the .XIIII. Day of December* (London: Jhon Day, 1550), sigs. D8–D8v.
49. Lever, *A Fruitfull Sermon made in Poules Churche*, sig. B8.
50. [Simon Fish], *A Supplication of the Poore Commons* (n.p., 1546) sig. b6.
51. Thomas Beacon, *The Jewel of Joy* in *The Seconde Part of the Bokes, which Thomas Beacon hath made* (London: [J. Day], 1560), sig. CCc5.
52. Brinkelow, *op. cit.*, sig. D3.
53. *Ibid.*, sigs. D3v–D4.
54. R. H. Tawney and Eileen Power, eds. *Tudor Economic Documents* (London, 1924), I. 301–2.
55. See, for instance, Thomas Lever, *A Sermon preached the Fourth Sundaye in Lente before the Kynges Majestie, and his Honorable Counsell* (London: John Day, 1550), sig. E1v.
56. *Ibid.*, sigs. E2v–E3.
57. Lever, *A Sermon preached at Pauls Crosse*, sig. D7v.
58. For an historic instance, see Tawney and Power, *op. cit.*, I, 19–29.
59. R. H. Tawney, *The Agrarian Problem in the Sixteenth Century* (London, 1912), p. 172.
60. *Ibid.*, pp. 151–52.
61. *Ibid.*, p. 166.
62. *Ibid.*, pp. 73–75.
63. *Ibid.*, p. 150.
64. *Ibid.*, p. 191.
65. *Ibid.*, p. 229–30.
66. *Ibid.*, pp. 114–15.
67. *Ibid.*, pp. 229–30.
68. *Ibid.*, pp. 279–80.
69. *Ibid.*, p. 310.
70. *Ibid.*, pp. 407–8.
71. *Ibid.*, p. 381.
72. *Ibid.*, pp. 214–15.
73. *Ibid.*, pp. 268–70.
74. Beacon, *The Jewel of Joy*, sig. CCc4v.
75. Latimer, *The Fyrste Sermon*, sigs. D4–D4v.
76. *Ibid.*, sigs. D2v–D3.
77. *Ibid.*, sigs. D5–D6.
78. Brinkelow, *op. cit.*, sig. A7.
79. R[obert] P[owell], *Depopulation Arraigned, Convicted and Condemned, by the Lawes of God and Man* (London: R. B., 1636), sig. E2v.
80. Lever, *A Fruitfull Sermon made in Poules Churche*, sigs, B4–B4v.
81. Fyshe, *The Supplication of Beggers*, sig. c8.
82. Fish, *A Supplication of the Poore Commons*, sig. b5.
83. Hemingius, *A Godlie Treatice concerning the Lawful Use of Ritches*, sigs. P4–P4v.
84. Lever, *A Sermon preached the Fourth Sundaye in Lente*, sigs. E3–E3v.
85. John Weever, *The Mirror of Martyrs* (London: V. S. for William Wood, 1601), sig. B8v.
86. Hughe Latemer, *The Fifte Sermon* (preached before the king, April 5, 1549), printed in collection of sermons with titlepage, *The Seconde Sermon of Master*

Hughe Latemer, whych he preached before the Kynges Majestie, within hys Graces Palayce at Westminster (March 15, 1549) (London: Jhon Daye and William Seres 1549), sigs. P7–P7v.

87. *Ibid.*, sigs. P7v–P8.
88. Lever, *A Sermon preached at Pauls Crosse*, sig. E1v.
89. Lever, *A Fruitfull Sermon made in Poules Churche*, sig. B7.
90. Fish, *A Supplication of the Poore Commons*, see above, ftn. 50.
91. *Ibid.*, sig. a8.
92. *Ibid.*, sig. a3v.
93. *Ibid.*, sig. a8.
94. *Ibid.*, sig. a2.
95. *Ibid.*, sig. b6.
96. Foxe, *op. cit.*, sig. Ii6v.
97. Brinkelow, *op. cit.*: see above, ftn. 36.
98. *Ibid.*, sig. F5v.
99. *Ibid.*, sig. G1v.
100. *Ibid.*, sigs. F4–F4v.
101. *Ibid.*, sig. F4v.
102. *Ibid.*, sig. F3.
103. *Ibid.*, sig. F5.
104. Robert Crowley, *The Way to Wealth* (London: Robert Crowley, 1550).
105. *Ibid.*, sig. B6v.
106. *Ibid.*, sig. A8v.
107. *Ibid.*, sig. B5.

Chapter IV

Social Radicalism and Religious Reform

1. [Robert Crowley], *An Informacion and Peticion agaynst the Oppressours of the Pore Commons of this Realms* (London: J. Day, 1548).
2. *Ibid.*, sig. A1.
3. *Ibid.*, sig. A2.
4. *Ibid.*, sigs. A3–A4.
5. *Ibid.*, sig. A4.
6. *Ibid.*
7. *Ibid.*, sigs. A7v–A8.
8. *Ibid.*, sig. B4 ff.
9. *Ibid.*, sig. A5.
10. *Ibid.*, sigs. B2–B2v.
11. *Ibid.*, sig. A5v.
12. *Ibid.*, sig. A8v.
13. *Ibid.*, sigs. B2v–B3.
14. For instance, John Bromyard, the thirteenth-century English Dominican. See G. R. Owst, *Literature and Pulpit in Medieval England* (Cambridge, 1933), p. 299.
15. Robert Crowley, *The Way to Wealth* (London: Robert Crowley, 1550).
16. R. H. Tawney, *The Agrarian Problem in the Sixteenth Century* (London, 1912), p. 318.
17. *Ibid.*, p. 383.

18. *Ibid.*, p. 316.
19. Frances Rose-Troup, *The Western Rebellion of 1549* (London, 1913), p. 167.
20. *Ibid.*, p. 7.
21. *Ibid.*, p. 407.
22. *Ibid.*, p. 229.
23. *Ibid.*, p. 347.
24. Tawney, *op. cit.*, p. 338.
25. Crowley, *The Way to Wealth*, sigs. B2v–B3.
26. Tawney, *op. cit.*, p. 330.
27. *Ibid.*, p. 333.
28. Thomas Lever, *A Fruitfull Sermon made in Poules Churche at London in the Shroudes, the Seconde Daye of Februari* (London: Jhon Daie and Wylliam Seres, 1550), sigs. B3v–B4.
29. Robert Wilkinson, *A Sermon preached at North-Hampton the 21. of June Last Past, before the Lord Lieutenant of the County, and the Rest of the Commissioners there assembled upon Occasion of the Late Rebellion and Riots in those Parts committed* (London: for John Flasket, 1607).
30. *Ibid.*, sigs. F2v–F3.
31. *The Life and Death of Jacke Straw, a Notable Rebell in England* (London: John Danter for William Barley, 1593), sigs. A3–A3v.
32. Hughe Latemer, *The Fourth Sermon . . . whyche he preached before the Kynges Majestye wythin hys Graces Palace at Westminster* (March 29, 1549), printed in collection of sermons with titlepage, *The Seconde Sermon of Master Hughe Latemer, whych he preached before the Kynges Majestie, within hys Graces Palayce at Westminster* (March 15, 1549) (London: Jhon Daye and William Seres, 1549), sig. K1.
33. William Wilkinson, *A Confutation of Certaine Articles delivered unto the Familye of Love* (London: John Daye, 1579), sigs. [hand] 3–[hand] 3v.
34. *Ibid.*, sig. [hand] 4v.
35. *The Defence of John Hales ayenst Certeyn Sclaundres and False Reaportes made of Hym*, Appendix to Introduction to John Hales, *A Discourse of the Common Weal of this Realm of England*, ed. Elizabeth Lamond (Cambridge, 1829), pp. lvi–lvii.
36. *Ibid.*, p. lvii.
37. *Ibid.*, pp. lvi–lvii.
38. Jhon Calvine, *A Short Instruction for to Arme All Good Christian People agaynst the Pestiferous Errours of the Common Secte of Anabaptistes* (London: Jhon Daye and William Seres, 1549), sigs. A5–A5v.
39. J[ohn] P[oynet], *A Shorte Treatise of Politike Power, and of the True Obedience which Subjectes owe to Kynges and Other Civile Governours* (n.p., 1556), sig. C8. See also Richard Turnbull, *An Exposition upon the Canonicall Epistle of Saint James* (London: John Windet, 1591), sig. P2.
40. Thomas Beacon, *The Jewel of Joy* in *The Seconde Part of the Bokes, which Thomas Beacon hath made* (London: [J. Day], 1560), sig. CCc6.
41. Hughe Latymer, *A Moste Faithfull Sermon preached before the Kynges most Excellente Majestye, and hys most Honorable Councel, in his Court at Westminster* (London: John Day, 1550), sig. B7.
42. Hugh Latimer, *The Fyrste Sermon . . . whiche he preached before the Kynges Majest. wythin his Graces Palayce at Westmynster* (March 8, 1549) (London: Jhon Daye and William Seres [,1549]), sig. D5v.
43. Thomas Lever, *A Fruitfull Sermon made in Poules Churche*, sig. B5.
44. Thomas Lever, *A Sermon preached the Fourth Sundaye in Lente before the Kynges Majestie, and his Honorable Counsell* (London: John Day, 1550), sig. F3.

45. William Langland, *The Vision of William concerning Piers the Plowman*, ed. W. W. Skeat (Oxford, 1886), pass. xx, ll. 271–74.
46. *Ibid.*, pass. xx. 1. 187.
47. [Henry Parker], *Dives and Pauper* (London: Richarde Pynson, 1493), sig. M6v.
48. *Ibid.*
49. Poynet, *op. cit.*, sig. E8.
50. Calvine, *op. cit.*, sig. A4.
51. *Ibid.*, sigs. F8v–G1.
52. Henrie Smith, *The Poore Mans Teares* (London: John Wolfe for William Wright, 1592), sig. A6v.
53. Lever, *A Fruitfull Sermon made in Poules Churche:* see above, ftn. 28.
54. *Ibid.*, sig. B2v.
55. *Ibid.*, sigs. B2v–B3v.
56. See above, pp. 111 ff.
57. Henry Brinkelow, *The Complaint of Roderyck Mors, sometime a Gray Fryre, unto the Parlament House of Ingland* (Geneve: Myghell Boys [London: A. Scoloker and W. Seres, 1548?]), sig. F5v.
58. Beacon, *The Jewel of Joy*, sigs. AAa2v–AAa3.
59. See, for example, *The Select Works of Robert Crowley*, ed. J. M. Cowper, E.E.T.S. (London, 1872), p. x.
60. Crowley, *The Way to Wealth*, sig. A4v.
61. *Ibid.*, sig. A5.
62. Lever, *A Sermon preached the Fourth Sundaye in Lente*, sig. B6v.
63. Langland, *op. cit.*, pass. xvi, 1.16 (C text).
64. Crowley, *The Way to Wealth*, sig. B1v.
65. Lever, *A Fruitfull Sermon made in Poules Churche*, sig. B3v.

CHAPTER V

Submission

1. For example, *The Fyrste Sermon of Mayster Hughe Latimer whiche he preached before the Kynges Majest. wythin his Graces Palayce at Westmynster* (March 8, 1549) (London: Jhon Daye and William Seres [,1549]), sigs. B7–B7v.
2. J. W. Allen, *A History of Political Thought in the Sixteenth Century* (New York, 1928), p. xiii.
3. Stephen Gardiner, *Obedience in Church and State*, ed. and trans. Pierre Janelle (Cambridge, 1930), p. xiv.
4. David and Gervase Mathew, *The Reformation and the Contemplative Life: a Study of the Conflict between the Carthusians and the State* (New York, 1934), p. 86.
5. Edward Allen Whitney, "Erastianism and Divine Right" in *The Huntington Library Quarterly*, II, No. 4 (July, 1939), p. 390.
6. Allen, *op. cit.*, p. 8.
7. Wyllyam Tyndale, *The Obedience of a Christen Man and how Christen Rulers Ought to Governe* (Marlborow in Hesse: Hans Luft [Antwerp], 1535).
8. *The Institution of a Christen Man* (London: Thomas Berthelet, 1537).
9. *An Homelie against Disobedience and Wylfull Rebellion* (London: Richard Jugge and John Cawood [,1571?]).
10. Tyndale, *op. cit.*, sig. D5.

11. See, for example, Richard Hooker, *Of the Lawes of Ecclesiasticall Politie* (London: John Windet [,1594?]), Book I, sec. 10, sig. F5v.
12. Tyndale, *op. cit.*, sig. D6.
13. *Ibid.*, sigs. D8v–E1.
14. See, for example, Sir John Fortescue, *A Learned Commendation of the Politique Lawes of England*, trans. Robert Mulcaster (London: R. Tottill, 1567), chap. viii, sigs. D2v–D3.
15. Tyndale, *op. cit.*, sig. F4v.
16. *Ibid.*, sig. E1v.
17. *Ibid.*, sig. E1v–E2.
18. *Ibid.*, sig. E4.
19. *Ibid.*, sigs. F6–F7.
20. *Ibid.*, sigs. D6–D6v.
21. *Ibid.*, sig. D8v.
22. *Ibid.*, sig. F1.
23. *Ibid.*, sig. D7.
24. *Ibid.*, sigs. D7–D8v.
25. *Ibid.*, sig. F6v.
26. *Ibid.*, sig. F5.
27. *Ibid.*, sig. F4v.
28. *Ibid.*, sigs. F5–F5v.
29. *Ibid.*, sig. F5v.
30. *Ibid.*, sig. F7v.
31. *The Institution of a Christen Man*, sig. a4v ff.
32. *Ibid.*, sig. Q4 ff.
33. *Ibid.*, sig. Q4.
34. *Ibid.*, sig. R2v.
35. *Ibid.*
36. *Ibid.*, sig. R3.
37. *Ibid.*, sig. R3v.
38. *Ibid.*
39. *Ibid.*
40. *Ibid.*
41. *Certayne Sermons, or Homelies appoynted by the Kynges Majestie, to bee Declared and Redde, by All Persones, Vicares, or Curates, Every Sondaye in their Churches, where they have Cure* (London: Rychard Grafton, 1547).
42. *Ibid.*, sig. R1 ff.
43. *Ibid.*, sig. R1v.
44. *Ibid.*, sig. R3v.
45. *Ibid.*, sigs. R4–S1v.
46. *Ibid.*, sig. R3.
47. *Ibid.*, sig. R3v.
48. *Ibid.*, sig. S2v.
49. *Ibid.*, sig. S3.
50. *Ibid.*, sig. S1v.
51. *Ibid.*, sigs. S1v–S2.
52. *Ibid.*, sig. S2.
53. *Ibid.*, sig. S4.
54. Thomas Cranmer, *The Remains of,* ed. Henry Jenkyns (Oxford, 1833), II, 248 ftn.
55. *Ibid.*, pp. 245–46.
56. *Ibid.*, p. 248 ftn.
57. *Ibid.*, p. 250.

58. *Ibid.*, p. 254.
59. *Ibid.*, p. 252.
60. *Ibid.*, p. 254.
61. *Ibid.*, pp. 260–61.
62. *Ibid.*, p. 256.
63. *Ibid.*, p. 257.
64. *Ibid.*, p. 253.
65. *Ibid.*, pp. 255–56.
66. *Ibid.*, p. 258.
67. *Ibid.*, pp. 257–58.
68. *Ibid.*, pp. 258–59.
69. *Ibid.*, pp. 259–60.
70. *Ibid.*, p. 261.
71. *Ibid.*, p. 263.
72. *Ibid.*, p. 260.
73. *Ibid.*, pp. 264–65.
74. *Ibid.*, pp. 264–67.
75. *Ibid.*, p. 268.
76. *Ibid.*
77. *Ibid.*, p. 269.
78. *Ibid.*, pp. 270–71.
79. *Ibid.*, p. 273.
80. [Sir John Cheke], *The Hurt of Sedicion howe Greveous it is to a Commune Welth* (London: John Daye, 1549).
81. *Ibid.*, sig. A1v.
82. *Ibid.*, sig. A2v.
83. *Ibid.*, sig. A3.
84. *Ibid.*, sig. A3v.
85. *Ibid.*, sig. A4.
86. *Ibid.*, sig. A4v.
87. *Ibid.*, sig. A6.
88. *Ibid.*, sig. A6v.
89. *Ibid.*, sigs. A7–A7v.
90. *Ibid.*, sig. A8.
91. *Ibid.*, sig. A8v.
92. *Ibid.*
93. *Ibid.*, sig. B1.
94. *Ibid.*, sig. E3.
95. *Ibid.*, sig. E4v.
96. *Ibid.*, sig. E6v.
97. *Ibid.*, sigs. F8v–G1v.
98. *Ibid.*, sig. G2v.
99. *Ibid.*, sigs. G7–G7v.
100. *Ibid.*, sig. H1.
101. Robert Crowley, *The Way to Wealth* (London: Robert Crowley, 1550).
102. *Ibid.*, sig. A2v.
103. *Ibid.*, sigs. A3–A3v.
104. *Ibid.*, sig. A4.
105. Sir John Fortescue, it will be remembered, attributed the wretchedness which he found in the kingdom of France in his day to the form of government of that unhappy realm, and in contrast drew a very prosperous picture of the England of his time. (Fortescue, *op. cit.*, chaps. xxxv and xxxvi, sigs. K7 ff. and L4v ff.)

106. Crowley, *op. cit.*, sig. A4.
107. *Ibid.*
108. *Ibid.*, sig. A5.
109. *Ibid.*
110. *Ibid.*, sig. B3v.
111. *Ibid.*, sigs. B3v–B4v.
112. *Ibid.*, sig. B5v.
113. Thomas Beacon, *The Jewel of Joy* in *The Seconde Part of the Bokes, which Thomas Beacon hath made* (London: [J. Day,] 1560), sig. HHh4v).
114. Thomas Lever, *A Fruitfull Sermon made in Poules Churche at London in the Shroudes, the Seconde Daye of Februari* (London: Jhon Daie and Wylliam Seres, 1550), sig. D2v.
115. *Ibid.*, sig. D3.
116. *Ibid.*, sigs. C2v–C3.
117. *Ibid.*, sigs. C6v–C7.
118. Crowley, *op. cit.*, sig. A7.
119. *Ibid.*, sig. B4v.
120. *Ibid.*, sig. B6v.
121. Thomas Lever, *A Sermon preached at Pauls Crosse, the .XIIII. Day of December* (London: Jhon Day, 1550), sigs. F1–F1v.
122. Crowley, *op. cit.*, sigs. A6–A7.
123. Lever, *A Sermon preached at Pauls Crosse*, sig. E8v.
124. *Ibid.*, sig. F1.
125. Lever, *A Fruitfull Sermon made in Poules Churche*, sigs. D1v–D2v.
126. Beacon, *op. cit.*, sig. CCc1.
127. J[ohn] P[oynet], *A Shorte Treatise of Politike Power, and of the True Obedience which Subjectes owe to Kynges and Other Civile Governours* (n.p., 1556).
128. *Ibid.*, sig. B4.
129. *Ibid.*, sig. B6.
130. Cf. Fortescue, *op. cit.*, chap. iii, sigs. B1v–B3v; chap. viii, sigs. D2v–D3v.
131. Sir Thomas Smyth, *De Republica Anglorum, the Maner of Governement or Policie of the Realme of England* (London: Henrie Midleton for Gregorie Seton, 1583), Bk. II, chap. i, sig. F1v; see also *ibid.*, Bk. I, chap. ix, sigs. C1–C1v.
132. Poynet, *op. cit.*, sig. G5v.
133. *Ibid.*, sig. F5.
134. *Ibid.*, sigs. H1v–H2.
135. *Ibid.*, sig. G1v.
136. See, for instance, Thomas Starkey, *A Dialogue between Cardinal Pole and Thomas Lupset, Lecturer in Rhetoric at Oxford* in *England in the Reign of King Henry the Eighth*, Part II, ed. J. M. Cowper, E.E.T.S. (London, 1878), p. 167.
137. St. Thomas Aquinas, *The "Summa Theologica,"* trans. Fathers of the English Dominican Province, Part II (Second Part), First Number, IX (London, 1918), Q. 42. Art. 2, 518.
138. Poynet, *op. cit.*, sig. G6.
139. *Ibid.*, sig. G7v.
140. *Ibid.*, sig. H3.
141. *Ibid.*, sig. G1.
142. *Ibid.*, sigs. K1–K1v.
143. *Ibid.*, sig. H6v.
144. *Ibid.*, sig. K7.
145. *Ibid.*, sig. M3.
146. *Ibid.*, sigs. C8–C8v.

147. *Ibid.*, sigs. C8v–D1.
148. [John Knox], *Certain Questions concerning Obedience to Lawful Magistrates, with Answers by Bullinger* in *The Works of,* ed. David Laing for the Bannatyne Club, III (Edinburgh, 1854), 219.
149. *Ibid.*, pp. 222–23.
150. *Ibid.*, pp. 223–25.
151. John Knox, *The First Blast of the Trumpet against the Monstrous Regiment of Women* in *The Works of,* ed. David Laing for the Bannatyne Club, IV (Edinburgh, 1855), 373.
152. *Ibid.*, pp. 381–82.
153. *Ibid.*, p. 415.
154. John Knox, *The Appellation of John Knoxe from the Cruell and Most Injust Sentence pronounced against him by the False Bishoppes and Clergie of Scotland, with his Supplication and Exhortation to the Nobilitie, Estates, and Communaltie of the Same Realme* in *Works*, IV, 471.
155. *Ibid.*, p. 472.
156. *Ibid.*, p. 473.
157. *Ibid.*, p. 495.
158. *Ibid.*, p. 517.
159. Christopher Goodman, *How Superior Powers Oght to be Obeyd*, reproduced from the Edition of 1558, with a Bibliographical Note by Charles H. McIlwain, for the Facsimile Text Society (New York, 1931), sigs. b3v–b4.
160. *Ibid.*, sig. b5v.
161. *Ibid.*, sigs. k4–k5.
162. *Ibid.*, sig. b6v.
163. *Ibid.*, sigs. n3v–n4.
164. *Ibid.*, sig. c1v.
165. *Ibid.*, sig. d3.
166. *Ibid.*, sig. f8v.
167. *Ibid.*, sig. g2.
168. *Ibid.*, sigs. d2v–d3.
169. Allen, *op. cit.*, p. 116.
170. Goodman, *op. cit.*, sig. d3.
171. Charles H. McIlwain, Bibliographical Note to Goodman, *op. cit.*
172. Goodman, *op. cit.*, sig. c3v.
173. *Ibid.*, sigs. a7v–b1.
174. *Ibid.*, sig. c8.
175. *Ibid.*, sig. g6v.
176. *Ibid.*, sig. g8v.
177. *Ibid.*, sigs. h2–h2v.
178. *Ibid.*, sig. f2v.
179. *Ibid.*, sigs. e6–e6v.
180. *Ibid.*, sig. e7.
181. *Ibid.*, sigs. e7–e7v.
182. *Ibid.*, sig. k1.
183. *Ibid.*, sigs. k2v–k3v.
184. *Ibid.*, sigs. l8v–m1.
185. *Ibid.*, sigs. m2v–m3.
186. *Ibid.*, sig. m5.
187. *Ibid.*, sig. n2v.
188. *Ibid.*, sigs. d1v–d2.
189. *Ibid.*, sigs. k5–k5v.
190. McIlwain, *op. cit.*

191. John Stockewood, *A Very Fruiteful Sermon preached at Paules Crosse the Tenth of May Last* (London: for George Bishop, 1579), sig. F2.

192. *A Profitable and Necessarye Doctryne, with Certayne Homelies adjoyned thereunto, set forth by . . . Edmonde Byshop of London* (London: Jhon Cawodde, 1550).

193. *Ibid.*, sig. A1v.

194. *Certaine Sermons appoynted by the Quenes Majesty, to be Declared and Read, by Al Parsons, Vicars, and Curates, Everi Sunday and Holiday, in their Churches* (London, 1653).

195. *An Homelie against Disobedience and Wylfull Rebellion*: see above, ftn. 9.

196. *Ibid.*, sigs. A1v–A2.

197. *Ibid.*, sigs. A3v–A4.

198. *Ibid.*, sig. C2v ff.

199. *Ibid.*, sig. D2v ff.

200. *Ibid.*, sigs. F1–F1v.

201. *Ibid.*, sig. F2 ff.

202. *Ibid.*, sig. F3.

203. *Ibid.*, sig. G1.

204. *Ibid.*, sig. G1v.

205. *Ibid.*, sig. G2.

206. *Ibid.*, sig. G4v.

207. *Ibid.*, sigs. H1–H1v.

208. *Ibid.*, sig. H2 ff.

209. *Ibid.*, sigs. H2v–H3.

210. *Ibid.*, sigs. H4v–I1.

211. *Ibid.*, sig. I3v.

212. *Ibid.*, sig. I4.

213. *Ibid.*, sigs. K2v–K3.

214. *Tom Tell Troath, or a Free Discourse touching the Manners of The Tyme* [London? 1630?], sig. B2.

215. *Ibid.*, sigs. C4v–D2v.

216. Robert Wilkinson, *A Sermon preached at North-Hampton the 21. of June Last Past, before the Lord Lieutenant of the County, and the Rest of the Commissioners there assembled upon Occasion of the Late Rebellion and Riots in those Parts committed* (London: for John Flasket, 1607).

217. *Ibid.*, sig. C3v.

218. *Ibid.*, sigs. F1v–F2.

219. *Ibid.*, sig. F1.

220. *Ibid.*, sig. F4.

221. *Ibid.*, sigs. F1–F1v.

222. Gervase Babington, *The Workes of* (London: George Eld by the assignement of Thomas Charde, 1615), sig. 2F3v.

223. Henrie Smith, *The Sermons of* (London: Richard Field for Thomas Man, 1593), sig. Zz3v.

224. John Carpenter, *A Preparative to Contentation* (London: Thomas Creede, 1597).

225. See, for instance, Hooker, *op. cit.*, sig. F5v.

226. Carpenter, *op. cit.*, sig. M5v.

227. *Ibid.*, sig. M6v.

228. Thomas Aquinas, *op. cit.*, Second Number, X (London, 1918), Q. 63. Art. 3, pp. 191–92.

229. John Calvin, *The Institution of Christian Religion* (London: Reinolde Wolfe and Richarde Harison, 1561), sig. Y2.

230. Carpenter, *op. cit.*, sig. N1v.
231. Edwin Sandys, *Sermons made by* (London: Henrie Midleton for Thomas Charde, 1585), sig. L6v.
232. William Perkins, *A Discourse of Conscience* in *The Workes of,* I (London: John Legatt, 1612), sig. Yy3.
233. *Ibid.*, sig. Yy4v.
234. William Perkins, *The Whole Treatise of the Cases of Conscience* in *The Workes of,* II (London: John Legatt, 1613), sig. H3v.
235. William Perkins, *A Godly and Learned Exposition upon the Whole Epistle of Jude* in *The Workes of,* III (London: Cantrell Legge, 1618), sig. Eeee6v.
236. Sandys, *op. cit.*, sig. B6.
237. *Ibid.*, sig. C3.
238. *Ibid.*, sig. N3v.
239. *Ibid.*, sig. C2v.
240. Robert Pricke, *The Doctrine of Superioritie, and of Subjection, contained in the Fift Commandement of the Holy Law of Almightie God* (London: for Ephraim Dawson and Thomas Downe, 1609), sigs. D1–D1v.
241. Babington, *op. cit.*, sig. o3.
242. Sandys, *op. cit.*, sig. C4.
243. Allen, *op. cit.*, p. 17.
244. *Ibid.*, p. 52.
245. Laurence Chaderton, *An Excellent and Godly Sermon preached at Paules Crosse the .XXVI. Daye of October 1578* (London: Christopher Barker [,1580]), sig. C3.
246. *Ibid.*, C4.
247. *Ibid.*
248. Smith, *op. cit.*, sig. Zz3.
249. Edward Dering, *A Sermon preached before the Queenes Majestie, the .25. Day of February . . . in Anno. 1569* (n.p. n.d.).
250. *Ibid.*, sig. H1v.
251. *Ibid.*, sig. B3v.
252. *Ibid.*, sig. C3.
253. Smith, *op. cit.*, sig. Yy5.
254. Chaderton, *op. cit.*, sig. A7v.
255. Stockewood, *op. cit.:* see above, ftn. 191.
256. *Ibid.*, sigs. A4–A5.
257. *Ibid.*, sig. A3.
258. *Ibid.*, sig. D2.
259. *Ibid.*, sigs. C3–C3v.
260. *Ibid.*, sig. I5.
261. Chaderton, *op. cit.*, sig. C3.
262. Dering, *op. cit.*, sig. E2.
263. Sandys, *op. cit.*, sigs. L4v–L5.
264. John Jewell, *The Works of* (London: John Norton, 1609), sig. [hand] I3v.
265. Babington, *op. cit.*, sig. g4.
266. Jhon Calvine, *A Short Instruction for to Arme All Good Christian People agaynst the Pestiferous Errours of the Common Secte of Anabaptistes* (London: Jhon Daye and William Seres, 1549), sig. D1.
267. Carpenter, *op. cit.:* see above, ftn. 224.
268. *Ibid.*, sigs. I4–I4v.
269. *Ibid.*, sig. K4.
270. *Ibid.*, sig. K5v.
271. *Ibid.*, sig. K7v.
272. *Ibid.*, sig. O7.
273. *Ibid.*, sigs. H5v–H6.

CHAPTER VI

Usury

1. William Perkins, *A Faithfull and Plaine Exposition upon the Two First Verses of the 2. Chapter of Zephaniah* in *The Workes of*, III (London: Cantrell Legge, 1618).
2. *Ibid.*, sigs. Qqq1v–Qqq2.
3. *Ibid.*, sig. Qqq2v.
4. William Perkins, *A Treatise of the Vocations* in *The Workes of*, I (London: John Legatt, 1612).
5. *Ibid.*, sig. Ttt5v.
6. *Ibid.*, sigs. Ttt5v–Ttt6.
7. *Ibid.*, Ttt6.
8. *Ibid.*
9. *Robin Conscience and his Father* [London: J. Audeley? 1560?].
10. *Ibid.*, sig. A2.
11. *Ibid.*, sig. A2v.
12. *Ibid.*
13. *Ibid.*, sig. A3.
14. *Ibid.*, sigs. A3–A3v.
15. *Ibid.*, sig. A3v.
16. [John Hales,] *A Discourse of the Common weal of this Realm of England*, ed. Elizabeth Lamond (Cambridge, 1929), p. xxxiii.
17. See above, pp. 171–73.
18. Charles Richardson, *A Sermon against Oppression and Fraudulent Dealing preached at Paules Crosse, the Eleventh of December* (London: George Purslowe for Joseph Browne and Thomas Harper, 1615), sig. R5.
19. Arthur Warren, *The Poore Mans Passions* (London: J. R[oberts] for R. B[ankworth], 1605), sig. A2.
20. George Phillips, *The Life and Death of the Rich Man and Lazarus* (London: for Edward White, 1600), sig. C4v.
21. H[enry] A[rthington], *Provision for the Poore, now in Penurie, out of the Store-House of Gods Plentie* (London: Thomas Creede, 1597), sig. C2.
22. Phillips, *op. cit.*, sigs. B7v–B8.
23. Richard Turnbull, *An Exposition upon the Canonicall Epistle of Saint James* (London: John Windet, 1591), sig. Mm5v.
24. *Tom Tell Troath, or a Free Discourse touching the Manners of the Tyme* [London? 1630?], sig. A2v.
25. See, for example, Nicolas Hemingius, *A Godlie Treatice concerning the Lawful Use of Ritches*, trans. Thomas Rogers (London: for Andrew Maunsell, 1578), sig. L3v.
26. Richardson, *op. cit.*, sig. D3v.
27. Arthington, *op. cit.*, sig. C2.
28. Thomas Wilson, *A Discourse upon Usury*, with an Historical Introduction by R. H. Tawney (London, 1924), p. 177.
29. Henrie Smith, *The Sermons of* (London: Richard Field for Thomas Man, 1593), sig. L8v.
30. Philippus Caesar, *A General Discourse against the Damnable Sect of Usurers*, trans. Thomas Rogers (London: for Andrew Maunsell, 1578).
31. *Ibid.*, sig. *4.

32. *Ibid.*, sig. **1v.
33. Wilson, *op. cit.*, p. 178.
34. R. H. Tawney, Historical Introduction to Wilson, *op. cit.*, p. 41.
35. *Ibid.*, pp. 134–54.
36. *Ibid.*, pp. 121–72.
37. Nicolas Sander, *A Briefe Treatise of Usurie* (Lovanii: apud Joannem Foulerum, 1568), sig. H5v.
38. Smith, *op. cit.*, sigs. N3v–N4.
39 Miles Mosse, *The Arraignment and Conviction of Usurie* (London: the Widdow Orwin for Thomas Man, 1595), sig. Aa1v.
40. Tawney, *op. cit.*, p. 111.
41. *Ibid.*
42. *Ibid.*, p. 119.
43. *Ibid.*, pp. 119–21.
44. Caesar, *op. cit.*, sig. H4.
45. *Ibid.*, sig. H4v.
46. Hemingius, *op. cit.*, sig. N4.
47. *Ibid.*, sig. N3.
48. *Ibid.*, sig. N3v.
49. Caesar, *op. cit.*, sigs. **2–**2v.
50. Hemingius, *op. cit.*, sig. N4.
51. Richardson, *op. cit.*: see above, ftn. 18.
52. *Ibid.*, sig. A3v.
53. *Ibid.*, sig. F2v–F3.
54. Gervase Babington, *The Workes of* (London: George Eld by the assignement of Thomas Charde, 1615), sig. Hh4v.
55. Caesar, *op. cit.*, sig. B2.
56. Smith, *op. cit.*, sig. M2.
57. John Jewell, *The Workes of* (London: John Norton, 1609), sig. [hand] G3v–[hand] G4.
58. Sander, *op. cit.*, sigs. A4–A4v.
59. St. Thomas Aquinas, *The "Summa Theologica,"* trans. Fathers of the English Dominican Province, Part II (Second Part), Second Number, X (London, 1918), Q.78. Art. 1, p. 330.
60. Caesar, *op. cit.*, sig. B1v.
61. Sander, *op. cit.*, sigs. H5–H5v.
62. *Ibid.*, sig. C4v.
63. *Ibid.*, sig. C7.
64. *Ibid.*, sig. G2.
65. Mosse, *op. cit.*, sigs. F4–F4v.
66. *Ibid.*, sig. K3v.
67. Thomas Aquinas, *op. cit.*, Q.78. Art. 2, pp. 336–37.
68. Caesar, *op. cit.*, sigs. F2v–F3v.
69. Henry Brinkelow, *The Complaint of Roderyck Mors, sometime a Gray Fryre, unto the Parlament House of Ingland* (Geneve: Myghell Boys [London: A Scoloker and W. Seres, 1548?]), sig. F3v.
70. Jewell, *op. cit.*, sig. [hand] G6v.
71. Babington, *op. cit.*, sig. Hh4v.
72. Smith, *op. cit.*, sig. N1.
73. *Ibid.*, sig. N2.
74. Caesar, *op. cit.*, sig. ***2v.
75. Hemingius, *op. cit.*, sigs. M2–M2v.
76. Mosse, *op. cit.*, sig. C2v.

77. Jewell, *op. cit.*, sig. [hand] G3v.
78. Smith, *op. cit.*, sigs. M1v–M2.
79. Babington, *op. cit.*, sig. 2H6v.
80. *Ibid.*
81. Caesar, *op. cit.:* see above, ftn. 30.
82. *Ibid.*, sigs. D1v–D2.
83. Thomas Aquinas, *op. cit.*, Q.78, p. 329.
84. Sander, *op. cit.:* see above, ftn. 37.
85. *Ibid.*, sig. H7v. For convenience the chapter numbers are here put before the headings instead of after on a separate line with the word "chapter" as in Sander, and the indications of foliation are omitted.
86. Richardson, *op. cit.:* see above, ftn. 18.
87. *Ibid.*, sig. B4.
88. Tawney, *op. cit.*, pp. 22–30.
89. *Ibid.*, pp. 21–22.
90. *Ibid.*, pp. 23–24.
91. Thomas Aquinas, *op. cit.*, Q.78. Art. 1, pp. 332–33.
92. Edwin Sandys, *Sermons made by* (London: Henrie Midleton for Thomas Charde, 1585), sig. L8v.
93. Richard Greenham, *Grave Counsels, and Godlie Observations* in *The Workes of* (London: Felix Kingston for Ralph Jacson, 1599), sig. F4v.
94. Hemingius, *op. cit.*, sig. L4v.
95. Mosse, *op. cit.*, sig. M2v.
96. *Ibid.*, sigs. N4–N4v.
97. Hemingius, *op. cit.*, sigs. N2v–N3v.
98. Caesar, *op. cit.*, sig. A2v.
99. Thomas Aquinas, *op. cit.*, Q78. Art. 4, pp. 340–41.
100. Babington, *op. cit.*, 2H6v.
101. Smith, *op. cit.*, sig. N7v.
102. *Ibid.*, sig. O1.
103. *Ibid.*, sig. O1v.
104. *Ibid.*, sig. O2v.
105. *Ibid.*, sigs. O2v–O3.
106. *Ibid.*, sigs. M7–N1.
107. Sander, *op. cit.*, sigs. A2v–A3.
108. *Ibid.*, sigs. A3v–A4.
109. *Ibid.*, sig. F8.
110. *Ibid.*, sig. F8v.
111. *Ibid.*, sigs. F8v–G1.
112. Jewell, *op. cit.*, sig. [hand] G4v.
113. Mosse, *op. cit.*, sig. P3v.
114. Henry Smith, *The Sinners Confession* in *Ten Sermons preached by* (London: Richard Field for Robert Dexter, 1596), sig. Bb1.
115. Caesar, *op. cit.*, sig. *4v.
116. Wilson, *op. cit.:* see above, ftn. 28.
117. *Ibid.*, p. 198.
118. *Ibid.*, p. 199.
119. *Ibid.*, p. 200.
120. *Ibid.*
121. *Ibid.*, p. 202.
122. *Ibid.*
123. *Ibid.*, pp. 207–8.
124. *Ibid.*, p. 208.

125. *Ibid.,* p. 215.
126. *Ibid.,* p. 216.
127. *Ibid.,* pp. 217–20.
128. *Ibid.,* pp. 223–26.
129. *Ibid.,* pp. 228–31.
130. *Ibid.,* p. 232.
131. *Ibid.,* p. 234.
132. *Ibid.,* p. 233.
133. *Ibid.,* p. 234.
134. *Ibid.,* p. 235.
135. *Ibid.,* p. 236.
136. *Ibid.,* p. 237.
137. *Ibid.,* p. 246.
138. *Ibid.,* p. 249.
139. *Ibid.,* p. 250.
140. *Ibid.,* p. 252.
141. *Ibid.,* p. 253.
142. *Ibid.,* p. 275 ff.
143. *Ibid.,* p. 275.
144. *Ibid.,* pp. 298–306.
145. *Ibid.,* p. 322 ff.
146. *Ibid.,* p. 329 ff.
147. *Ibid.,* p. 341.
148. *Ibid.*
149. *Ibid.*
150. *Ibid.,* pp. 351–52.
151. *Ibid.,* p. 352.
152. *Ibid.,* p. 360.
153. *Ibid.,* p. 362.
154. *Ibid.,* p. 365.
155. *Ibid.,* p. 372.
156. *Ibid.,* p. 374.
157. *Ibid.,* p. 378.
158. *Ibid.,* p. 379.
159. *Ibid.,* p. 381.
160. *Ibid.,* pp. 196–97.
161. Phillips, *op. cit.,* sig. A7v.

Chapter VII

Contentation

1. John Jewell, *The Works of* (London: John Norton, 1609), sig. [hand] G4–[hand] G4v.
2. Amintore Fanfani, *Catholicism, Protestantism and Capitalism* (London, 1935), pp. 21–22.
3. Max Weber, *The Protestant Ethic and the Spirit of Capitalism,* trans. Talcott Parsons with a Foreword by R. H. Tawney (London, 1930), p. 53.
4. Fanfani, *op. cit.,* pp. 34–35, 41 ff.
5. Henrie Smith, *The Benefit of Contentation* in *Three Sermons made by* (London: James Roberts for Nicholas Ling, 1599), sig. Blv.

6. Jewell, *op. cit.*, sig. [hand] G4.
7. Smith, *op. cit.*, sig. A3.
8. Richard Turnbull, *An Exposition upon the Canonicall Epistle of Saint James* (London: John Windet, 1591), sig. Mm5v.
9. Smith, *op. cit.*, sig. A2.
10. Richard Greenham, *Meditations* in *The Workes of* (London: Felix Kingston for Ralph Jacson, 1599), sig. Olv. Cf. Nicolas Hemingius, *A Godlie Treatice concerning the Lawful Use of Ritches,* trans. Thomas Rogers (London: for Andrew Maunsell, 1578), sigs. K3–K3v.
11. William Perkins, *The Whole Treatise of the Cases of Conscience* in *The Workes of,* II (London: John Legatt, 1613), sig. L3.
12. *Ibid.*
13. Hemingius, *op. cit.*, sigs. N4–N4v.
14. John Calvin, *A Little Booke . . . concernynge Offences,* trans. Arthur Goldinge [London: W. Seres, 1567], sig. C5.
15. Gervase Babington, *The Workes of* (London: George Eld by the assignement of Thomas Charde, 1615), sig. aa3v.
16. Richard Greenham, *Grave Counsels, and Godlie Observations* in *Workes,* sig. C2.
17. Perkins, *op. cit.*, sig. L3.
18. Philippus Caesar, *A General Discourse against the Damnable Sect of Usurers,* trans. Thomas Rogers (London: for Andrew Maunsell, 1578), sig. Alv.
19. Smith, *op. cit.*, sig. A3v.
20. Henrie Smith, *The Sermons of* (London: Richard Field for Thomas Man, 1593), sigs. N6–N6v.
21. *Ibid.*, sig. N7v.
22. William Perkins, *How to Live, and That Well: in All Estates and Times* in *The Workes of,* I (London: John Legatt, 1612), sig. Ss1.
23. St. Thomas Aquinas, *The "Summa Theologica,"* trans. Fathers of the English Dominican Province, Part II (Second Part), Second Number, X (London, 1918), Q.55. Art. 7, p. 96.
24. William Perkins, *A Treatise of the Vocations* in *Workes,* I, sig. Vvvl.
25. Hughe Latemer, *The Seconde Sermon . . . whych he preached before the Kynges Majestie, within hys Graces Palayce at Westminster* (March 15, 1549), (London: Jhon Daye and William Seres, 1549), sig. A6.
26. Robert Crowley, *The Way to Wealth* (London: Robert Crowley, 1550), sig. B6.
27. Robert Crowley, *The Select Works of,* ed. J. M. Cowper, E.E.T.S. (London, 1872), p. 89.
28. [Robert Crowley], *An Informacion and Peticion agaynst the Oppressours of the Pore Commons of this Realme* [London: J. Day, 1548], sig. B1.
29. See above, pp. 98–99.
30. Latimer, *op. cit.*, sig. D7.
31. *An Homelie against Disobedience and Wylfull Rebellion* (London: Richard Jugge and John Cawood [,1571?]), sig. G4v.
32. William Perkins, *A Godly and Learned Exposition upon the Whole Epistle of Jude* in *The Workes of,* III (London: Cantrell Legge, 1618), sig. Eeee6v.
33. Perkins, *A Treatise of the Vocations,* sig. Ttt5.
34. *Ibid.*, sigs. Ttt5–Ttt5v.
35. William Perkins, *A Discourse of Conscience* in *Workes,* I, sig. Zz3v.
36. Henrie Smith, *The Poore Mans Teares . . . treating of Almesdeeds, and Releeving the Poore* (London: John Wolfe for William Wright, 1592), sigs. A8v–B1.
37. Edwin Sandys, *Sermons made by* (London: Henrie Midleton for Thomas Charde, 1585), sig. Z3.

38. Perkins, *A Treatise of the Vocations*, sig. Sss3v.
39. H[enry] A[rthington], *Provision for the Poore, now in Penurie, out of the Store-House of Gods Plentie* (London: Thomas Creede, 1597), sig. C2.
40. "A Farewel, cauld, Churcheyeards, Rounde," in *Ballads and Broadsides chiefly of the Elizabethan Period,* ed. Herbert L. Collmann for the Roxburghe Club (Oxford, 1912), p. 80.
41. Arthur Warren, *The Poore Mans Passions* (London: J. R[oberts] for R. B[ankworth], 1605), sigs. G4v–H1.
42. Charles Richardson, *A Sermon against Oppression and Fraudulent Dealing preached at Paules Crosse, the Eleventh of December* (London: George Purslowe for Joseph Browne and Thomes Harper, 1615), sig. C2
43. *Ibid.,* sigs. C2–C2v.
44. Smith, *The Poore Mans Teares,* sig. B3.
45. *Ibid.,* sig. C2v.
46. *Ibid.*
47. Matt. 19:23–24.
48. R[obert] P[arsons], *A Booke of Christian Exercise, appertaining to Resolution . . . Perused, and accompanied now with a Treatise tending to Pacification,* by Edmund Bunny (London: for John Wight, 1585), sig. C5.
49. Smith, *The Poore Mans Teares,* sig. C1.
50. Turnbull, *op. cit.,* sigs. L15v–L16.
51. Hemingius, *op. cit.,* sig. K3.
52. Greenham, *Grave Counsels, and Godlie Observations,* sig. D1.
53. Perkins, *A Discourse of Conscience,* see above, ftn. 35.
54. *Ibid.,* sig. Zz3.
55. *Ibid.,* sigs. Zz3–Zz3v.
56. See, for instance, Fanfani, *op. cit.,* pp. 28–29 and Weber, *op. cit.,* pp. 170–71.
57. Perkins, *The Whole Treatise of the Cases of Conscience,* sig. L3.
58. *Ibid.*
59. *Ibid.*
60. *Ibid.*
61. *Ibid.*
62. Perkins, *A Discourse of Conscience,* sig. Zz3.
63. Weber, *op. cit.,* p. 172.
64. Perkins, *A Treatise of the Vocations,* sig. Ssslv.
65. See above, pp. 140–41.
66. Robert Pricke, *The Doctrine of Superioritie, and of Subjection, contained in the Fift Commandement of the Holy Law of Almightie God* (London: for Ephraim Dawson and Thomas Downe, 1609).
67. *Ibid.,* sig. M5v.
68. Perkins, *A Treatise of the Vocations,* sig. Sss4.
69. For instance, *ibid.,* sig. Ttt5.
70. Turnbull, *op. cit.,* sig. P1.
71. *Ibid.,* sig. P2.
72. *Ibid.,* sig. A2.
73. *Ibid.,* sigs. P2–P2v.
74. Perkins, *A Godly and Learned Exposition upon the Whole Epistle of Jude,* sig. Dddd5.
75. Greenham, *Grave Counsels, and Godlie Observations,* sig. F6v.
76. Perkins, *A Treatise of the Vocations,* sig. Sss2.
77. *Ibid.*
78. *Ibid.,* sigs. Vvvl–Vvv2v.

79. John Carpenter, *A Preparative to Contentation* (London: Thomas Creede, 1597), sig. B1.
80. *Ibid.*, sig. A1.
81. *Ibid.*, Z8v.
82. Smith, *Sermons*, sigs. Pp1–Pp2.
83. Richard Greenham, *Seven Godlie and Fruitfull Sermons* in *Workes*, sig. H4v.
84. Carpenter, *op. cit.*, sig. a1.
85. *Ibid.*, sigs. Aa4–Aa5v.
86. Turnbull, *op. cit.*, sig. Oo6v.
87. Babington, *op. cit.*, sig. Ee1v.
88. *Ibid.*, sig. Fff4.
89. Arthington, *op. cit.*, sigs. C1v–C2.
90. See above, pp. 5–6.
91. Babington, *op. cit.*, sig. aa2v.
92. George Phillips, *The Life and Death of the Rich Man and Lazarus* (London: for Edward White, 1600), sig. C4v.
93. Perkins, *A Godly and Learned Exposition upon the Whole Epistle of Jude*, sig. Eeee6v.
94. Hughe Latymer, *A Moste Faithfull Sermon preached before the Kynges most Excellente Majestye, and hys most Honorable Councel, in his Court at Westminster* (London: John Day, 1550), sig. G2v.
95. Smith, *The Benefit of Contentation:* see above, ftn. 5.
96. *Ibid.*, sig. A3.
97. *Ibid.*, sig. B4.
98. Perkins, *How to Live, and That Well*, sig. Ss1.
99. See, for instance, Jewell, *op. cit.*, sig. [hand] H2v.
100. Babington, *op. cit.*, sig. 2I2v.
101. Perkins, *A Treatise of the Vocations*, sig. Sss4.
102. Smith, *Sermons*, sigs. Pp2–Pp2v.
103. Perkins, *The Whole Treatise of the Cases of Conscience*, sig. L3v.

CHAPTER VIII

Alms

1. F. R. Salter, ed., *Some Early Tracts on Poor Relief* with a Preface by Sidney Webb (London, 1926), p. xvi ff.
2. *Ibid.*, p. xviii.
3. Sidney Webb, Preface to Salter, *op. cit.*, p. x.
4. Salter, *op. cit.*, pp. 120–21.
5. *Ibid.*, pp. 32–36, 120–21.
6. *Ibid.*, p. 32.
7. *Ibid.*
8. *The Forme and Maner of Subvention or Helping for Pore People Devysed and Practysed i the Cytie of Hypres in Flanders*, trans. William Marshall (London: Thomas Godfray, 1535), reprinted in Salter, *op. cit.*, pp. 36–76.
9. *Ibid.*, p. 38.
10. *Ibid.*, p. 41.
11. *Ibid.*, p. 43.

12. *Ibid.*, p. 45.
13. *Ibid.*, p. 47.
14. *Ibid.*
15. *Ibid.*, p. 48.
16. *Ibid.*, p. 50.
17. *Ibid.*, p. 52.
18. *Ibid.*, p. 53.
19. *Ibid.*, p. 54.
20. *Ibid.*
21. *Ibid.*, p. 55.
22. *Ibid.*, pp. 56–57.
23. *Ibid.*, pp. 58–59.
24. *Ibid.*, p. 60.
25. *Ibid.*, pp. 68–69.
26. *Ibid.*, pp. 71–72.
27. D. Andreas Hyperius [Gerardus], *The Regiment of the Povertie*, trans. H[enry] T[ripp] (London: F. Coldock and H. Bynneman, 1572).
28. *Ibid.*, sig. A2.
29. *Ibid.*, sig. A2v.
30. *Ibid.*, sig. A7.
31. *Ibid.*, sigs. G5v–G7v.
32. *Ibid.*, sig. G7v.
33. *Ibid.*, sig. C1.
34. *Ibid.*, sigs. B6v–B8.
35. *Ibid.*, sigs. H3v–H4.
36. Henrie Smith, *The Poore Mans Teares . . . treating of Almesdeeds* (London: John Wolfe for William Wright, 1592), sig. A8.
37. Hyperius, *op. cit.*, sigs. C5–C5v.
38. *Ibid.*, sigs. C6v–C7v.
39. Bruges was the adopted home of Vives, and though Mr. Salter says that the city "did nothing till 1560, and then not very much" (Salter, *op. cit.*, p. 34), this provision may be due to Vives' influence.
40. Hyperius, *op. cit.*, sigs. G2–G2v.
41. *Ibid.*, sigs. C4–C4v.
42. *Ibid.*, sig. H8v.
43. *Ibid.*, sig. H6.
44. *Ibid.*
45. *Ibid.*, sigs. H8–H8v.
46. *Ibid.*, sig. H8v.
47. *Ibid.*, sigs. I4–I4v.
48. *Ibid.*, sig. I1v.
49. *Ibid.*, sig. K6.
50. *Ibid.*, sigs. K6–K6v.
51. *Ibid.*, sigs. D3–D3v.
52. *Ibid.*, sig. D3v.
53. *Ibid.*, sig. D4.
54. *Ibid.*, sig. A3v.
55. See above, pp. 237–239.
56. Nicolas Hemingius, *A Godlie Treatice concerning the Lawful Use of Ritches*, trans. Thomas Rogers (London: for Andrew Maunsell, 1578), sigs. K4–L1.
57. William Perkins, *The Whole Treatise of the Cases of Conscience* in *The Workes of*, II (London: John Legatt, 1613), sigs. L3v–L4v.
58. *Ibid.*, sig. L4v.

59. Edwin Sandys, *Sermons made by* (London: Henrie Midleton for Thomas Charde, 1585), sig. L4.
60. George Phillips, *The Life and Death of the Rich Man and Lazarus* (London: for Edward White, 1600), sig. A4v.
61. Richard Turnbull, *An Exposition upon the Canonicall Epistle of Saint James* (London: John Windet, 1591), sig. Mm4v.
62. H[enry] A[rthington], *Provision for the Poore, now in Penurie, out of the Store-House of Gods Plentie* (London: Thomas Creede, 1597), sig. C4v.
63. *An Homely of Almes Dedes, and Mercyfulnesse towarde the Poore and Nedye* in *Certaine Sermons Appoynted by the Quenes Majesty, to be Declared and Read, by al Parsons,* etc. ([London,] 1563).
64. *Ibid.,* sig. Zz3.
65. Hemingius, *op. cit.,* sigs. O2v–O3.
66. Smith, *op. cit.,* sig. A5.
67. St. Thomas Aquinas, *The "Summa Theologica,"* trans. Fathers of the English Dominican Province, Part II (Second Part), First Number, IX (London [,1918]), Q.32, p. 407.
68. *Ibid.,* Q.32. Art. 1, p. 407.
69. *Ibid.,* p. 409.
70. *Ibid.,* Q.32. Art. 5, p. 417.
71. *Ibid.,* p. 418.
72. *Ibid.,* Q.32. Art. 6, p. 420.
73. *Ibid.,* Q.32, Art. 10, p. 430.
74. "Mock-Begger's Hall" in *A Book of Roxburghe Ballads,* ed. John Payne Collier (London, 1847), p. 50.
75. "Christmas' Lamentation" in *A Book of Roxburghe Ballads,* p. 13.
76. Sandys, *op. cit.,* sig. V1v.
77. Smith, *op. cit.,* sig. B6v.
78. *Ibid.,* sigs. B6v–B7.
79. See Sandys, *op. cit.,* sig. M2v; William Perkins, *How to Live, and That Well: in All Estates and Times* in *The Workes of,* I, (London: John Legatt, 1612), sig. Ss5; Laurence Chaderton, *An Excellent and Godly Sermon preached at Paules Crosse the .XXVI. Daye of October 1578* (London: Christopher Barker [,1580]), sig. C5v.
80. N. D[oleman, i.e. Robert Parsons], *The Third Part of a Treatise Intituled Of Three Conversions of England* (n.p., 1604), sig. *7.
81. Arthington, *op. cit.,* sig. E3.
82. Nicolas Sander, *A Briefe Treatise of Usurie* (Lovanii: apud Joannem Foulerum, 1568), sig. B2v.
83. Sandys, *op. cit.,* sig. K8v.
84. Gervase Babington, *The Workes of,* (London: George Eld by the assignement of Thomas Charde, 1615), sig. 2Ff5.
85. Chaderton, *op. cit.,* sigs. C6v–C7.
86. William Perkins, *A Salve for a Sicke Man* in *Workes,* I, sig. Vv2v.
87. Richard Greenham, *Of Murmuring,* in *The Workes of* (London: Felix Kingston for Ralph Jacson, 1599), sig. H4.
88. Richard Greenham, *Grave Counsels, and Godlie Observations* in *Workes,* sig. B3.
89. Jhon Calvin, *The Institution of Christian Religion* (London: Reinolde Wolfe and Richarde Harison, 1561), sig. Kk4v.
90. *Wicklieffes Wicket . . . and the Testament of Wyllyam Tracie Esquire, expounded by Willyam Tyndall, and Jhon Frythe,* ed. M.C. [John Daye and William Seres, 1548?], sig. d7.
91. *An Homely of Almes Dedes,* sigs. Zz7v.–Zz8.

92. *Ibid.*, sig. Zz8v.
93. *Ibid.*, sig. Aaa1.
94. *Propositions and Principles of Divinitie, Propounded and Disputed in the Universitie of Geneva, by Certaine Students of Divinitie there, under M. Theod. Beza, and M. Anthonie Faius* [trans. J. Penry] (Edinburgh: Robert Waldegrave, 1591), sig. I2v.
95. Turnbull, *op. cit.*, sig. T4v.
96. Chaderton, *op. cit.*, sig. C5.
97. *Ibid.*, sig. C6.
98. *Ibid.*, sig. C7.
99. *Ibid.*, sig. E7v.
100. Sandys, *op. cit.*, sig. V1v.
101. William Perkins, *The Whole Treatise of the Cases of Conscience* in *Workes*, II, sigs. M6–M6v.
102. William Perkins, *A Warning against the Idolatrie of the Last Times*, in *Workes*, I, sig. Ooo6.
103. Sandys, *op. cit.*, sig. P5.
104. Hemingius, *op. cit.*, sig. O3v.
105. *Ibid.*, sigs. O4–P1.
106. Perkins, *A Warning against the Idolatrie of the Last Times*, sig. Ooo6v.
107. *Ibid.*
108. Phillips, *op. cit.*, sig. B5.
109. *An Homely of Almes Dedes*, sig. Aaa3 ff.
110. *Ibid.*, sigs. Aaa4v–Aaa5.
111. *Ibid.*, sig. Aaa6.
112. Smith, *op. cit.*, sigs. A2v–C4v.
113. Sandys, *op. cit.*, sig. N4v.
114. Perkins, *How to Live, and That Well*, sig. Ss5.
115. Hemingius, *op. cit.*, sigs. P1v–P2.
116. Perkins, *The Whole Treatise of the Cases of Conscience*, sigs. N1v–N2.
117. John Stockewood, *A Very Fruiteful Sermon preached at Paules Crosse the Tenth of May Last* (London: for George Bishop, 1579), sigs. I2v–I3.
118. Smith, *op. cit.*, sigs. C3–C3v.
119. Babington, *op. cit.*, sig. 2Ff4.
120. Smith, *op. cit.*, sig. C4.
121. Arthur Warren, *The Poore Mans Passions* (London: J. R[oberts] for R. B[ankworth], 1605), sig. B3.
122. *Ibid.*, sig. B4.
123. *An Homely of Almes Dedes*, sigs. Zz3–Zz6.
124. Turnbull, *op. cit.*, sig. P1.
125. *Ibid.*, sig. P4v.
126. John Jewell, *The Works of* (London: John Norton, 1609), sig. [hand] G3v.
127. Abraham Fleming, *A Memoriall of the Famous Monuments and Charitable Almesdeedes of the Right Worshipfull Maister William Lambe Esquire* ([London:] Henrie Denham for Thomas Turner [,1580]).
128. *Ibid.*, sigs. B2v–B3.
129. *Ibid.*, sig. C3v.
130. *Ibid.*, sig. D4v.
131. *Ibid.*, sigs. D3v–D4.
132. *Ibid.*, sig. C1v.
133. *Ibid.*, sigs. C1v–C2.
134. *Ibid.*, sig. C2v.
135. *Ibid.*, sig. C3.

136. *Ibid.,* sig. C3v.
137. *Ibid.,* sig. D3v.
138. Abraham Fleming, *An Epitaph, or Funerall Inscription, upon the Godlie Life and Death of the Right Worshipfull Maister William Lambe Esquire* (London: Henrie Denham for Thomas Turner, 1580).
139. Abraham Fleming, *The Diamond of Devotion* (London: Peter Short, 1602).
140. "A Living Remembrance of Master Robert Rogers, Marchaunt Adventurer and Leatherseller of London Deceased," etc. in *Ballads and Broadsides, Chiefly of the Elizabethan Period*, ed. Herbert L. Collmann for the Roxburghe Club (Oxford, 1912), No. 79, pp. 227–29.

INDEX

319